WHEN SOCIAL WORKERS IMPACT POLICY AND DON'T JUST IMPLEMENT IT

Research in Social Work series

Series Editors: **Anna Gupta**, Royal Holloway, University of London, UK and **John Gal**, Hebrew University of Jerusalem, Israel

---

Published together with The European Social Work Research Association (ESWRA), this series examines current, progressive and innovative research applications of familiar ideas and models in international social work research.

Also available in the series:

The Origins of Social Care and Social Work
By **Mark Henrickson**

Social Work Research Using Arts-Based Methods
Edited by **Ephrat Huss** and **Eltje Bos**

Critical Gerontology for Social Workers
Edited by **Sandra Torres** and **Sarah Donnelly**

Involving Service Users in Social Work Education, Research and Policy
Edited by **Kristel Driessens** and **Vicky Lyssens-Danneboom**

Adoption from Care
Edited by **Tarja Pösö**, **Marit Skivenes** and **June Thoburn**

Interprofessional Collaboration and Service User Participation
Edited by **Kirsi Juhila**, **Tanja Dall**, **Christopher Hall** and **Juliet Koprowska**

The Settlement House Movement Revisited
Edited by **John Gal**, **Stefan Köngeter** and **Sarah Vicary**

Find out more at:
policy.bristoluniversitypress.co.uk/research-in-social-work

Research in Social Work series

Series Editors: **Anna Gupta**, Royal Holloway, University of London, UK and **John Gal**, Hebrew University of Jerusalem, Israel

---

International Editorial Board:

Find out more at:

policy.bristoluniversitypress.co.uk/
research-in-social-work

Research in Social Work series

Series Editors: **Anna Gupta**, Royal Holloway, University of London, UK and **John Gal**, Hebrew University of Jerusalem, Israel

---

Forthcoming in the series:

Migration and Social Work

Edited by **Emilio J. Gómez-Ciriano, Elena Cabiati** and **Sofia Dedotsi**

Find out more at:

policy.bristoluniversitypress.co.uk/
research-in-social-work

WHEN SOCIAL WORKERS IMPACT POLICY AND DON'T JUST IMPLEMENT IT

A Framework for Understanding Policy Engagement

John Gal and Idit Weiss-Gal

First published in Great Britain in 2023 by

Policy Press, an imprint of
Bristol University Press
University of Bristol
1–9 Old Park Hill
Bristol
BS2 8BB
UK
t: +44 (0)117 374 6645
e: bup-info@bristol.ac.uk

Details of international sales and distribution partners are available at
policy.bristoluniversitypress.co.uk

British Library Cataloguing in Publication Data
A catalogue record for this book is available from the British Library

ISBN 978-1-4473-6475-7 hardcover
ISBN 978-1-4473-6477-1 ePub
ISBN 978-1-4473-6478-8 ePdf

Cover design: Bristol University Press
Front cover image: iStock/antishock
Bristol University Press and Policy Press use environmentally responsible
print partners.
Printed in Great Britain by CPI Group (UK) Ltd, Croydon, CR0 4YY

Contents

List of figures and tables

Figures

Tables

Acknowledgements

The idea to write this book originally emerged nearly immediately after our article on the 'The "why" and the "how" of policy practice: an eight-country comparison' was published in the *British Journal of Social Work* in 2015 (Gal and Weiss-Gal, 2015). Our sense then, as it is now, was that a better understanding of why and how social workers seek to influence policy requires a much longer and more empirically and theoretically based discussion. In the years since, we have been thrilled to see how the discourse on the engagement of social workers in policy has billowed and generated ever-better analyses and thinking on the part of colleagues across the world. Hopefully, this book succeeds in presenting a useful take on the subject that incorporates not only our own thinking and work, but also that of all the scholars, social workers and students who have contributed to this discourse and, indirectly, to a greater social work role in social policy formulation and change.

Most of this book was written during an extraordinary sabbatical year that included COVID-19 lockdowns at our home in Tel Aviv and two very fruitful (and enjoyable) stays in St. Gallen and in Florence. We are thus extremely grateful to our colleagues Professor Stefan Köngeter at The University of Applied Sciences of Eastern Switzerland and Dr Riccardo Guidi at the University of Pisa for both hosting us and participating in lively discussion on social work, social policy and the interface between them during our stays. We are also grateful to Stéphane Beuchat, Tobias Kindler, María-Asunción Martínez-Román and Simone von Wattenwyl for sharing their unique perspectives on the policy engagement of social workers with us. In addition, we want to thank our students, ranging from undergraduate through to doctoral, for the dialogue with them that raised questions and contributed thoughts and ideas that enriched our thinking and contributed to the book. Similarly, we have learnt much from the many social workers that we have met over the last decades in Israel and elsewhere who expressed an interest in the topic of our work – social workers as policy actors – and who told us of their own experiences and the factors that impacted their efforts to influence policy.

As always, it has been a pleasure working with the team at Policy Press. The professional inputs of Isobel Bainton, Emma Cook and Helen Flitton have all made the process of publishing this book much less complicated than it could have been. Thanks are also due to Professor Anna Gupta, John's co-editor of the Research in Social Work series, who facilitated the inclusion of the book in a rapidly growing series of books.

Finally, thanks to Eli Deitch and Anat Ifergan for their help in preparing the book and its content for publication.

We very much hope that this book will contribute to a better understanding of the role of social workers as policy actors and perhaps encourage more social workers to take the first steps along one of the various routes to policy engagement. In doing so, we and they will contribute to a more just, equal, inclusive and caring society that can indeed create a greater sense of well-being and further human rights.

1

Introduction

Introduction

The relevance of social policy for social workers hardly needs to be emphasised or reiterated. It has been the subject of much discussion within the profession, it is a topic integral to the education process of social workers and the relevance of social policy for social workers has been the focus of ample scholarly attention across the world (Dickens, 2010; Simpson and Connor, 2011; Colby et al, 2013; Jaswal and Kshetrimayum, 2020). Suffice it to say at this point that social policy has an enormous impact on: the people with whom social workers work; the problems of individuals, families and communities that they seek to prevent, mitigate or solve; the circumstances of their work environment; and the resources available for them to undertake their tasks and duties effectively and ethically. Moreover, social workers are often the key professionals in many of the various welfare state institutions and affiliates that create and implement these policies.

In the past, an implicit assumption that emerged from much of the academic literature concerning the interface between social policy (and social policymakers) and social workers was that the primary role of social workers is to implement policies decided upon by others (Denney, 1998; Adams, 2002). In this still-prevalent, top-down model of the policy process, social workers are obviously required to understand the nature of social policies and the context in which they operate, but they have little impact or say with regard to which problems policies should address or the forms that policies adopted actually take. While the work of Michael Lipsky (2010) and others on the role of street-level bureaucrats introduced a crucial caveat to this assumption, the focus of attention in this body of work has generally been on the ways in which individual social workers seek to impact the implementation of policies (Gofen, 2014; Evans, 2016a) and, in some cases, to resist their negative implications (Greenslade et al, 2015; Schiettecat et al, 2018; Trappenburg et al, 2020). However, regardless of the success or originality of these acts of resistance to policies, from this perspective, social workers are still generally perceived less as participants in the formal policy formulation process and more as irreverent policy implementers, seeking to undermine policies that they judge to be inappropriate or unjust and are unwilling to adopt as is. In short, social workers are seen as implementors of policies, and their impact on the formulation of policies is diminished or unrecognised.

This rigid top-down view of the social worker–social policy nexus has been challenged by a growing volume of research which reveals that social workers – either individually or collectively and either as citizens or as professionals – not only implement policies, but also, in fact, affect the design of policies. They play an active role in formulating policies or effecting change in them that goes well beyond implementation (and engaging in individual resistance to it) (Harris Rome and Hoechstetter, 2010; Weiss-Gal, 2017a; Lavee and Cohen, 2019; Guidi, 2020; Aviv et al, 2021). Indeed, this policy role can take diverse forms and occur on different policy levels and in varying stages of the policy formulation process (Klammer et al, 2020).

To a certain degree, this emphasis on social workers' policy role should not surprise us. The social work profession has traditionally distinguished itself from other helping professions by the centrality of its commitment to social justice and social change through active participation in efforts to influence public policies on behalf of vulnerable populations. This sentiment is clearly expressed formally in social work's codes of ethics and the definitions of the profession formulated by its international and national bodies. The International Association of Schools of Social Work/International Federation of Social Workers' definition of social work begins with an emphasis on the promotion of 'social change and development, social cohesion, and the empowerment and liberation of people' (IFSW, 2014). The code of ethics of the National Association of Social Workers (NASW) in the US asserts that 'social workers pursue social change, particularly with and on behalf of vulnerable and oppressed individuals and groups of people. Social workers' social change efforts are focused primarily on issues of poverty, unemployment, discrimination, and other forms of social injustice' (NASW, 2017). In the same vein, the code of ethics of the British Association of Social Work notes that social work interventions 'include agency administration, community organisation and engaging in social and political action to impact social policy and economic development' (BASW, 2019: 8).

Moreover, texts authored by social work academics and professionals have long adhered to a person-in-environment ethos that views the social and physical environment of individuals and families as a primary source of their disadvantages (Hare, 2004; Weiss-Gal, 2008). This understanding of the role of the social work profession was put succinctly 30 years ago by British social worker and academic Bill Jordan (1990: 77), who noted that 'clients are not isolated individuals, nor are their problems theirs alone'. The inevitable consequence of this perspective is a recognition that social workers need to focus their interventions not only on individuals, families and communities, but also on the environment that affects them (Mmatli, 2008; Haynes and Mickelson, 2009; Reisch, 2017; Jansson, 2018; Hoefer, 2019a). Social policies often play a key role in constructing or affecting this environment.

A retrospective view of the history of social work across the globe offers numerous examples of the role social workers have played in the creation and adoption of social policies. An overview of the contribution of social workers to the development of social welfare in the US by Michael Sherraden and others (2015) underscored this by noting the policy achievements of social workers in that country, such as Florence Kelley, Julia Lathrop, Grace Abbott, Jeanette Rankin and Dorothy Height, during the 20th century. The same can be said of, say, the role played by Eileen Younghusband in formulating policy with regard to social services in the UK in the 1950s and 1960s (Lyons, 2003), that undertaken by Gerda Meyerson and Agda Montelius in the emergent years of the Swedish welfare state (Thorén and Salonen, 2013), and that played in recent years by Medha Paktar in advocating for environmental justice in India (Pawar and Pulla, 2015).

Social change has, of course, always been identified with, at least, one major stream within social work: community social work or community practice (Rothman, 2007). With its origins in the Settlement House Movement (Gutiérrez and Gant, 2018; Gal et al, 2021), community social work has often tended to attract practitioners with a commitment to harnessing the energies of communities and groups to bring about changes in policies (Makaros and Weiss-Gal, 2014). Indeed, the unique emphasis within this type of social work practice has been on the ways in which members of communities engage in 'autonomous collective action' in order to bring about change in their lives (Twelvetrees, 2008: 1). As such, community social workers have sought to 'mobilize disenfranchised people to advocate on their own behalf in relationship to some power structure in order to achieve needed change' (Pyles, 2014: 13).

Similarly, radical social work in its various forms (which often emerged from within community social work) has struggled to move the focus within the profession away from individuals and their pathology to a focus on the social structures that create and maintain inequality and disadvantage (Specht and Courtney, 1994; Reisch and Andrews, 2001). In their classic edited volume, Roy Bailey and Mike Brake (1975) bemoan the overemphasis on psychological and clinical orientations in social work, and urged social workers to embrace a critical stance with regard to the state and the role of their profession. Robert Mullaly (1997) advocates moving beyond a critical perspective by discussing the practical implications of this radical approach (or, in his terms, 'structural social work'). These include an array of practices, all with the ultimate goal of transforming society. More contemporary work in the radical tradition has sought to identify ways in which social workers, including those employed by the state, can seek to move this agenda forward in a neoliberal era (Ferguson and Woodward, 2009). This effort to bring about change in social policies and institutions can take various forms, ranging from that of resistance by individual social workers in their workplace, to working with social movements and service users on the local, national and global levels (Dominelli, 2002; Ferguson and Lavalette, 2007; Strier and Bershtling, 2016). In recent years, policy engagement has also been incorporated in the emergent poverty-aware practice paradigm (Krumer-Nevo, 2016, 2020; Timor-Shlevin, 2021) and anti-poverty practice (Strier, 2009, 2019), both of which offer a critical, holistic social work approach to working with people living in poverty, as well as in the notions of radical incrementalism advocated by Sanford Schram (2015) and disruptive social work forwarded recently by Guy Feldman (2021).

Thinking about social workers' impact on policy

Despite social work's formal commitment to social change, the role that leading social workers have played in the making of social policy and the development of the welfare state, and the place of engagement in efforts to seek policy change in community and radical social work, the current discourse around the policy involvement of social workers diverges markedly from the past. It offers a new perspective on the social work–social policy nexus, which does not assume that social workers' impact on policy is, or should be, limited to that of the activities of a small number of exemplary professional leaders who perceive of the policy arena as their prime field of activity. Nor does it concentrate on the relatively narrow domain of community organisers within social work, who inevitably (and importantly) link changes in social policy to the organisation of communities. Finally, it does not limit itself to the confines of a radical social work that perceives of policy engagement as a conflictual endeavour that inevitably seeks to challenge policymakers and the structure of the existing state, and to lead to social transformation.

Rather, the emerging discussion of the policy engagement of social workers widens significantly the boundaries of our understanding of this type of practice. Thus, attention has moved to the policy role that social workers – be they caseworkers, community social workers, supervisors and managers (Levin et al, 2013; Weiss-Gal and Gal, 2014; Lustig-Gants and Weiss-Gal, 2015; Jansson et al, 2016; Lavee et al, 2019; Weiss-Gal et al, 2020), civil servants (Gal and Weiss-Gal, 2011), elected officials (Gwilym, 2017; McLaughlin et al, 2019; Amann and Kindler, 2021) or academics (Gal and Weiss-Gal, 2017) – play in seeking to influence policies. This discussion views policy engagement as an avenue for social change that is not limited to specific fields or service-user groups, but should be integrated into the professional and civil repertoire of social workers regardless of where, or with whom, they work. This perspective perceives of policy as being part and parcel of the professional behaviour of social workers. Since policy is determined not only by formal decision-makers on the national level, but also by policymakers on the local and organisational levels, it is in all these diverse policymaking arenas that social workers can, and do, have an impact on policy.

While this approach clearly incorporates radical challenges to existing policies that are seen as oppressive, unjust and discriminatory, and to attempts to roll back existing services and benefits, it moves beyond these goals and forms. As such, the new perspective also encompasses efforts to work with decision-makers or to serve as decision-makers in order to address lacunae in existing policy and to improve them, or to identify new social problems and to invent policies to overcome them. Thus, this discussion embraces a wide range of interventions, from the adversarial to the consensual, including: voting and organising protest activities; legislative advocacy and lobbying through the use of media; policy analysis; participation in policy committees and consultations; and undertaking formal policymaking positions (Ritter, 2008; Harris Rome and Hoechstetter, 2010; Weiss-Gal, 2017a). It incorporates the actions of social worker policy entrepreneurs (Aviv et al, 2021) and the added value that social workers can bring to the activities of broad policy coalitions (Lavee and Cohen, 2019). The goal of this book is to enhance thinking about the wide universe of policy involvement of social workers by offering a conceptual framework that will identify factors associated with this type of activity and by providing a (sufficiently) convincing theoretical and empirical basis for explaining the levels and forms that it takes.

The origins of the more contemporary discussion of the involvement of social workers in the policy process can be found in the discourse on 'policy practice' that emerged in the mid-1980s in the US, primarily due to the efforts of University of Southern California social work academic Bruce Jansson (1984). In the years since, it has enjoyed growing attention in the literature. Not surprisingly, scholars and social work educators in the US have played a pioneering role in efforts to better articulate the form that social workers' policy involvement should take. Initially, much of the literature was geared primarily to the needs of educators seeking to incorporate this type of practice into social work training (Weiss-Gal, 2016). Over the last two decades, the policy involvement discourse has grown in volume and sophistication (Weiss-Gal, 2017a). In addition, it has attracted the interest of scholars beyond North America, who have brought distinctive perspectives to this discussion that are influenced by the political, social and professional contexts within which they work (Fargion, 2018; Feldman, 2019; Klammer et al, 2020; Pawar, 2019; Corte and Roose, 2020; Guidi, 2020; Lombard and Viviers, 2020; Nouman et al, 2020; Cai et al, 2021).

The social work policy discourse

One major strand in the burgeoning volume of literature pertaining to the policy involvement of social workers comprises efforts to establish a solid normative foundation for this and to describe strategies and routes by which social workers can impact policy (Haynes and Mickelson, 2009; Kam, 2014; Bent-Goodley, 2015; Reisch, 2017; Weiss-Gal, 2017b; Jansson, 2018; Pawar, 2019). Given the persistent dominance of the micro emphasis in social work and the, often hostile, political environments in which social workers practise, this effort remains a very necessary one.

A second emphasis in the literature has been on the ways in which social work education can best provide future social workers with the values and the practical infrastructure required to influence policies (Pritzker and Lane, 2014; Bernklau Halvor, 2016; Weiss-Gal, 2016; Lim et al, 2017; Brierton Granruth et al, 2018; Lane et al, 2018; Elmaliach-Mankita et al, 2019; Schwartz-Tayri et al, 2020; Meehan, 2021; Collins et al, 2022). The main impetus for this work in the US has been the inclusion of policy practice as one of the competencies required by the Council on Social Work Education for the accreditation for social work training in that country (CSWE, 2015). This literature has underscored the use of innovative experiential didactic methods to enable social work educators to convince future social workers of the need to engage in policy formulation processes and to equip them with the knowledge necessary to become a policy actor. No less important a goal of this body of work is to offer budding social workers a sense of internal and external political efficacy by familiarising them with the political arenas in which policy is discussed and created, and with the tools that need to be employed while doing so.

Another facet of the social work policy discourse is the empirical effort to assess the level of social workers' engagement in policy change (Weiss-Gal, 2017a) and the ways and forms that it takes (Chandler, 2009; Mendes et al, 2015). Most of the quantitative studies seek to assess the extent of social workers' engagement in policy, generally using a retrospective, self-report design. Often, they have researched social workers' practice in general and, within this, the extent to which social workers engage in policy (Teare and Sheafor, 1995; Gibelman and Schervish, 1997; Thompson et al, 1999; Dudziak and Coates, 2004; Koeske et al, 2005; Weiss-Gal, 2008). Social workers' engagement in social advocacy, broadly defined, has also been a subject of research (Epstein, 1981; Ezell, 1992, 1994; Herbert and Mould, 1992; Hardina, 1995; Herbert and Levin, 1996; McLaughlin, 2009; Necel, 2019). Social advocacy includes activities that social workers engage in to change policies within the framework of their employment and beyond (McCullagh, 1987; Ezell, 1992). Finally, a number of recent studies focus specifically on the on-the-job policy-change efforts of social workers that were undertaken as part of their formal employment (Gewirtz-Meydan et al, 2016; Weiss-Gal and Gal, 2020; Weiss-Gal et al, 2020). These studies, which typically adopt a retrospective, self-report design, are distinctive, in that they employ scales pertaining explicitly to on-the-job policy-related activities and query a wide range of such activities.

Despite the many differences in their design, the studies measuring the extent of social workers' engagement in policy report moderate or low levels of engagement. Research on social advocacy has found that social workers engage in this considerably less than case advocacy on behalf of individual clients. In a similar vein, content analyses of social workers' involvement in policy processes in the US have found that only a very small number of social workers give testimony at public hearings, send written comments on a proposed legislative change (McCullagh, 1987) or make use of opportunities to impact regulations (Beltran et al, 2022). The same is true of the presence of social workers in the discourse on policy in the national media in the US (Leigh Bliss and Ginn, 2019). More encouragingly, quantitative content analyses undertaken in Israel found that as part of their social work practice, 667 social workers participated in 14 per cent of the deliberations of all legislative committees in the parliament between 1999 and 2006, and in over 43 per cent of the deliberations in five of them (Gal and Weiss-Gal, 2011). However, the levels of social worker participation in meetings of committees dealing with financial issues were much lower (Weiss-Gal and Nouman, 2016).

Moving beyond more general examinations of the levels of policy engagement, studies have explored the various strategies and activities that social workers adopt when they do involve themselves in policy. The first of these is legislative advocacy. While historical studies in the US describe social workers as having served as advisors to policy committees and having testified before legislative committees in the first half of the 20th century (Coombs-Orme, 1988; Rodems et al, 2011), more contemporary, quantitative studies in different countries (Reeser and Epstein, 1990; Lai, 2004; Douglas, 2008; Weiss-Gal et al, 2020) reveal that this type of practice typically includes contacting legislators or public officials, or being consulted by them on policy issues or social problems.

Social action has also been the subject of a number of studies. This incorporates efforts with an external focus, for example: forming or participating in broad-based coalitions for policy change; organising or participating in social action groups to resolve policy problems; organising conferences or public meetings; working through professional associations and agency boards; and using the media (Heffernan, 1964; Lai, 2004; Douglas, 2008; Ioakimidis et al, 2014; Lundälv, 2019). Studies have also examined social workers' social action with internal foci, such as assisting communities to organise collective actions for policy change or educating individuals, families or groups about policy problems in order to encourage them to be involved in policy-change activities (Ezell, 1992; Weiss-Gal et al, 2020).

Research and documentation are another facet of efforts by social workers to influence the policy process. Historical studies (Coombs-Orme, 1988; Rodems et al, 2011) show that in the first decades of the 20th century, research by social workers played a crucial role in promoting policies to combat infant mortality and improve maternal health in the US. A recent study in the US indicates that this effort continues today as well (Allen et al, 2018). Only two studies, one in the US and the other in Hong Kong, have asked social workers directly whether they conduct research as part of their advocacy efforts. In the US, Ezell (1994) found that very few of the workers queried conducted research on specific issues. In Hong Kong, Lai (2004) found that more than 60 per cent of the sample engaged in needs assessments, analyses of client group or social problems, or policy evaluations.

Finally, social workers have also reported participating in advocacy activities aimed at making changes in the policies of their own organisations or of other organisations in order to improve services. Ezell (1992, 1994) found that the most frequent advocacy activity is arguing for better services within organisations. Other studies report that high percentages of social workers seek to influence fellow social workers' opinions on organisational policy, advocate for change in services by meeting with subgroups in the agency and providing them with knowledge on the problem, or organise a group to work on an agency-related policy problem (Gray et al, 2002; Dudziak and Coates, 2004; Levin et al, 2013).

Social workers frequently collaborate with service users and work alongside them to impact policies. This was examined with regard to Spain during the joint efforts by social workers and service users to prevent the implementation of austerity policies in the wake of the Great Recession (Guidi, 2019). Similarly, in a study on a struggle during the second decade of the millennium, social workers, community activists and advocacy organisations in Israel undertook a decade-long struggle to bring about the introduction of legislation to ensure the basic right to electricity and to prevent electricity cuts due to arears (Saeid, 2019).

Alongside the empirical facet regarding the extent and the form that policy involvement has taken, a number of studies have addressed the factors associated with the social workers' (and social work students') engagement in policy (Ritter, 2008; Jansson et al, 2016; Lavee et al, 2019; Makaros et al, 2020; Kulke et al, forthcoming). This is a fourth emphasis in the literature (for reviews, see Weiss-Gal, 2017a; Mattocks, 2018; Ostrander et al, 2018). Most of the factors identified in this body of work can be described as individual factors and are based, explicitly or implicitly, on the civic voluntarism model (CVM), which was developed by Sidney Verba and his colleagues (1995) to explain the involvement of the citizens of a democratic society in politics. The factors found in these studies in social work include personal resources (seniority, tenure and policy skills), psychological engagement in politics (interest in politics and political efficacy), belonging to a recruitment network, the social worker's occupational role, policy practice training and professional and socio-economic perceptions. Other factors focus more on the organisational context of social workers and include the agency auspices of the social worker and the organisational culture in which social workers operate (Jansson et al, 2016).

In recent years, scholars have sought to move beyond an effort to explicate the normative pillars upon which social workers' policy engagement is based in order to evaluate and influence social work training related to policy, to assess levels of engagement in policy by social workers, or to identify specific factors associated with various forms of policy involvement. Drawing upon insights from other disciplines, in particular, the political and policy sciences, some of the most exciting recent work on policy involvement has sought to establish a more solid and broader theoretically grounded infrastructure in order to reflect upon the engagement of social workers in policy.

One feature of this effort is an attempt to draw upon public policy and political science models in order to primarily 'highlight the strategies and actions through which they could intervene during different phases of the policy cycle to realize their social justice agenda' (De Corte and Roose, 2020: 236). In this sense, authors have sought to encourage engagement in policy on the part of social workers by identifying the possibilities for interventions. Drawing upon key models in this literature, such as John Kingdon's multiple stream framework, the advocacy coalition framework and Steven Lukes' three dimensions of power, or by employing a policy stages approach, this literature has sought to flesh out facets of the interaction between social workers and social policy, and to offer more analytical insights into these (Almog-Bar et al, 2015; Krings et al, 2019; De Corte and Roose, 2020; Cai et al, 2021). In other work, leading political science theories have been employed to distinguish between the different forms that social workers' policy engagement can take (Feldman, 2019).

Another focus of the recent scholarship on social workers' policy engagement has endeavoured to study social work actors from different organisational perspectives and address such questions as: 'How does social work affect social policy along different stages of the policy cycle?'; and 'What explains success or failure?' In a recent edited volume, Klammer, Leiber and Leitner (2020) drew upon knowledge from diverse disciplines to respond to these questions. Written from a primarily European perspective, the editors and case-study authors incorporate insights regarding the impact of distinctive political and welfare regimes to explore the ways in which social workers impact policy. Crucially, the impact of dominant social policy paradigms found within the social policy discourse enabled the editors to identify the contexts in which the social work–social policy interface exists and the impact of this on the forms that policy engagement takes.

A third facet of the emerging, more theoretically grounded, contemporary discourse, and the focus of this book, seeks to concentrate on the factors that explain social workers' engagement in policy and the forms that this takes. As noted earlier, the initial efforts to explore factors related to the involvement of social workers in policy processes tended to draw heavily on the CVM. While these efforts generally focused more on the participation of social workers in the formal political process as citizens (Hamilton and Fauri, 2001; Ritter, 2008), the model has also been employed to explain policy activities that social workers undertake as professionals within their workplace context (Douglas, 2008; Broers, 2018; Weiss-Gal and Gal, 2020).

In this book, we seek to extend the boundaries of the discourse on the policy role of social workers and their contribution to social justice. We endeavour to think more broadly about when social workers impact policy and to move towards a theory of policy engagement in social work. While the evidence points to the fact that social workers can, and do, impact policies, we still do not have a good understanding of why, how and when this occurs. It is similarly unclear what the conditions are that lead social workers to engage in policy processes in order to affect the social policies.

The policy engagement conceptual framework

Drawing upon findings from a cross-national study of social workers' engagement in policy practice, the authors of this book took an initial step towards explaining social workers' policy engagement by developing the policy practice engagement (PPE) conceptual framework (Gal and Weiss-Gal, 2015). This framework is comprised of three categories of factors, which we called: opportunity, facilitation and motivation. *Opportunity* focuses upon how accessible the social policy process is to social workers. *Facilitation* refers to the degree to which the organisational context in which social workers operate enables employees to engage in policy-related activities. *Motivation* encompasses a number of individual-level factors that influence the willingness of social workers to engage in policy-related activities.

In the years since the initial publication of the PPE conceptual framework, we have witnessed a significant volume of research that has sought to employ the framework within social work in different contexts and in relation to diverse routes of policy engagement beyond on-the-job policy engagement by social workers, which we termed 'policy practice' (see, for example, Boehm et al, 2018; Fargion, 2018; Pawar, 2019; Weiss-Gal and Gal, 2019a, 2020; Guidi, 2020; Nouman, 2020; Shewell et al, 2021; Nouman and Azaiza, 2021a; Webster, 2021). In addition, there has been an initial effort to employ it in other related disciplines, such as nursing (Bar Yosef et al, 2020). This had led us to assume that the framework can be employed to better understand not only policy practice, but also other routes through which social workers seek to affect policy (discussed at length in the Chapter 2).

In addition, our work and that of others in the years since the original formulation of the framework has convinced us that we need to incorporate a fourth category of factors in the framework, which are termed the

Figure 1.1: The basic PE conceptual framework

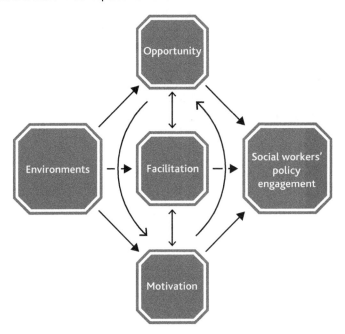

'*environments*'. These refer to a group of factors linked to the broader structural, social and professional environment of social workers that research indicates have an impact on one or more of the categories of factors included in the original PPE framework (see Chapter 3). The revised framework, the policy engagement (PE) conceptual framework, is presented in Figure 1.1.

As can be seen in Figure 1.1, our main claim is that the engagement of social workers in the policy process through diverse policy routes is directly affected by opportunity, facilitation and motivational factors. In addition, opportunity, facilitation and motivational factors impact each other. The three categories of factors are directly influenced by the environments. In other words, while the environments impact the policy engagement of social workers, this is mediated by opportunity, facilitation and motivation.

We believe that the framework described in this book offers us a way of thinking more systematically about the various factors that determine how social workers seek to influence policies in very diverse arenas and forms. However, given the wide diversity of the types of policy engagement that social workers engage in as professionals and citizens, we note that not all of the components of the framework are relevant to each and every route of policy engagement. We will return to this issue in Chapter 7.

A foundation for a discussion of the PE conceptual framework will be offered in Chapter 2. It will provide a more detailed overview of the social work–social policy nexus in which the policy-related activities of social workers are undertaken and the ways in which social workers seek to affect social policies that have relevance to service users and to professionals. Each of the four following chapters will be devoted to one of the four categories of factors in the framework. Finally, Chapter 7 will bring together the components of the framework, examine their interfaces and explore the challenges and possible venues for research, practice and teaching that the PE conceptual framework offers.

2

On the social work–social policy interface

Introduction

Social policies seek to address human needs. Although there is wide debate over how this can best be achieved, the prime stated objective of these policies is to improve the social welfare of individuals, families, groups and communities, and to tackle the social problems that affect them. Social policies are comprised of relatively identifiable ideas, assumptions, rules and procedures that determine the role of relevant authorities in the distribution of social resources intended to promote social welfare (Midgely and Livermore, 2009; Reisch, 2014; Green and Clarke, 2016). Obviously, these policies can provide very diverse types of resources, ranging from cash benefits, through different forms of services, to symbolic resources of the type that Nancy Fraser (1995) alluded to when she wrote about 'recognition'. This chapter explores various aspects of the interface between social policies and social work, and, in doing so, creates a conceptual infrastructure for the following chapters, which deal with the factors that impact social workers' engagement with the social policy formulation process.

The nexus between social policies and social workers lies, of course, at the very heart of the discussion in this book. Social policies impact nearly every aspect of the 'social work' that social workers engage in as agents of the welfare state, whether they are employed directly by it or indirectly by non-profits and for-profit enterprises, or even if they are self-employed. Policies have a crucial impact on the social problems that adversely affect the well-being of the people that social workers are committed to, as well as the severity, scope and intensity of these problems. Moreover, to a large extent, social policies determine not only whom social workers can serve, but also what they can do for these people, the time they can devote to them and the resources that they have at their disposal to engage in practice. Indeed, in modern welfare states, it is difficult to imagine social work without social policies.

A useful starting point for a discussion on the engagement of social workers in the social policy formulation process is to think, more generally, about the interface between social policy and social work. Clearly, as alluded to in Chapter 1, this interface is broader and more complex than the traditional perception that social workers are little more than the foot soldiers of the welfare state that seek to implement, in full and unconditionally, policies that were formulated by a small group of decision-makers and are intended to alleviate the suffering of their service users. Rather, it is a two-way process that is influenced by diverse factors, can take a variety of forms and can develop in different ways over time.

Social workers will ultimately seek to impact policies that they regard as a legitimate part of their professional remit. This is certainly the case for those policy routes that can be seen as integral to social workers' professional role. However, social work definitions or codes of ethics do not usually offer a definitive answer to what these policies are or what should be changed in them (Banks, 2012). These documents tend to emphasise the broader goal of furthering 'social justice' or to note that social workers should challenge discrimination, recognise diversity, distribute resources and challenge unjust policies and practices (BASW, 2019). In some cases, the codes also identify certain routes for engaging in policy change. However, they often do not go much beyond these generalisations. Thus, official documents do not offer much assistance in understanding the intricacy of the social work–social policy nexus.

A useful and comprehensive way to approach this nexus is to think about: the policy levels, arenas and stages where social workers can impact policy; the modes of policy change that they pursue; the types of social policies that social workers are likely to interact with; and the routes through which they participate in the social policy formulation process. Our guiding assumptions at this stage can be summed up in the following way:

• The social policies that social workers will seek to influence will be those that relate to problems (or create problems) that affect relevant service users or that directly or indirectly affect the social workers themselves.
• Social workers' decisions as to if, and how, they seek to influence social policies will depend much on the degree to which social workers are motivated to engage in this and the sense that they have a viable option to do so.

In order to flesh out these assumptions, we begin by touching upon some facets of the social policy formulation process and, in particular, their relevance to the policy engagement of social workers.

Stages in the social policy process

The policy process is the context in which social workers' policy engagement takes place. Efforts to better understand the policy process, its structure and the factors that impact it have been a key focus in the policy sciences and, more specifically, in the social policy literature. The goal at this point in the discussion is to explain how social workers can impact policy and to identify the stages in the policy process in which social workers interact with actors in this process and, employing different routes and strategies, can have a potential impact on the eventual formulation of social policy. As such, we follow in the path of Ute Klammer, Simone Leiber and Sigrid Leitner (2020), Joris De Corte and Rudi Roose (2020) and Richard Hoefer (2021b) in drawing upon the policy cycle framework (Hupe and Hill, 2006) to clarify the points in the policy process at which we expect social workers to have an impact. In particular, this heuristic construction is valuable in identifying four stages in the social policy process at which social workers, in their various roles, are likely to affect policy: agenda setting; policy formulation; implementation; and evaluation.

Agenda setting, or problem setting – that is, efforts to define and frame problems as issues that require public intervention and to place them on the public agenda in order to eventually lead to a process of policy change (Birkland, 2020) – is an obvious policy role for social workers. This is particularly relevant to front-line social workers and managers providing social services, who have unique knowledge about the needs of service users. This is because they have a close interface with service users, are privy to the problems that service users encounter or the adverse implications of policies that they endure, and can thus draw public conclusions from the private challenges faced by individuals and families. This is also the case for social workers employed by advocacy organisations, whose raison d'être is to draw policymakers' attention to issues that affect the populations they seek to assist and to create the political pressure that will lead to action being taken. A study of the participation of social workers in parliamentary committees in Israel did indeed find that initiatives to place matters on the committee agenda were common and undertaken both by central and local government social workers and by social worker representatives of advocacy organisations, though this was more often the case for the latter group (Weiss-Gal and Gal, 2014).

Often, this process of agenda setting will be undertaken through collaboration between street-level professionals (employed by the state or non-state service providers), service users and professional and civil society organisations. An interesting example of this is the way in which interorganisational networks created by social workers in two Belgian cities led to initiatives and joint efforts by the members of these networks that enabled them to raise awareness of the severity of homelessness in these cities among local policymakers (De Corte et al, 2017). An effort by social workers in Connecticut to place the issue of domestic minor sex trafficking on the public agenda and to redefine the problem as a consequence of the environment rather than individual choice also reflects this collaborative agenda-setting process (Werkmeister Rozas et al, 2019). In a 13-year effort led by the Trafficking in Persons Council (which comprised social workers from different sectors), these social workers managed to frame the problem of minor sex trafficking as one affecting a large number of domestic youth, whose engagement in prostitution was involuntary and typically the result of coercion, and to make clear that paying for sex with minors was a serious crime. This effort resulted in changes of legislation and of practices by the Department of Children and Families, the agency responsible for addressing this issue.

Social workers in diverse roles also engage in the formulation of policies, the stage at which policy is constructed to address problems that are perceived as requiring solutions by policymakers. Social workers can play a role in the concrete formulation of policy as elected officials and as bureaucrats who play a formal role in the translation of ideas into policy, as academics in advisory roles, as practitioners contributing ideas to policy processes, and as representatives of professional or service user organisations. These efforts can take place on different policy levels. Social workers representing international social work federations or transnational organisations have contributed to the formulation of policies on the global and regional levels (Jones and Truell, 2012). More often, this takes place on the national level, in which deliberations in legislative institutions, formal commissions and bureaucratic forums lead to the detailed formulation of legislation or administrative decisions concerning social policy. In their historical overview of the grand accomplishments of social work in the US, Sherraden et al (2015) describe how social workers, often serving as senior officials in state or federal administrations, contributed to the adoption of significant social policies throughout the 20th century. These included services for children and families, measures to reduce maternal and infant mortality, social insurance, employment protection, women's rights, and anti-poverty policies.

This can also take place on the local level, as reflected in the following example from Switzerland. A social worker employed by a small non-profit social service provider working with foster families and the head of the organisation (also a social worker) participated in a canton-level consultation process concerning the adoption of new federal legislation aiming to move the funding of foster-care families and agencies to the cantonal context. While the social workers' efforts to include in the legislation health insurance coverage for the foster families were unsuccessful, they did manage to add an additional layer to the existing policy. This took the form of an amendment of the law on the canton level to incorporate support for the participation of foster parents in courses on child psychology and parenting prior to their fostering of children beginning. In its efforts to influence the policy process, the non-profit adhered to a non-confrontational and often behind-the-scenes approach, particularly with regard to its interactions with the state bureaucracy, which funded and regulated its activities. This was reflected in the policy practice efforts of the social worker and the head of the organisation. The consultation process was primarily informal and consisted of the back and forth of suggested changes to the legislation by way of phone calls, emails and informal face-to-face meetings with canton officials.

Implementation of social policy is, of course, what most social workers do, and this is the stage where the interface between street-level social workers and policies is greatest. This is where social workers are expected to execute policies or where they can observe at close quarters the impact of social policies on service users. As such, this is not only the arena in which social workers are motivated to engage in policy practice and raise issues that need to be addressed by policies, but also the place where social workers can, and do, have a direct impact on actual policies on the ground. The role that social workers play as street-level bureaucrats, and their impact on policy implementation, is one of the burgeoning fields of inquiry in the social work literature in recent years (Nothdurfter and Hermans, 2018). In particular, scholars have questioned the degree to which social workers do indeed comply with formal policy directives in their street-level activities (Evans, 2020). Both our research and that of others have identified the multiple ways in which social workers who are street-level managers or caseworkers employ either the formal discretion that they enjoy or, in many cases, discreet and informal efforts to interpret and change policies in order to address the needs of their service users (Schiettecat et al, 2018; Gjersøe et al, 2020; Trappenburg et al, 2020; Sery and Weiss-Gal, 2021; Tzadiki and Weiss-Gal, 2021).

A final policy stage relevant to our discussion is that of evaluation, the process by which the impact of existing policies is assessed and conclusions regarding it and future policies are reached. Evaluations of social policies take diverse forms, and their impact on the social policy formulation process is not clear-cut. Indeed, despite advances in the methodologies employed in evaluations and the incorporation of wider participants in the process, policymakers need not, and often do not, heed the findings of evaluations of existing policies or base their decisions on new policies on the best evidence available (Greve, 2017). Nevertheless, efforts to reach conclusions about the impact of social policies on service users are crucial, and social workers can, and do, play a role in this stage of the policy formulation process. This is, of course, an obvious role for social work academics, who often have the theoretical and empirical tools to engage in evaluation studies and the collection of evidence as a basis for practice and policy (Weiss-Gal and Gal, 2019a). However, professional social workers can also participate in the evaluation of policies, as shown in a recent Italian example. Here, social workers joined other professionals in the evaluation of a pilot project of innovative anti-poverty steps introduced between 2013 and 2015 in municipalities across the country. The project linked personalised projects by service users with the provision of social services. The introduction of the experimental measure, *Carta Aquisti Sperimentale*, was then evaluated through institutional round tables in which social workers participated as part of the process of formulating a national policy (D'Emilione et al, 2019).

Where policy is made: policy arenas

A second crucial aspect of the social work–social policy nexus focuses on the arenas and the levels where social policies are determined and enacted, and the implications of this for social workers. Here, the focus is on the settings in which social workers in diverse capacities can have an impact on the social policy formulation process.

Contemporary welfare states, within which social policies are determined and implemented, comprise a complex 'mixed economy of welfare' that includes a very diverse array of providers of the benefits and services involved (Powell, 2007). Thus, alongside the more traditional provision of welfare by the state (be it on the national/federal, the state, the regional or the local levels), there is also a myriad of for-profit and non-profit agencies and organisations that today play significant roles in the welfare state. The diversification of the provision of welfare today inevitably raises issues concerning the role of the state in both funding and regulating this system.

Social policies are, then, determined in different arenas. International organisations, such as the United Nations (Palattiyil et al, 2019), are one such arena in which global policy principles and guidelines intended to further social and human rights are formulated. Clearly, the source of many of the policies that affect social workers and their service users is the welfare state and policymakers on the national level (for example, legislative bodies or national bureaucracies). However, to paraphrase the old Buffy Sainte-Marie (1964) song, it is also the case that the 'orders come from far away no more. They come from here and there and you and me.' Policies that are relevant to the work of social workers and the lives of service users are often formulated or reformulated by regional and local authorities, and by administrators within the (state or non-state) social service organisations that employ social workers. Not surprisingly, then, social workers are not indifferent to the policies that impact them, and, as we will show later, they often seek to affect them in those arenas in which the policies are formulated.

Various developments within welfare states and their political systems in recent decades have undermined, to a certain extent, the degree to which social policy decisions are taken by a small centralised group of decision-makers, be they politicians or senior civil servants, and then conveyed to a highly disciplined professional workforce through a hierarchical state bureaucracy. As such, the options for social workers to affect the policy process have become greater, which requires us to widen the scope of our investigation so as to include additional sites in which the policy engagement of social workers can take place.

One key contributing factor in the emergence of additional arenas in which social policy is formulated is the accelerated process by which policymaking has been decentralised in welfare states (Toubeau and Wagner, 2015). It is true that social policies have always been implemented at different levels. However, the decentralisation of social policy refers not only to the fact that the implementation of social policies has been increasingly devolved to subnational levels, but also to the idea that the policy process is being influenced, to a greater degree, by subnational actors, particularly in federal political systems (Bonoli et al, 2019). Contemporary interest in this process was initially triggered by the enhanced decentralisation of safety nets under welfare reform in the US in the mid-1990s and by the efforts to assess its impact (Pierson, 1995; Brodkin, 1997; Bruch et al, 2018). Yet, it is not only in federalised states that the power to determine social policy has moved (at least, partially) from central to subnational governments. Rather, this process has taken place across welfare states (Kleider, 2018).

One important manifestation of this decentralisation process is the emergence of localism, which refers to the 'devolution of power and/or functions and/or resources away from central control and towards front-line managers, local democratic structures, local institutions and local communities, within an agreed framework of minimum standards' (Evans et al, 2013: 405). This has led to the growing relevance of local welfare systems in addressing social problems (Johansson and Panican, 2016). Although the causes and the implications of this process are the subject of debate and research, it would appear that decentralisation has created additional spaces on the local level, in particular, for social policy formulation and variation (Mosley, 2013; Kutsar and Kuronen, 2015; Kleider, 2018; Trætteberg and Grødem, 2021).

A second, and related, process that has contributed to the broadening of the social policy formulation process in tandem with the devolution of social policy decision-making is the growing diversity of policy actors present in the policy formulation process. This reflects the enhanced role of third sector and for-profit organisations in the provision of welfare, and the inability of the state to effectively coordinate and control these organisations (Bar-Nir and Gal, 2011; Hustinx et al, 2014). Moreover, observers have noted a growing blurring of the previously clear-cut distinctions between formal decision-makers and providers (Ahonen et al, 2006). As such, deliberations over the content of policy (as well as its implementation) have moved beyond the traditional 'core executive' to include not only additional levels of government, but also an array of actors and institutions (Kooiman, 2003). Relating specifically to social policy, Ingo Bode (2006) described this as a 'disorganized welfare mix', in which more volatile and heterogeneous public–private partnerships have emerged, and there is more creative civic action. This body of research has underscored the role of local authorities and non-profits in the provision of welfare services, emphasised self-governance (that is, the increasing role of service users in decisions pertaining to social services), and stressed the impact of professional providers at various stages in the policy process (Hill and Hupe, 2006; Bifulco and Centemeri, 2008; Newman et al, 2008).

The decentralisation of social policy and the emergence of a more diverse mix of welfare provision have obvious implications for the social work–social policy nexus. The arenas in which decisions about social policy are made have become much more diverse and, crucially, are likely to be more accessible to social workers. As we will see in the discussion in the following chapters of this book, they can include: the institutions of local government and the professional units within them; the organisations that provide social services and the sites in which these interact with the state; regional-level agencies and political bodies; and, of course, the national or federal political and bureaucratic decision-making forums. They can also include the public arenas – virtual or physical – in which the political and public discourse takes place. Playing a role in these policy processes are additional actors that include advocacy organisations, social movements, political parties and professional bodies. The likelihood of social workers being present in these arenas and taking part in decisions made within them, or being able to influence decision-makers, is much greater than in the past.

Obviously, these processes do not guarantee that social workers will necessarily be party to decision-making. However, the fact that social workers are likely to be the key professionals in state and local social services, in non-profits and for-profits providing services, and in advocacy organisations, and to be undertaking roles in various levels of the government bureaucracies determining policies, does offer diverse options for policy engagement. As such, our discussion regarding the scope of social workers' engagement in policy will have to be broad enough to encompass not only efforts to affect policies determined in formal, national-level arenas, but also attempts to influence those policies that are determined by regional and local governments or formulated in the social services in which social workers are employed. Thus, we can find social workers seeking to impact policies in policy arenas that include social welfare providers on the ground, local government, state and national parliaments, and administrative units on these levels.

Modes of policy change

Moving beyond a descriptive examination of the link between the impact of policies, the levels and stages at which these are formulated, and the involvement of social workers in the policy process, it is useful to think about the modes of policy decisions that social workers will seek to bring about. Policy efforts by social workers can be undertaken to prevent, what they perceive of as, detrimental policy change (this is particularly the case during periods of retrenchment). In addition, they can also engage in changing existing policies or in seeking to introduce new policies to address previously non-existent, unobserved or ignored social problems or needs, as in the case of changing local policy in one municipality in Israel to create services for foreign immigrants and asylum seekers (Aviv et al, 2021).

Policy change can take diverse forms. In seeking to better explain the nature of developments within the welfare state, political scientists like Peter Hall (1993), Jacob Hacker (2004) and, in particular, Kathleen Thelen (2004) have devoted much thought to the modes of policy change that take place in the social policy arena. The work by Thelen and her associates (Streek and Thelen, 2005; Mahoney and Thelen, 2010) offers a useful conceptual framework for thinking about the modes of policy change. Employed frequently in the years since its originally conceptualisation in the social policy discourse to better understand institutional change (Béland and Powell, 2015), this framework was incorporated into the social work policy engagement discourse by Feldman (2019).

This discussion is not only particularly pertinent to the role of social workers as policy actors because it is obviously social policies that social workers generally seek to affect. Rather, it is also relevant to understanding the policy engagement of social workers due to the diverse roles played by social workers participating in the policy formulation process. Social workers engaging in social policy can be: employed by advocacy or professional organisations as lobbyists or as community organisers; administrators in non-profit or for-profit service providers; elected or appointed officials at different levels within government agencies; academics; self-employed clinicians; or street-level professionals employed by local or state governments in social welfare agencies, hospitals or an array of institutional settings. The policies that social workers can, and do, seek to affect can range from those within their own organisation all the way through to policies determined by national decision-making bodies. This diversity in the roles of social workers and the level of their policy intervention requires us to conceive of a broad spectrum of policy decisions sought by social worker policy actors. Often, the mode of change sought by social workers will be determined by the boundaries and the authority of their professional role. Thus, for example, a front-line administrator will act differently in the policy arena and probably seek types of policy change that diverge from those sought by a social worker employed in an advocacy organisation or professional association.

Five modes of policy change have been identified: displacement, layering, conversion, drift and exhaustion (Streek and Thelen, 2005). The first three of these modes describe active efforts to bring about policy change, while the last two (drift and exhaustion) relate to change that results primarily from a lack of active change and, consequently, in a widening, sometimes unsustainable, disconnect between existing policy and the relevant policy environment. Given that the goal of this discussion is to understand proactive policy engagement on the part of social workers, the focus here will be on the first three modes of change. Together, they offer a wide spectrum of potential changes to existing policies.

Displacement refers to the removal of existing rules and the introduction of new ones. This is the most radical of the modes of policy change and describes a major revision of existing policy. As such, it is a consequence of an overt decision to bring about policy change. Welfare reform enacted in the US in 1996 is a useful example of the way in which an existing policy was indeed changed dramatically. Similarly, the outsourcing of social services and the introduction of New Public Management (NPM) principles into social welfare services in many welfare states reflect the displacement that has taken place in services in which social workers are employed. The adoption of the first piece of legislation identifying social services and medical care for people with HIV in the US, the Ryan White CARE Act 1990, is an example of efforts to bring about a dramatic change in policy by a coalition of organisations in which social workers played a major role (Poindexter, 1999). Another interesting effort by social workers to promote a policy change of this proportion was undertaken in Australia during the first decade of the millennium. Concern over the country's mandatory offshore policy towards asylum seekers led the Australian Council of Heads of Schools of Social Work and practitioners to undertake a highly publicised campaign to expose the consequences of this policy and, ultimately, to bring about policy change. This included a citizen-driven People's Inquiry into Detention that consisted of public hearings in ten cities and culminated in a report released at a national social work conference (Mendes, 2013; Briskman, 2020).

A second mode of policy change, layering, does not entail the removal of a policy and its replacement by an alternative, but rather takes the form of adding new elements on top of, or alongside, the components of an existing social policy (van der Heijden, 2011). This can take the form of incorporating new elements into existing policies, such as a private pillar in pensions or healthcare (Capano, 2018), or adding programmes, such as new plans for supporting disadvantaged children in education policy (Hardy and Woodcock, 2014) or adopting additional layers of governance in long-term care (Arlotti and Aguilar-Hendrickson, 2018). A useful example of this type of change is the policy process that led to the introduction of a child development account policy in Israel in 2017 (Grinstein-Weiss et al, 2019). Based on the assets-building model (Sherraden, 1991), this policy had been advocated for over a decade by social workers holding high-level administrative positions within the Israeli Ministry of Welfare, social work academics from Israel and the US, and economists within the social security system. It sought to encourage savings for children in order to further social mobility during early adulthood. The policy was finally adopted by adding an additional policy layer to the existing universal child benefits. Following an increase in the level of child benefits, most of the amount was required to be placed in a savings account and invested on behalf of the child. The parents choose the type of investment and can top up the mandatory amount saved with additional funds from this benefit (Mandelkern and Rosenhek, 2021). Mahoney and Thelen (2010) note that while layering takes the form of amendments, revisions or additions to existing policy, it has the potential to lead to major change if these changes overshadow the original intention of the policy.

Finally, conversion refers to changes that occur when existing rules remain the same but the manner by which they are interpreted changes (Thelen, 2004). Thus, policy will effectively change not necessarily due to an explicit effort by social workers to replace or add to an existing policy, but rather through their interpretation of the policy and the discretionary form in which they translate this understanding into practice (D'Eon, 2017). An example of this type of policy change emerges from a study of the practices of Flemish social workers dealing with the needs of service users living in poverty. Schiettecat, Roets and Vandenbroeck (2018) detail the ways in which front-line social workers and, in some cases, their organisations and teams reinterpret or subvert existing rules and regulations to provide families living in poverty with access to services or resources. In particular, the researchers discovered how social workers explicitly and skilfully utilised ambiguities and uncertainties in existing policies to better address needs. Similar evidence has emerged of the ways in which street-level managers and professionals in outsourced services in Australia employ discretion as a means of ensuring that policies reflect professional values, as they do not have the possibility to change these policies formally (Carson et al, 2015), as well as the efforts by social service managers in Canada to expand the reach of services to excluded populations while working within the confines of existing policy (Aronson and Smith, 2010).

Types of social policy

After discussing the stages, levels, arenas and modes of policy change, we want to identify the different types of policies social workers seek to address. The policies that impact social workers, either directly or indirectly, are broader than what would appear to be, at first sight, part of their natural sphere of activity. This is, of course, pertinent to our discussion because the types of policies that social workers regard as relevant to them as professionals or as

Table 2.1: Examples of types of policies relevant to social workers' policy engagement

	Directly impact service users	Indirectly impact service users
Directly impact social workers	Preventing cuts in funding for mental health services	Establishing a masters in social work programme
Indirectly impact social workers	Raising the minimum wage	Solidarity with migrants and refugees

citizens are also liable to be those in which they will be most likely to engage in policy-related activities.

We can identify four different types of policies in which social workers are involved in their creation or change by employing two axes: one focusing on the impact of policies on service users; and a second relating to the impact of policies on social workers themselves. A schematic exposition of examples of each of the four different types of policies is summarised in Table 2.1.

The first of these types of policies (in the bottom-left corner), and those that would appear to be closest to the issues alluded to in the profession's official documents, are policies that relate to social problems affecting services users. Here, the scope of decisions by policymakers can range from efforts to address new social problems or persistent social problems that have not been addressed (or have not been adequately addressed) in the past, to instituting changes in existing policies that have an impact on the scope or the form of these policies.

Social workers will typically seek to affect these decisions because they perceive of the issues that are the target of these policies as being directly related to the well-being of their service users (Aviv et al, 2021) or, to use social work jargon, as falling into the broad category of 'social justice' (Craig, 2002; Reisch, 2002; Postan-Aizik et al, 2020). The impact of these policies upon social workers is indirect. It does not directly affect their status or work conditions, but rather has relevance to them because the policies have a direct impact upon the well-being of the members of social groups to whom social workers are committed or upon social problems that social workers identify. Such policies as those that determine the adequacy and the conditions related to cash benefits, the form that activation programmes take, the quantity and the quality of public housing stock or of childcare centres, the level of access of asylum seekers to health and welfare services, or the degree to which the design of social policies is attentive to the cultural sensitivities of minority ethnic groups are all typical examples of policies of this type.

A pertinent example of social workers' activities in relation to this type of policy is a campaign undertaken by social work academics and students in Nevada to raise the minimum wage in that state in 2001. A report entitled 'Working hard, living poor' and authored by social work scholars served as the trigger for a four-year campaign, in which social work educators and students actively participated as advocates, which eventually culminated in a number of raises in the minimum wage in that state (Chandler, 2009). The policy change did not directly affect the professional interests of social workers, but it did have a direct impact on the incomes of people employed in an estimated 17.4 per cent of jobs in Nevada that paid less than a liveable hourly wage.

In Switzerland, a recent struggle over the level of social assistance in the Canton of Bern was led by a coalition formed by social workers, service users and advocacy organisations. It also focused on an issue that did not affect social workers directly, but had a very potentially detrimental effect on their service users. A proposal passed in the cantonal parliament sought to cut financial assistance to service users by 10 per cent and, in doing so, to below the non-binding recommendations of the Swiss conference on social welfare. In 2018, the cantonal government's final draft on the cuts in benefits was accepted by a majority in the parliament. In response, a broad social work-led coalition collected enough signatures to hold a referendum on the issue. A social worker member of parliament, the national social work professional association, heads of social welfare agencies and individual social workers were actively involved in the campaign to reject the legislation and indeed played a crucial role in establishing the coalition that led it. These efforts were ultimately successful, and in 2019, the citizens of the Canton of Berne voted against the reduction in social assistance.[1]

A joint struggle in which social workers worked alongside service users in Jerusalem in Israel to prevent cuts in the water supply to low-income households with debts also reflects this type of policy. Following pressure by service users across the city to stop the water utility company from using stoppages in the water supply as a means to pressure clients to cover their debts, the social services established a 'water forum' to bring about change in policy. The forum, which comprised service users, social workers and advocacy organisations, engaged in social action and legislative advocacy over a six-year period to lower the costs of water to low-income families and to curtail cuts in water due to debts (Sirkis and Moskovitz, 2015).

Not surprisingly, given the nature of the social work profession and the social groups with whom social workers work, there is a significant overlap between service users and social workers with regard to the impact of social policies. In other words, policy decisions that improve the well-being of service users will often also have a direct and positive impact on social workers. This is a second type of policy that directly affects both social workers and service users (see the top-left corner of Table 2.1), and given the overlap, it may be that this is the type of policy that is most likely to inspire joint efforts by social workers and service users to engage in policy-related activities.

Thus, social workers engaged in advocating for such policies or seeking to prevent detrimental changes in these types of policies will be not only fulfilling their commitment to social work's social justice goals, but also furthering professional objectives that serve their own interests – status, employment conditions, job options and so on. A dramatic increase in the number of people living in poverty and the retrenchment of resources for social programmes during the Great Recession was the impetus for this type of situation in Spain, and it led to a number of efforts on the part of social workers to influence social policies (Martinez-Román, 2013). Most striking, perhaps, was what Riccardo Guidi (2019: 112) describes as a 'large-scale, innovative and pronounced professional mobilization' of social workers in that country in order to protest against the loss of jobs and budget for social services. The launching of the *Marea Naranja* (Orange Tide) in 2012 brought together social workers, social work educators and service users to engage in a series of public protests intended to prevent the implementation of additional cuts in social spending and the restructuring of local social services (Pastor Seller et al, 2019). In the UK, a turn towards the outsourcing of mental health services, the individualising of treatment through a growing emphasis on the recovery approach and, finally, major cuts in spending on mental health services during the Great Recession led to the mobilisation of social workers by the Social Work Action Network (SWAN), an alliance of social workers, services users, carers, trade unionists and academics (Simpson, 2013; Smith, 2019). A Charter for Mental Health, published by SWAN, served as a tool for campaigners in their diverse efforts to oppose these changes on the national and local levels. One successful result of these efforts was the prevention of the closure of local authority mental health resource centres in Liverpool (Moth and Levalette, 2019). In both of these cases, the policy-related activities of social workers were aimed at achieving policy objectives that would provide more accessible services for service users and, at the same time, ensure jobs and better working conditions for the social worker professionals employed in these services.

One caveat should be mentioned here. While the impetus for social workers to intervene in such policies is clear, the fact that policies directly impact both service users and social workers need not necessarily imply that the direction of the impact will be similar. There may well be cases when policies, or policy changes, will advance service users but not necessarily social workers. The introduction of cash-for-care schemes in the UK from the late 1990s onwards is a good example of this (Ellis, 2007). Although the adoption of direct payments for services for different service user groups had been strongly supported by advocacy organisations representing diverse social groups, it also generated much criticism within the social work profession. Thus, while personalisation enhanced the control by service users over the services provided to them, thus granting them much more choice and autonomy, it also led to a reduction in the number of social workers working with adults and the elderly, and undermined their professional role (Lymbery, 2014). Situations of this type will inevitably lead to difficult choices by social workers with regard to questions as to whether they seek to engage in the policy process and, if so, what the goal of their efforts will be.

A third type of policy will be that which directly impacts social workers but has limited, or only indirect, impact on service users (the top-right corner of Table 2.1). These have been described as 'the promotion of professional self-interest' and were found to be prominent in the policy activities of local branches of the NASW (Brown et al, 2015) in the US. Here, the policies adopted, or advocated for, will be very clearly and obviously focused upon social workers, while the logic of their impact upon service users will typically be opaque. Thus, it will be assumed that if social workers are better trained, enjoy better remuneration or work in better conditions, then they will be able to provide more professional and more accessible services to their clients.

The mobilisation of social workers in South Dakota between 2006 and 2009 to advocate for the establishment of the first masters in social work (MSW) programme in that state is a good example of this type of policy (Peffer Talbot, 2014). Employing a variety of advocacy tactics, including building a broad coalition, lobbying and giving testimony to the state assembly, participating in town meetings, and initiating media coverage, the NASW state chapter managed to successfully bring about the adoption of legislation funding an MSW programme. While the existence of an MSW programme in South Dakota would clearly have the potential to lead to better-trained professionals in the state, the benefit to service users is indirect.

A campaign to prevent the cancellation of Medicare rebates for accredited mental health social workers by Australian social workers organised by the Australian Association of Social Workers (AASW) can be seen in a similar light. Although the campaign to reverse this decision by the Australian government was portrayed by the AASW as an effort to secure access to mental health services by clients, particularly those in rural areas, its ultimate goal was to ensure that the government continued to cover a major part of the cost of mental health interventions provided by social workers who were private practitioners (Mendes et al, 2015). In other words, the decision to cancel the rebates would have had a direct impact on the livelihoods of social work private practitioners providing this service. Indirectly, it would have had a negative impact on service users, in the sense that it would require them to seek help from other professionals, which may have led to less accessible or more expensive services. Not surprisingly, this ultimately successful campaign gained much traction among individual social workers but did not attract many service user participants.

Finally, policies that have only an indirect impact on both social workers and their specific service users may nevertheless lead to social worker policy engagement. Calls for social workers to participate in international efforts to support migrants and refugees are an example of this type of policy engagement. In a publication on global social work, Iain Ferguson, Vasilios Ioakimidis and Michael Lavalette (2018) draw on the long history of social work involvement in addressing the needs of migrants and refugees in order to urge social workers and international social work organisations to support efforts to address the implications of the contemporary refugee crisis. Apart from working with migrants and refugees in their own countries, the authors describe efforts by social workers to join solidarity networks intended to support work with refugees in other countries and to advocate for policies that ensure safe passage for refugees, oppose incarceration, support unaccompanied minors and uphold rights to family unification and to work for adults. A similar call was made by international social work organisations in collaboration with health organisations to engage in activities aimed at ensuring global equitable access to vaccines in the wake of the COVID-19 pandemic (IFSW, 2021). The mobilisation of social workers in these types of campaigns reflects a policy-related commitment that rises above the concrete interests of either their direct service users or the social workers themselves.

The discussion of what types of policies social workers seek to impact requires us to address a related, and often untouched, issue: what we can describe as the 'ethics of policy engagement'. It is, of course, possible to conceive of policies that social workers implement or even seek to advance that are unethical and immoral, and that contradict any reasonable interpretation of the values of the profession. A particularly useful discussion of these can be found in a recent article by Vasilios Ioakimidis and Nicos Trimikliniotis (2020), which relates to the role of social workers in the Nazi regime in Germany, Francoist Spain and the South African apartheid system, alongside the complicity of social workers in the forced assimilation of native populations in colonial societies. Yet, alongside these extreme cases, the moral aspects of social workers' policy engagement are less straightforward than they may sometimes seem. As social policy, and indeed social work practice, is often concerned with the allocation of resources and recognition, as well as with questions of how best to do this and to whom to distribute the resources, there are inevitably losers and winners. Values, contexts and institutional affiliation will play a role in determining the stands adopted by social workers engaging in policy formulation and can, indeed, create ethical dilemmas for social workers. Even if the result does not contradict the values of the professions, it may well lead to the privileging of one group of service users over another, or a certain interpretation of social justice over another. Nevertheless, the underlying assumption in this book is that, broadly speaking, social workers will generally seek to advance policies that align with the values of the profession.

Policy engagement routes

The final section of this chapter focuses on a component of the explanatory framework that is central to this book: the routes by which social workers impact policy. In other words, these are the routes through which social workers choose to respond to problems and policies by engaging in policy formulation. Thus, we can identify not only diversity in the stages, levels, modes and types of policy in which social workers can, and do, intervene, but also rich variation in the routes that social workers choose to take in order to do so.

Our research indicates that it is possible to discern (at least) six possible routes for the policy involvement of social workers (Weiss-Gal, 2017b). As can be seen in Figure 2.1, two of these occur in the civic sphere, with social workers acting as citizens in the formal political process, while an additional four routes are those in which social workers engage as professionals. The civic routes are voluntary political participation and holding elected office (Lane and Pritzker, 2018). The professional routes are: policy practice;

Figure 2.1: Policy routes

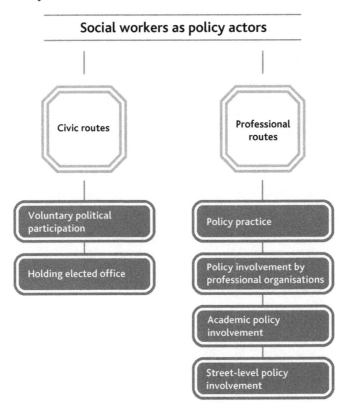

policy involvement by social work organisations, either by proxy or through recruitment networks; academic policy involvement, through university–community partnerships, teaching and/or individual engagement; and street-level policy involvement. The conceptualisation of these routes serves as a map of social workers' policy involvement and a basis for our discussion of the factors that impact the engagement of social workers in policy.

Voluntary political participation

Voluntary civic political participation describes any type of 'activity that has the intent or effect of influencing government action – either directly by affecting the making or implementation of public policy or indirectly by influencing the selection of people who make those policies' (Verba et al, 1995: 38). Social workers engaged in this type of activity do so voluntarily as private citizens and not in their formal capacity as professional social workers. Voluntary political participation can include: voting in elections; engaging in electoral activities, such as campaigning for, or contributing financially to, a candidate or party; undertaking non-electoral activities, such as writing to or talking directly with officials, joining local, national or global social movements, or participating in political meetings or in groups that work on policy problems; and taking part in protest activities, such as sit-ins, marches or demonstrations (Ritter, 2008).

Voluntary political participation exists in the civic sphere beyond the boundaries of the social workers' employment setting. In principle, social workers may thus act with relative autonomy and more or less as they see fit when embarking on this route. However, although undertaken outside their work settings, the degree and form of their voluntary political participation may be affected by government rules and regulations pertaining to the political participation of employees in public and non-profit organisations. The Hatch Act in the US is an example of this (Rocha et al, 2010).

Research shows that social workers engage, to one degree or another, in all the categories of voluntary political participation (Hardina, 1995; Domanski, 1998; Gray et al, 2002). A review of studies undertaken between 1964 and 2015 (Weiss-Gal, 2017b) showed that voluntary political participation by social workers was the topic of 23 studies undertaken in the US, Canada, Australia, New Zealand, South Africa, Egypt and Israel. Most (14) of the studies were undertaken in the US during the 1980s and 1990s. As such, much of the knowledge on the voluntary political participation of social workers relates to the specific US context and is, to a certain degree, dated. In recent years, additional studies on voluntary political participation have been undertaken in the US, Switzerland and Israel (Ostrander et al, 2021; Darawshy et al, 2021).

Studies in the US have found that social workers are more politically active than the general public (Hamilton and Fauri, 2001; Ritter, 2008; Felderhoff et al, 2016). Indeed, in a number of studies, the researchers concluded that approximately 50 per cent of the participants demonstrated high levels of voluntary political participation (Ezell, 1993; Harris Rome and Hoechsteitter, 2010). Cross-national studies have shown that social workers demonstrate distinctive levels of political participation in different countries. For example, a sample of social workers in New Zealand tended to be more politically active than their counterparts in Australia, South Africa (Gray et al, 2002) and Hong Kong, while those in the latter were the least politically active (Chui and Gray, 2004).

Holding elected office

By holding an elected office, whether at the local, county, state or federal level, social workers become formal policy actors and influence the policy formulation process from within (Haynes and Mickelson, 2009; Gwilym, 2017; McLaughlin et al, 2019; Miller et al, 2021; Amann and Kindler, 2021; Binder and Weiss-Gal, 2021; Pence and Kaiser, 2022). As is the case for voluntary political participation, this route is rooted in the notion of democratic citizenship, which encourages members of society to play an active political role. The policy involvement may, but not necessarily, entail remuneration and tends to be more intensive than in the case of voluntary political participation.

Scholars and social work organisations in the US and Canada have encouraged, and indeed sought to prepare, social workers to run for political office, and describe holding such office as a viable career option for social workers (Cummins et al, 2011; Haynes and Mickelson, 2009; Strandberg and Marshall, 1988; Lane et al, 2018; Meehan, 2019; Miller et al, 2021). In the US, the NASW encourages social workers to run for office, explaining that 'social workers are a profession of trained communicators with concrete ideas about how to empower communities. Social workers understand social problems and know human relations, and the commitment to improving the quality of life brings a vital perspective to public decision-making.'[2]

Evidence of the degree to which social workers adopt this route, their reasons for this and how social work values are reflected in their elected roles is limited but has been growing over the last few years. Although there is some data on social workers who run for elected office in a range of partisan and non-partisan bodies, from school boards, to city and county councils, to state legislatures, and to Congress in the US (Leighninger, 2001; Haynes and Mickelson, 2009; Lane and Humphreys, 2011; Miller et al, 2021), Canada (McLaughlin et al, 2019; Greco, 2020), the UK (Gwilym, 2017),

Switzerland (Amann and Kindler, 2021) and Israel (Binder and Weiss-Gal, 2021), this area of research is still in its infancy.

The available studies show that social workers choose to run for office and see this route as a viable career path. For example, Lane and Humphreys (2011) identified 467 social workers who had run for elected office at the federal, state or local level. Of the 270 social workers who participated in their study, half were holding office at the time of the survey, 39 per cent had held office in the past and 10 per cent had run for office but were not elected. The largest group (69 per cent) had been office holders or candidates at the local level, with almost a third (29 per cent) at the state level. McLaughlin and her colleagues (2019) interviewed eight Canadian social workers who were elected in 2015 as representatives of the New Democratic Party to the Alberta provincial legislative assembly. When asked about the reasons for their political engagement, the social workers talked about a combination of factors. They spoke about the contribution of their families in creating their commitment to social justice, public citizenship and involvement in the public sphere. They attributed their transition to politicians to values and knowledge acquired in their social work education, especially a macro or systemic perspective on social problems. They also reported that social work education provided them with the relevant and necessary skills for their work as politicians. An additional factor was a professional environment that supported politics as a career choice.

Policy practice

Policy practice refers to one-off or ongoing intentional professional activities undertaken by social workers, either on their own initiative or that of others, as an integral part of their professional work in diverse fields and types of practice. These activities aim to impact the formulation of new policies, as well as existing policies and suggested changes to them. They can take place on the organisational (Levin et al, 2013), local (Aviv et al, 2021; Gilboa and Weiss-Gal, 2022) or national levels (Weiss-Gal et al, 2020). These activities are sometimes termed 'cause', 'class', 'policy' or 'social advocacy' (Ezell, 2001; Hoefer, 2019a) or 'job-related political advocacy' (Ritter, 2008: 64). In contrast to the two previously mentioned routes, social workers engaging in policy practice do so in their work setting. That is to say, they do not play a voluntary political role, but undertake policy-related activities as professional employees who receive remuneration for it.

Policy practice can be conducted both by social workers whose prime professional task is to deal with policy issues as policy experts and by front-line social workers, be they direct, clinical or community social workers, whose prime professional tasks do not necessarily focus on active engagement in the policy process (Wyers, 1991; Lavee and Cohen, 2019;

Weiss-Gal et al, 2020). In both cases, social workers employ their knowledge and expertise to influence policy. Social workers whose prime professional task is to deal with policy issues may hold positions in government or civil society (Jansson, 2018). In government, such social workers may serve on the staff of a politician, have a major policy formulation role in the civil service or have a designated policy remit within a social service. In civil society, they may have jobs that mainly require engaging in lobbying on behalf of an advocacy organisation or in policy analysis in a think tank or policy centre (Cummins et al, 2011).

Direct, clinical or community social workers engage in policy practice when they integrate policy-change activities into their routine practice (Gal and Weiss-Gal, 2011; Nouman et al, 2019; Weiss-Gal et al, 2020; Gilboa and Weiss-Gal, 2022). Their interactions with service users and communities, and their familiarity with the day-to-day difficulties they encounter, enable the social workers to identify flaws in policies and their implementation, and to engage in on-the-job policy activities aimed to affect these policies (Aviv et al, 2021).

Whatever the position of the social worker, policy practice features a variety of policy activities and strategies that can be incorporated into direct or macro social work practice (Figueira-McDonough, 1993; Rocha, 2007; Gal and Weiss-Gal, 2011; Gewirtz-Meydan et al, 2016; Jansson, 2018; Lavee and Cohen, 2019; Aviv et al, 2021; Saxena and Chandrapal, 2021; Gilboa and Weiss-Gal, 2022). These include: research on and documentation of the social or policy problem and policy analysis; the acquisition of political knowledge and sharing it with service users and other stakeholders; social action (client empowerment, working with community groups to influence policy and organising or participating in coalitions); legislative advocacy (writing to, speaking with or meeting with legislative staff, elected politicians or members of legislature bodies, as well as testifying in legislative committees); working with administrators and officials in local or central government (organising meetings or forums with them, as well as organising meetings between them and people that are affected by the problem); use of the media (blogs and other social media, opinion pieces, and participation in press conferences, radio or television programmes); and judicial policy practice (by which the courts are perceived as a targeted system for change or as avenues for changing another branch of the government or a private organisation).

As social workers who engage in policy practice do so as paid employees, they inevitably represent the organisation that employs them. This necessarily affects the policies they choose to affect and the policy strategies they choose to employ (Gilboa and Weiss-Gal, 2022). Moreover, the levels and types of policy practice activities social workers undertake are affected by regulations and laws that may restrict the political activities of organisations and their employees (Haynes and Mickelson, 2009; Rocha et al, 2010).

In recent years, there has been growing evidence of social workers employed by local government who act as policy entrepreneurs (Lavee and Cohen, 2019). These social workers do not focus on improving the implementation of existing policies or limit themselves to specific ad hoc policy activities. Rather, they are energetic actors engaged in long-term, ongoing and diverse policy activities, working with others in and around policymaking venues, and directing efforts and resources in order to engage in policy change. A study undertaken in Israel showed how these efforts led to the adoption of local policy changes that reflected innovative policy ideas: integrating social considerations into urban planning; incorporating employment policies into local social services; and providing social services for migrant workers (among them, undocumented migrants), despite the lack of central government legitimation or support (Aviv et al, 2021).

Policy involvement by, and through, professional organisations

Social workers may be involved in policy through their professional organisations, which can serve them as proxies or as recruitment networks (Gal and Weiss-Gal, 2013). In policy involvement by proxy, social workers do not engage in policy processes directly, but are involved indirectly through the policy engagement of the professional organisations that represent them. In acting as proxies, the organisations relieve rank-and-file members of the need to be involved directly in the policy process. This is an especially important option for social workers whose place of employment places restrictions on policy-change activities (Weiss-Gal, 2017b).

Studies have shown that professional associations and organisations worldwide are involved in policy-change activities as initiators, leaders or participants in policy-change coalitions, as well as engaged more directly in the political process through the endorsement and financial support of candidates for political office. These organisations undertake their policy-change activities on behalf of, and as proxies for, their social worker members and, in doing so, facilitate more collective efforts to affect policies. For example, the NASW and its state chapters in the US (Scanlon et al, 2006; Talbot and McMillin, 2014), the British Association of Social Workers (BASW) (Payne, 2002; Smith, 2019), SWAN[3] in the UK and in other countries (Jones et al, 2007 [2004]; Moth and Lavalette, 2019), the Italian Consiglio Nazionale Ordine Assistenti Sociali (CNOAS), the Spanish Consejo General del Trabajo Social (CGTS) (Guidi, 2020) and the AASW (Mendes et al, 2015) were all involved in activities aimed to impact policies and were proxies for their members.

When they function as recruitment networks, professional organisations enable social workers to engage more directly in voluntary political activities. For example, using its Social Workers Advocacy list,[4] the NASW encourages its members to vote for and/or donate money to specific candidates, to contact senators and representatives on policy issues, and to participate in social action. Studies show that social work organisations recruit social workers for diverse political actions. A majority of NASW chapters reported that they encourage social workers and students to advocate for or against specific pieces of legislation and organise social workers to testify on specific pieces of legislation (Beimers, 2015).

Academic policy involvement

Academic policy involvement refers to the involvement of social work faculty and students in policy-related activities (Gal and Weiss-Gal, 2017). The literature suggests a number of ways in which this can occur. Two are collaborative. One collaborative form is through university–community partnerships, whether ongoing or ad hoc, which are established by schools of social work to promote policies that further social justice (Sherraden et al, 2002; Kaufman, 2004; Chandler, 2009; Patterson et al, 2014; Strier, 2019). Such collaborations provide students, faculty, members of the community and social workers in the field with opportunities to engage in policy-change processes through research, formulating policy proposals, establishing and serving on committees, participating in legislative advocacy and lobbying, using the media, litigation, and organising groups in the community.

Academic policy involvement can also take a more didactic form. Over the years, scholars have initiated and developed courses in which social work students were required to be involved in policy-change activities in the real world (Heidemann et al, 2011; Weiss-Gal and Savaya, 2012; Ferguson and Smith, 2012; Elmaliach-Mankita et al, 2019). These activities, which include, for example, writing op-eds on policy problems for newspapers (Weiss-Gal and Peled, 2009), enable faculty and students to mutually engage in activities aimed at affecting policies at different levels.

Finally, social work scholars can play policy roles as individuals (Weiss-Gal et al, 2017; Gal and Weiss-Gal, 2017; Weiss-Gal and Gal, 2019a). They can do so by taking part in policy activities, such as organising or serving on policy-related committees, giving press interviews or writing op-eds, or advising advocacy organisations and policymakers. They can also affect policy by conducting relevant research and distributing its findings to stakeholders so that they can form a basis for policy change. Indeed, a study undertaken in Canada showed that practitioners and decision-makers used the findings of social work research more than the findings of research in other social science disciplines (Landry et al, 2001).

A recent quantitative cross-national study (Weiss-Gal and Gal, 2017) that examined the policy practice of social work academics in 12 countries found that social work academics do indeed engage in this type of activity.

The academics were most likely to participate in public, rather than more traditional academic, forms of policy-related activities. Thus, they sought to influence policy more through protest activity, giving press interviews, serving on policy-related committees and engaging in activities aimed at affecting policy in conjunction with social work partners (students, service users and practitioners) than by sending publications to decision-makers, formulating policy papers and serving as policy advisors. Similar findings have emerged in studies undertaken in Canada (Shewell et al, 2021) and in Ethiopia (Baynesagn, 2020).

While the findings of the aforementioned study led us to conclude that the level of engagement in policy on the part of social work scholars in the different countries ranged from low to moderate (Weiss-Gal and Gal, 2017), a comparison with faculty in other helping professions (education and healthcare) in the Israeli case offered a different perspective on this (Weiss-Gal and Gal, 2019b). The members of the three groups reported similar levels of articulating an opinion, which was one of the three forms of policy engagement examined, and similar levels of engagement in all but one of the policy stages examined. However, social work educators were more involved in institutional policy (for example, working directly with policymakers and serving on committees that discussed policy) and in social action (working with students, service users and practitioners, as well as participating in coalitions and protests) than their colleagues. They were also more likely to place social problems on the public agenda than their counterparts in healthcare and in education.

Street-level policy involvement

The last route, termed here 'street-level policy involvement', consists of social workers' involvement in impacting policies through their actions and decisions as front-line practitioners or as mangers of social services who implement policies (Lipsky, 2010; Wyers, 1991; Evans, 2016b; Northdurfter and Hermans, 2018). Social workers and the street-level organisations that employ them are pivotal policy players during the process of policy implementation through producing policy on the ground at the point of service delivery (Gofen, 2014; Trappenburg et al, 2020; Sery and Weiss-Gal, 2021; Tzadiki and Weiss-Gal, 2021).

This is because: the policies that social workers translate into concrete services are frequently ambiguous; social workers can use their discretion to interpret the policies, rules or procedures that they implement; and they often have authority to make decisions on issues of eligibility, access and sanctions (Sery and Weiss-Gal, 2021). The decisions and actions taken on a daily basis by social workers and managers of social services turn them into 'policymakers' who engage in 'direct service policymaking' (Dolgoff,

1981: 285) that affects the actual contents of the policy and types of services that service users receive (Lipsky, 2010; Brodkin, 1997; Maynard–Moody and Portillo, 2010; Virtanen et al, 2018). On the ground, front-line practitioners and managers may interpret policies in a way that strays from their original intention (Gofen, 2014; Schiettecat et al, 2018; Sery and Weiss-Gal, 2021).

Similarities and differences between the policy routes

The six policy routes identified here are similar in their goals, nature and activities, and the skills they require. In all of them, social workers seek to influence policy (whether on an organisational, local, state or federal level) by becoming policy actors, whether in an official (that is, in elected office as policy experts in government agencies) or unofficial capacity (as individual citizens engaged in voluntary political participation or by undertaking policy practice as social workers in advocacy groups). All the routes are political since they involve power relationships, conflict and the struggle over the allocation of resources, public recognition, rights, access, opportunities and status (Haynes and Mickelson, 2009; Reisch and Jani, 2012; Jansson, 2018). Thus, they necessitate an understanding of power and the structure of oppression, which shape the well-being of people and actions that address the root causes of injustice (Simpson and Connor, 2011).

While some of the routes are characterised by unique activities (for example, voting in the case of voluntary political participation), most share a wide spectrum of similar activities. Indeed, social workers can engage in the same activities in different routes. For example, they can contact public officials, work with others on a policy problem, write op-eds or blogs, participate in committees dealing with policy problems, and form groups to solve policy or social problems as private citizens (voluntary political participation), as elected officials, as professionals in their job setting in macro or micro positions (policy practice), as academics, or as part of a social work professional organisation.

Finally, all the six routes require social workers to develop a vision and to draw upon at least four basic skills: analytical (for example, to analyse policies and power relationship, to evaluate social problems, and to develop policy ideas); political (being able to gain and use power); interactional (building personal power and relationships with others); and ethical (the ability to engage in ethical reasoning) (Jansson, 2018).

Alongside these similarities, there are also major differences between the policy routes across five dimensions. The first of them pertains to the sphere in which social workers engage in policy formulation. Voluntary political participation and holding elected office by social workers transpire in the civic sphere. This is a sphere in which citizens exercise their democratic right to participate in determining the direction their society takes by participating in the policy formulation process. This can take the form of engagement in the formal political process or in less formal efforts within civil society or on an individual level. In engaging in policy-related activities in this sphere, citizens are free agents and their actions will primarily reflect their personal values and opinions. By contrast, the other routes of social workers' policy engagement take place in the professional sphere. Here, activities relate more directly to those undertaken by social workers in their capacity as professionals, who are identified as such and are bound to a defined set of professional values and ethics. These can be undertaken by social workers in the context of their workplace or in their affiliation with a professional association.

Clearly, the boundaries between these two spheres are often blurred and are sometimes not easily distinguished. This will be the case when a social worker volunteers to participate after working hours in an effort undertaken by an advocacy organisation to change policies (for example, reform policies relating to domestic violence) that relate directly to the social workers' clients (abused women). In such cases, social workers inevitably bring to bear their social work values, knowledge and professional identity. The cause they choose to further may well have implications for the problems encountered by their service users. However, they will not engage in the activity in a professional capacity and will not be bound by the limitations placed upon individuals engaging in professional activities in the context of their workplace.

The second difference relates to the policy stage in which the policy intervention takes place. Whereas the focus of activities (whether intentional or not) in the case of street-level policy involvement will typically be on the implementation of policies, the other routes for policy engagement will be directed at diverse stages of the policy process. Obviously, in some cases, actions undertaken on the street level will permeate to other levels and lead to changes in the policies themselves. However, this will rarely be the intended aim of the efforts by street-level social workers who engage in discretionary activities seeking to change the ways policies are applied. In other situations, social workers may consciously engage in activities intended to change policies, drawing upon insights from their implementation experience. When this occurs, they will be engaging in another route to policy change, for example, policy practice.

The third difference is the organisational context. When social workers engage in voluntary political participation, seek political office or are recruited by their professional organisation, they act as citizens outside their work setting. When they engage in policy practice, academic policy involvement or street-level policy involvement, they do so as employees within their work setting. The organisational context is crucial due to the restrictions that it entails, the forms of policy involvement that it prescribes and the opportunities that it offers (see Chapter 5). Clearly, social workers engaging in voluntary political participation, holding political office or acting by, and through, professional organisations face relatively fewer legal or organisational restrictions than they do when engaging in policy practice, academic policy involvement or street-level policy involvement as employees. Formal organisations have rules, norms and modes of activity, and certainly in the case of government entities, they are bound by legislation and regulations (Rocha et al, 2010). At the same time, this organisational context can also offer social workers opportunities to impact policies from within or to draw upon their professional power, expertise and the legitimisation that their organisational and professional affiliation confers upon them when seeking to affect policies (Jansson, 2018).

The fourth difference concerns representation. When social workers engage in voluntary policy participation, they express their own views and ideas, and seek to further their personal concerns or interests. As elected officials, they will inevitably speak and act on behalf of their constituencies, while as appointed officials, they are expected to further the common good. As professionals employed in an agency and engaging in policy practice or in street-level policy engagement, their agendas and goals will primarily be a reflection of the aims and interests of that organisation and its service users. Finally, when social work academics engage in policy as formal representatives of their institutions, it is generally incumbent upon them to express views and undertake activities that broadly reflect the perceptions and interests of those institutions. However, the unique nature of academia, as well as the academic freedom and the relative job security enjoyed by scholars, offers possibilities for engagement in the policy process where it is not the institution in which they are employed that they represent, but rather their own individual agendas.

The fifth, and last, difference is in the autonomy that social workers enjoy in deciding whether and how to engage in policy. In the two civic routes and in policy involvement by and through social work organisations, social workers enjoy greater autonomy since they are relatively unimpeded by legal and organisational constraints. In policy practice and street-level policy involvement, social workers have less autonomy since their choices are inevitably affected by the institutional and legal environments. In academic policy involvement, social workers will enjoy greater autonomy when they act as individuals, but this will not be the case when they engage in policy processes through university–community projects or courses.

The social work–social policy nexus: some conclusions

The discussion in this chapter clearly reveals that the social work–social policy nexus offers an expanse in which social workers seek to affect social policy that is wider and more nuanced than is generally assumed. Here, we have depicted diverse facets of the activity in this expanse that are particularly relevant to our efforts to explain the factors that determine this type of activity. In particular, we have sought to elaborate on the stages in the policy process in which social workers are most likely to intervene, on the very diverse policy arenas that can be open to their policy efforts and on the modes and types of policies that will be advocated by social workers. Finally, we sought to describe, and distinguish between, the policy routes that social workers are likely to adopt in their policy efforts. Chapter 3 describes the first of four categories of factors related to the policy-related efforts of social workers (see Figure 1.1). It focuses on the issue of the environments that create the context within which these efforts are (or are not) undertaken.

3

The environments

Introduction

Efforts by social workers to influence policies, regardless of the stage, arena, level, mode and route that is taken to engage in this activity, or the type of policy sought (see Chapter 2), will take place in a specific context. Given that the contexts in which social workers practise differ, it is reasonable to expect that the degree to which they engage in policy-related activities, and the forms that this will take, will also diverge. These contexts can differ between countries, within countries and over time. An initial way of thinking about these contexts is to focus on the environments within which the social problems exist and in which efforts to address them through the adoption of social policies take place. In other words, there is a need to observe the structural, social and professional environments that have a potential impact on decisions by social workers to engage (or not) in the diverse policy routes and the forms that this will take.

In this chapter, we discuss four distinctive environments that have an impact on the policy engagement of social workers. While a cross-national comparative perspective is arguably the best way to understand the impact of environments, the difficulties entailed in employing this type of approach in studying social work and social work practice (Meeuwisse and Swärd, 2007), and, consequently, its limited use in studies (Hämäläinen, 2014), require us to draw upon national case studies as well.

The four environments are: the welfare regime; policies and problems; the profession; and people. The notion advanced here will be that a strong case can be made for claiming that all of these environments have an impact on the six different routes of policy engagement of social workers (see Figure 3.1). This impact is indirect and mediated by way of the three categories of factors described in the following chapters of the book: opportunity, facilitation and motivation. The direction of this impact is not unidirectional, and there is often much overlap between the environments themselves and between other factors that impact social workers' policy involvement. Indeed, given the state of the existing research, it is exceedingly difficult to unravel all their impacts. Nevertheless, the environments clearly contribute to a better understanding of the level and form of the policy engagement of social workers, and each of them offers a crucial context within which this policy engagement emerges.

Figure 3.1: Environments and the PE conceptual framework

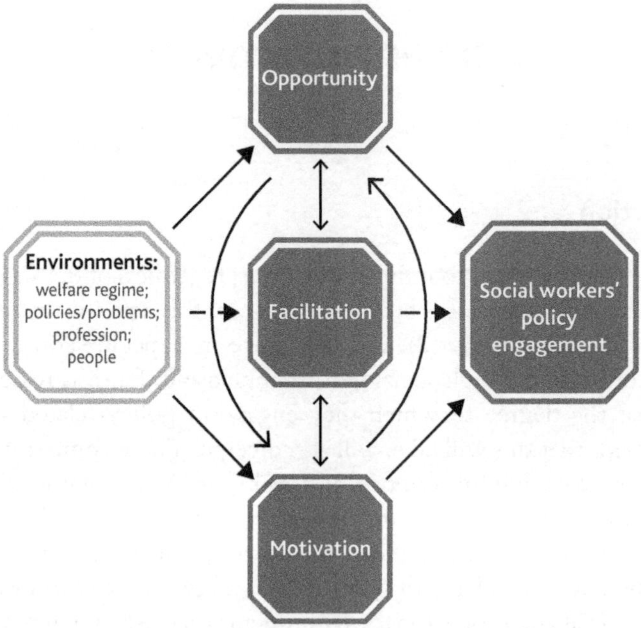

The welfare regime

As the focus of this book is on policies, *the state* – the political body that determines policies, either directly or indirectly – is clearly an obvious place to begin a discussion of the environments affecting the policy engagement of social workers as professionals and as citizens. The state is the formal context within which efforts by social workers to influence policy takes place. That the extraordinary and sustained growth in the social work profession during the last century occurred in tandem with the institutionalisation of social rights in the form of formal state responsibility for addressing social problems through the establishment of social security institutions and social services underscores the relevance of this. Indeed, the recent COVID-19 pandemic reminded us of the crucial role played by the welfare state, as it not only provided health services to tackle the threat of the virus, but crucially alleviated the social and economic implications of the pandemic and its impact on the employment, livelihoods and well-being of people (Béland et al, 2021).

Yet, even prior to the pandemic, the role that states play in addressing social rights was clear. Suffice it to note that social protection is a prime goal of government effort in industrialised societies. On average, these nations devote around a fifth of their resources to providing social protection (OECD, 2020). In the Global South, the spending level is lower (between

7 and 15 per cent on average) but has also been steadily growing (Bastagli et al, 2012). As noted previously, social workers tend to be incorporated within state bureaucracies or in agencies that are either dependent upon the state or, at the very least, regulated by it. In short, the growth of social work is clearly intertwined with the emergence of the welfare state and the transformations that it has undergone.

However, if the state is the context in which social workers' policy efforts are undertaken, making sense of the impact of this context on these policy efforts is complex and often frustrating. Although the process of state intervention with the goal of addressing social problems was a key defining process of the last century and continues during the current century, even a cursory glance at the breadth of this effort, at the form that it takes and at the results achieved by it reveals its cross-national diversity. Within industrialised nations, state social spending ranges from less than 15 per cent to just over 30 per cent (OECD, 2020), with nations differing greatly regarding how they use resources, how social services are organised and who gets what. Moreover, the results of state efforts in the social domain diverge, as is reflected in the levels of poverty and inequality across welfare states. This wide variation makes any attempt to explore the welfare state–social work policy engagement nexus extremely difficult. Moreover, in of themselves, social expenditure levels, which reflect a wide variety of factors, do not offer any plausible explanation for differences in levels or forms of policy engagement on the part of social workers. The search for a link between the welfare state and the policy engagement of social workers requires a broader and more robust perspective of the role of the welfare state.

A prevalent approach to exploring differences between welfare states and their impact on social policy discourse is that of welfare regimes. Moving beyond the funding of social protection and investment, it focuses on the ways in which welfare states actually work. Commonly, the welfare states in advanced liberal democracies have been divided into social-democratic, conservative, liberal and Mediterranean welfare regimes (Esping-Andersen, 1990; Gal, 2010), while scholars have distinguished between informal security and insecurity regimes in the Global South (Gough and Wood, 2004). This approach has also been employed by scholars within social work to distinguish between various models of social work practice across nations (Lorenz, 1994; McDonald et al, 2003; Rush and Keenan, 2014). The welfare regime approach invites us to examine the interface between states, markets and families in welfare provision (the 'regime') in order to seek patterns in the forms that social policy takes in different types of regimes with regard to its underlying goals and the ways in which these are reflected in the logic of social protection systems and social services. These patterns have an obvious impact upon social spending levels and the effect of policy upon social problems and the people affected by them, and this has been reflected in a wealth of studies in recent decades (Ferragina and Seeleib-Kaiser, 2011).

It can be assumed that the structuring of social welfare systems in a nation, the level of spending devoted to social protection and social services, and the effect that these have on the severity of social problems will have an impact not only on citizens and service users, but also on social workers and their engagement in the social policy formulation process. However, the nature of the impact of welfare regimes on the policy engagement of social workers is difficult to unravel. We can assume that a well-integrated social work presence in a highly developed welfare state will contribute to greater involvement by social workers in policy processes due to the central role of social workers in the social welfare services provided by the welfare state, which will, in turn, provide them with greater access to structured decision-making institutions. In this sense, it will offer them with, what we term, 'opportunity' (see Chapter 4). On the other hand, the positioning of social workers in state bureaucracies with rigid hierarchies and procedures may limit the degree to which there is facilitation, meaning support by the workplace for social workers' policy engagement (see Chapter 5). Moreover, in this type of setting, social workers may have a sense that social problems are already being addressed (to a greater or lesser degree of success), and this may inhibit or deter social work efforts to influence policy or, put another way, weaken the motivation (see Chapter 6) of social workers to influence policy.

Alternatively, a lack of strong social protection mechanisms and of a dominant social work presence in social services may both motivate social workers to engage in policy change due to the perceived severity of problems, and facilitate this because social workers affiliated with non-state entities and free of the constraints that state employment entails will be able to engage in policy-related activities in an effort to galvanise support for policies that promote social justice. Yet, the lack of adequate state social welfare systems or of possibilities for employment within these may also weaken the social work presence in a country and effectively limit social workers' access to decision-making arenas, thereby minimising opportunities to influence decision-makers and thus discouraging efforts (motivation) to further policy change.

Scholarly efforts to discern a clear link between welfare regime type and the level of social workers' policy engagement reflect the ambiguous nature of this discussion. In a study of eight different advanced industrial societies that was based on reports by country experts (Gal and Weiss-Gal, 2013), it emerged that in two of the three Mediterranean welfare states included in the study (Israel and Spain), policy practice was clearly present in the professional discourse and, compared to the other cases, policy engagement was relatively high. By contrast, the place of policy engagement in the discourse and practice of social workers in Italy, the third Mediterranean welfare state in the study, was limited. Similarly, policy practice was found to be an integral part of the discourse in all the three liberal welfare states included in our study, though far less prevalent in practice in the UK and in Australia than in the US. In the sole social-democratic welfare state in the study (Sweden), policy practice was found to be minimal in discourse and practice. In Russia, the final nation included in the study, it was very weak.

A second relevant study, which drew upon questionnaires distributed among national experts in ten nations, focused specifically on the velocity of professional debate within social work on social policies adopted in the nations and on the role of professional organisations in promoting that debate within social work (Sicora and Citroni, 2021). Here, the intensity of the debate was strongest in Brazil, Spain and the UK, and weakest in China, Russia and Turkey. The debate on social policy within social work was moderate in its intensity in India, Italy, Portugal and South Africa. While the debate on social policies was stronger in more established welfare states, there are marked differences between them.

What emerges from the limited data that currently exist is that while the welfare state offers a crucial context in which social policy is formulated and implemented, as well as where social workers are often employed, the manner in which this context actually affects the involvement of social workers in the policy formulation process is not clear-cut. The existing data indicate that social worker engagement in policy is more likely in developed welfare states, perhaps due to the opportunities for policy engagement that a larger social protection system (and hence a greater social work presence) creates, but that within them, there is marked variation in the form and level of this. One takeaway from this is that while the complexities of the patterns of interaction between the welfare state and the engagement of social workers in its policies makes cross-national comparisons difficult, these also offer fertile grounds for national studies, as the interaction between welfare state structures and other factors may offer useful insights into the policymaking role of social workers. A second implication is that there is clearly a need to explore other environments if we seek a fuller understanding of the impact of environments on social workers' policy engagement.

Policies and problems

If the relatively stable context of the welfare state does not offer a conclusive explanation for variation in levels and forms of social worker engagement in policy processes, a related context may conceivably do so. Here, the

45

claim is that it is not only the structure or effectiveness of the welfare state that impacts social workers' policy involvement. Rather, it is the severity of social problems and the policies adopted to address them (or vice versa) that will ultimately have an impact on the engagement of social workers in activities aimed to affect policy because this will impact the opportunities that social workers have to play a policy role, the options that the workplace offers them to do so and the degree to which social workers are motivated to impact policy.

The establishment of the Children's Bureau in the US in 1912 – apparently the first governmental office in the world devoted specifically to the welfare of children – reflects the impact of the severity of a social problem on social workers' policy engagement (Combs-Orme, 1988; Lindenmeyer, 1997; Branco, 2019). Growing Progressive Era concerns with the structure of families and the acute impact of poverty upon children and their health (Almgren et al, 2000), as well as intensive lobbying from women's organisations and, in particular, from social workers to address these concerns, led to the decision by the US Congress to create the office. Led by Julia Lathrop and Grace Abbott, and supported by Settlement Movement figures like Jane Addams, the establishment of the Children's Bureau offered social workers a unique opportunity to initiate and impact policies pertaining to maternal and children's health, child labour, and cash assistance to families with children (Lindenmeyer, 1997; Cohen, 2017).

The more contemporary adoption of policies to deal with poverty in Israel also reflects this process. The emergence of poverty as a key social problem followed an unprecedented wave of social protests by people living in poverty across the country in early 1971. Seeking to placate public opinion and to formulate social policies to address issues of poverty and inequality, the government established a wide-ranging commission in July of that year. Since social workers from academia and the field had been actively engaged in policy practice and in voluntary political participation intended to promote anti-poverty policies on the local and national levels in the years prior to the protests and in the protest movement itself (Torczyner, 1972; Kaufman, 2019), poverty was perceived as the professional domain of social work. This was manifested in the decision by policymakers to include social workers in the policy formulation process. The coordinator of the commission was a social worker (then the head of the social security administration) and a number of social work academics, government officials and street-level practitioners were members of the commission (Medzini, 2017). A similar process occurred in the second decade of the new millennium. Growth in poverty levels due to benefit cuts and widespread public criticism of the inability of government to deal with this social problem led to an initiative by the minister of welfare to establish a state commission to formulate a strategy to combat poverty. In this case, social workers and social work academics comprised a quarter of the commission members, and they played a dominant role in the formulation of its recommendations (Gal and Madhala-Brik, 2016). In both these cases, pressure to address the issue of poverty, the degree of the policy engagement of social workers in issues related to poverty prior to the decisions to establish the commissions, the legitimacy enjoyed by the commissions and the timing of the processes provided the opportunity for social workers to contribute to the policy formulation stages of the processes in order to both displace some existing policies with others and to engage in layering through the introduction of new elements in existing anti-poverty policies.

The claim that social problems and the policies adopted to address them have an impact on the engagement of social workers in policy processes has emerged in the social work discourse in the past, particularly in the wake of rising social problems or the threat of policies that are perceived to undermine the capacity of the welfare state to address these. Michael Reisch (2018), for example, has shown how problems (the rediscovery of poverty and racism), the perceived lack of adequate policies to address these and prevalent ideas (the emergence of a radical discourse) in the 1960s in the US led to growing calls for dramatic change in social work policy, practice, education and research in the later years of that decade. A similar process occurred in Australia during the same period of time, in which the perseverance of poverty and a sense that the state was unable to adequately address this led to a decade of policy activism on the part of the Victorian branch of the AASW (Mendes, 2003).

In recent decades, this type of claim linking policies to social workers' readiness to engage in policy activism typically emerged in the discourse around efforts to retrench the welfare state and cut social spending, and the impact of these on social work and service users. In the US, this was most clearly the case during the years of the Reagan administration in the 1980s. The efforts by this administration to implement, what were then described as, New Right policies, which underscored the perceived crisis of the US welfare state and advocated undermining its key elements, sparked a wave of opposition among social work leaders and academics, or, in the terms of the framework described in this book, impacted their motivation to affect policy. These urged their colleagues to engage more in policy-related activities in order to oppose the administration's policies. In an overt effort to motivate social workers to act, Mimi Abramovitz and Tom Hopkins (1983: 574) concluded an article discussing the policies adopted during this period and the social problems arising as a consequence with a vigorous call to arms for social workers: 'the most effective professional response to Reaganomics is to organize against it'.

Some evidence of the impact of the attempts to mobilise social workers to influence the policy arena during this period has emerged. For example, in a comparison of data on the engagement of social workers in various forms of voluntary political participation prior to, and during, the Reagan era in the US, Mark Ezell (1993) found evidence of an increase in this. Similarly, Karen Haynes and James Mickelson (1992: 179) claim that Reagan-era policies and their 'devastating effect on public social services' led to an upsurge in the motivation among social workers to engage in policy, which took the form of an increased recruitment of social workers to advocacy work by professional organisations and a growing willingness by social workers to run for public office.

Yet, efforts to retrench the welfare state during this period did not lead to clearly observable change in the policy-related activities of social work in another context: the UK. Thus, despite a similarly concerted effort to undermine the welfare state in the UK during the Thatcher years, Graeme Simpson (2013) notes that this did not lead to a major increase in the policy engagement of social workers. Indeed, it would appear that after a period of active involvement of social workers in social change during the 1960s and 1970s at both the national and local levels, government efforts during the 1980s to undermine not only the welfare state, but also social work, led to a marked decline in the involvement of social workers in policy-related efforts. In a critical review of social work during the Thatcher years, Chris Jones and Tony Novak (1983: 200) wrote that 'social work's active resistance to the restructuring of the welfare system has been negligible. Instead of offering a sustained opposition to the government's welfare reforms, it would appear that British social work has been overwhelmed and to a large extent routed.' Thus, while the severity of social problems in the US and cuts in social spending during this period led to greater motivation to impact the policy process, the 'bombardment' of social workers within state social services in the UK appears to have significantly undermined their willingness to actively engage in any type of policy efforts. Here, it would appear not only that the motivation of social workers had been dampened by the dominance of neoliberalism in public discourse, but that the weakening of social services significantly reduced the readiness of administrators to facilitate any form of policy engagement by social workers.

More recently, there has been a flurry of studies within the social work literature that have focused on the impact that the Great Recession and, in particular, that the neoliberal-inspired responses to this economic crisis had on social policy, social work and the policy engagement of social workers. The combined impact of the Great Recession and austerity, which defined the policy measures adopted in the wake of this economic crisis, offers fertile ground to explore the role of social problems and policies on the policy engagement of social workers.

The economic crisis that erupted in 2007–08 led to a sharp downturn in economic activity in nations across the world, particularly in developed economies. As a result, gross domestic product (GDP) contracted and unemployment grew in those countries deeply affected by the crisis (Ólafsson and Stefánsson, 2019), which had a devastating impact on the lives of people, particularly those living in poverty. Austerity policies, seen as drawing upon a neoliberal perspective and adopted in diverse welfare states as a response to the crisis, sought to achieve balanced budgets without tax increases by introducing spending cutbacks on social protection, structural reforms and efforts to introduce greater flexibility in labour markets (Taylor-Gooby et al, 2017). Consequently, the disposable incomes of households dropped and poverty levels grew across most welfare states (OECD, 2015).

However, the discourse pertaining to the impact of neoliberalism on social work and the role of social workers in the policy process is characterised by the same ambivalence that emerges when assessing the impact of welfare regimes on social workers' policy engagement. The discussion on the effect of neoliberalism within social work has underscored the dominance of this discourse in welfare states and the impact that the policies that it spawned have had on social protection and social services. Neoliberalism is generally seen to have had a major negative effect on social services, service users and social workers (McDonald and Reisch, 2008; Spolander et al, 2014; Pastor Seller et al, 2019). However, while some social work scholars regard neoliberalism as a trigger for the greater involvement of social workers in policy-related activities, such as social action (Ioakimidis et al, 2014; Pastor Seller et al, 2019) and a greater readiness to seek political office (Gwilym, 2017), others see it as a dampener that severely restrains efforts to engage in policy (Karger and Hernández, 2004).

Roni Strier and Guy Feldman (2018) adopt a more nuanced approach that underscores the contradictory impact of neoliberalism on the policy practice of social workers. They assert that the social problems that neoliberalism has brought in its wake, the pressure on service users that have been generated by individualistic neoliberal policy changes and the sense of alienation that NPM principles have created among the employees of social services have all galvanised social workers and led to innovative efforts to push back against the perceived destructive effects of neoliberalism. At the same time, neoliberalism has created major constraints that limit social workers' policy involvement. The downsizing and restructuring of social services along lines advocated by NPM have not only created a lack of job security and dependency among social workers, but also often redefined their roles in a very limited way that focuses on specific and closely monitored tasks that preclude involvement in policy processes. Moreover, the strong culture of marketisation and, what they call, the 'valorisation of entrepreneurship' has undermined public support for state intervention through social policies and has placed the onus for addressing need on the individual rather than society and its service providers. In short, Strier and Feldman identify two contradictory processes, while the crisis and the neoliberal policies adopted have an impact on the motivation of social workers to engage in policy, they claim that the adoption of NPM within social services has had a detrimental effect on the degree to which these services facilitate social workers' engagement in policy-related activities.

So, do the severity of problems and the nature of policies adopted to address them impact the levels and forms of social worker engagement in policy? In a study focusing on three Mediterranean welfare states (Greece, Portugal and Spain), which were strongly impacted by the crisis and neoliberal austerity measures, Vasilios Ioakimidis, Clara Cruz Santos and Ines Martinez Herrero (2014) find support for, what they describe as, a 'profound (re)politicization' of social work in these countries that includes a greater readiness on the part of social workers to both engage in social action as citizens and to demand more radical stands and actions on the part of professional organisations. While Ioakimidis, Santos and Herrero's study is based on limited empirical data, a study by Enrique Pastor Seller, Carmen Verde Diego and Anna Lima Fernandez (2019), which draws upon two sets of survey data, does offer support for this conclusion, at least in the Spanish case. The authors note that nearly half of the Spanish social workers surveyed participated in social action under the auspices of the CGTS (General Council of Social Work), their representative professional organisation. Engaging in policy through their professional organisations, the social workers participated in demonstrations calling for better social services. Two thirds supported the protest activities initiated by social work organisations in order to protest the neoliberal policies of the government.

By contrast, a more recent study on social work in Greece reaches a different conclusion and indicates that efforts to encourage greater engagement by Greek social workers in policy, particularly more radical activity, have remained marginal and primarily on an academic level (Karagkounis, 2017). Similarly, an examination of social work in two additional nations that suffered significantly from the recession and austerity – Italy and Ireland – does not offer any evidence of a marked increase in the policy engagement of social workers in these nations (Garrett and Bertotti, 2017).

What appears to emerge from this discussion is that social crises, as well as the adoption of policies that undermine social protection and exasperate social problems, can indeed motivate social workers to increase their engagement in policy, particularly in the form of either voluntary political participation, elected office or pressure on professional organisations to adopt more activist positions. However, this appears to be the case in only some of the nations, while in others, efforts to activate social workers appear to have failed dismally.

The profession

Social workers' profession, or rather the legacies, the institutions, the education system, the values and the practices associated with the social work profession, and its societal status can be, and indeed have been, identified as having an impact on the levels and forms that social workers' engagement in policy takes. This is true with regard to their impact on: social workers' motivation to engage in policy change; facilitation, that is, the ways organisations employing social workers regard the place of this engagement; and opportunity, that is, the access that social workers and their professional organisations have to the policy process.

Social work is a global profession and its phenomenal growth during the 20th century and into the current century reflect, among other things, an extended process of cross-national learning of practices and ideas (Healy, 2012). Indeed, there is clear evidence that the social work profession does have a common core that creates similarities between members of this profession across the globe (Weiss, 2005). The profession's commitment to promoting social change and furthering social justice by influencing structures is a key component of that common core. The international definition of social work created jointly by the International Federation of Social Workers and the International Association of Schools of Social Work clearly reflects this (IFSW, 2014). However, alongside the similarities that can be found in various facets of the profession, it is also true that the way in which social work has developed over time in diverse national contexts and the form that it takes differ markedly (Weiss and Welbourne, 2007; Ornellas et al, 2019). Indeed, this is even the case in nations that have common heritages and values (McDonald et al, 2003). The ways in which these differences are manifested in the social work–social policy nexus across countries will be explored in the following.

The assumption here is that differences across nations in the contours of the profession and the degree to which it regards social change as a key role of social work, the inclusion of this goal in processes of professional socialisation and discourse, and the way in which the profession in various nations incorporates the values and tools relevant to policy engagement in them will lead to differences in the motivation of social workers to engage in policy, the forms that this engagement takes and its goals. If social workers hold key administrative positions in social services, then these differences will also be reflected in the degree to which they can facilitate policy engagement among their social worker employees. The diverging degree to which the profession is embedded in a specific society and the level of support that its representative organisations enjoy among social workers will have a similarly divergent impact on both the opportunities that social workers have to impact policy through various routes and the degree to which social workers' engagement in policy is seen as legitimate and should be supported by the profession.

An initial insight into the role of discourse within the profession and it impact on the policy engagement of social workers emerges from a series of studies published in the early 2000s by Mel Gray and her colleagues (Gray et al, 2002; Chui and Gray, 2004). Seeking to understand the levels and forms that the political participation of social workers took in four different countries (Australia, Hong Kong, New Zealand and South Africa), the authors explored a wide range of political activities by employing a questionnaire covering both voluntary political participation, such as voting or contacting government officials on a local or national government problem of personal concern, and policy practice, including making efforts in a professional capacity to influence opinion among co-workers about a policy problem or organising a professional or community group to work on a government policy problem. The findings revealed that, at the time, social workers in New Zealand tended to be more politically active than their counterparts in Australia, South Africa and Hong Kong, and that the latter were the least politically active. While the authors of the studies attributed these differences to diverse structural factors and to dominant political ideologies in the various countries, they also linked them to the specific features of the social work profession in these countries. Notably, in the New Zealand case, the greater tendency on the part of social workers to engage in policy-related activities that stretched beyond voluntary political participation was related to the internal discourse within the profession and a propensity to emphasise structural, rather than individual, causes of distress. More specifically, major motivational elements with regard to policy engagement by social workers are seen to be the extent to which a structural understanding of individual problems and the place of critical perspectives are prominent in the profession, and the extent to which policy engagement is depicted as an integral part of the social work repertoire.

The degree to which social workers do indeed adhere to the values relevant to policy engagement is linked to their professional socialisation. This term is most often employed to describe the ways in which members of a profession internalise its values, beliefs and tools (Sadeghi Avval Shahr et al, 2019), and it has been the subject of scholarly scrutiny and debate within social work over the years (Barretti, 2004; Weiss et al, 2004a; Guy, 2011; Fruend et al, 2017). The assumption is that professional socialisation in social work impacts social work professionals' values, attitudes, knowledge, skills, professional identity and sense of efficacy. This process occurs in the period prior to social work students beginning their studies, then more formally through their education, and afterwards through the practice setting and the professional associations to which professionals are exposed (Weidman et al, 2001; Miller, 2010). As such, professional socialisation can play a crucial role in determining the ways in which social workers relate to policy engagement and its goals during their careers. The degree to which this process is effective and the extent to which the knowledge, values, perspectives and tools relevant to the policy engagement of social workers are embedded in the professional socialisation of social workers can be expected to have a major impact on the motivation to engage in policy (Butler and Coleman, 1997; Saulnier, 2000; Droppa, 2007; Dickinson, 2007; Tower and Hartnett, 2010).

Professional discourse is similarly crucial, in that it indicates the ways in which the social work profession perceives the sources of individual difficulties, as well as its tasks and roles in general and with regard to policy engagement in particular. Thus, the manner in which the written texts and oral communications of the social work profession relate to these issues signals to social workers whether engagement in the social policy formulation process is a legitimate and desirable component in social work practice or is considered deviant, unprofessional, irrelevant or the domain of members of other professions. Clearly, social workers operating in a legitimising professional environment will be more motivated to engage in policy as an integral part of their professional activity than those in contexts where professional signals indicate that this engagement is located outside of the professional endeavour.

The evidence of the impact of professional socialisation in social work on the engagement of social workers in policy is diverse and comes from different sources, relates to different routes of policy engagement and draws upon various methodologies. A literature review on this subject (Weiss-Gal, 2016) indicated that the results of evaluations of training efforts to enhance the policy practice of social workers offer support for this claim. It draws upon some, albeit generally small-scale, empirically based studies that found support for the claim that motivation and intention to engage in various aspects of policy among social work students can be enhanced through the adoption of effective didactic methods and content (Rocha, 2000; Zubrzycki and McArthur, 2004; Anderson and Harris, 2005; Weiss-Gal and Savaya, 2012; Broers, 2018).

The perceived levels of actual involvement in different policy-related activities were also found to have been the outcome of specific educational initiations (Weiss–Gal, 2016; Elmaliach-Mankita et al, 2019). Rocha (2000), for example, found that graduates who had participated in a policy practice course scored significantly higher in practising six of 16 activities, among them, working on a specific change effort and becoming a member of a committee or a coalition, than did graduates who had not. Similarly, research offers support for the claim that professional socialisation in policy engagement can also have an impact on the intention of social work students and indeed of practitioners to engage in voluntary political participation and to consider running for political office in the future (Lane et al, 2018; Witt et al, 2020).

A recent study that employed a pre-/post-test research design to study the impact of a policy advocacy course for bachelor in social work (BSW) students in two schools of social work in Israel offers strong support for the place of social work socialisation. The components of the course were theories and values, skills and strategies, and practical examples, which illustrate that policy change is feasible. The study's finding revealed that the course had indeed enhanced the participants' knowledge about policy practice and political efficacy, which led to an increase in their policy-related skills and, finally, to growth in their motivation to engage in policy practice (Schwartz-Tayri et al, 2020).

An additional facet of the role of the profession in policy engagement by social workers is revealed in a review of social work across nations that explores the degree to which support for policy engagement is incorporated within the professional discourse and the activities of social work representatives. In their comparative work mentioned earlier, Sicora and Citroni (2021) address one aspect of this nexus by examining the extent to which social workers in ten different countries (Italy, Spain, Turkey, Portugal, the UK, Brazil, Russia, India, China and South Africa) participated in a public debate on policy and reform. The findings drew upon the results of the responses by local informants to a series of questions. The focus here was upon the nature and extent of the professional debate on social policy, and the role of professional organisations in promoting that debate. The key finding that emerged from the study is that the more established the social work profession in terms of its historical development and the existence of a formal registration system, the more intense the debate within the profession on social policy and the participation in the public discourse on social policy by social work organisations.

A particularly compelling comparative study on the impact of the profession upon social workers' engagement in policy is that undertaken by Guidi (2020). Struck by the differences in the form and intensity of the response by social workers to the impact of austerity in Spain and in Italy, Guidi focused his study on the role of social work professional organisations and the discourse within them. Distinguishing between an emphasis on the predominant logic of the key professional organisations in the two countries, he notes that the Italian CNOAS was driven primarily by an effort to defend the professional status of social work during this period, reflecting the relatively weak professional status of social work within the country and a perceived need to ensure social work's standing and the rights of its practitioners. Although the CNOAS took a more active public stand during austerity than beforehand, it tended to depend more on activities by the organisation's staff and less upon the recruitment of the membership to engage in policy-related activities. By contrast, the Spanish CGTS focused more on, what Guidi describes as, a 'social justice first logic', which took the form of extensive grass-roots campaigns aimed at protecting public social services against cuts and retrenchment. He links this to a legacy of commitment to the post-Francoist social welfare system established in the 1980s and to the traditional ties between the profession and the Socialist Party that established this system. He concludes that social work professional organisations 'affect the connections between the micro (preferences, motivations, etc.) and the macro (opportunities) levels of social workers' policy practices, but in different ways. The organisation's policy actions, which connect social workers with political and institutional systems, influence the intensity and forms of individual policy practice' (Guidi, 2020: 1053–4).

In our own cross-national volume on the engagement of social workers in policy practice (Gal and Weiss-Gal, 2013), we concluded that the level of policy practice by social workers was apparently highest in the US, Israel and Spain among the countries examined. These three countries are also those (along with Australia) in which policy engagement is most discussed in the professional discourse. It is referred to in codes of ethics, in documents published by professional social work organisations, in the academic literature and in social work education. With regard to the Israeli case, in the last decade, we have seen a dramatic increase in the presence of policy engagement in the literature (see, for example, Feldman, 2019; Nouman and Azaiza, 2021a, 2021b) and education (see, for example, Elmaliach-Mankita et al, 2019), certainly above what was reported by us in 2013, which strengthens the claim. As for Australia, the disconnect between the place of policy engagement in the discourse and an apparently lower level of policy engagement (in comparison with the three other countries) can be attributed to the fact that social work is not a registered profession and membership in the AASW is small. Moreover, the places of employment of many social workers and the past leadership of the AASW were government departments or government-funded agencies, which restricted them from speaking out against government policies (Mendes, 2013).

The findings of these comparative studies enable us to draw some conclusions regarding the link between professional facets of social work and the three categories of factors (motivation, facilitation and opportunity) that impact directly the engagement of social workers in policy formulation. Social workers' motivation to engage in policy and, as a result, their actual policy engagement will be influenced by the degree to which policy issues and the involvement of social workers in them are prevalent within the profession, that is, in its publications, official documents and training systems. As Gray and her co-authors (2002) note, the more key elements within the profession adopt a structural understanding of social problems and regard policy engagement as an integral part of social work's role in addressing these, the more likely that members will seek to act on this. It can be assumed that a more prominent policy discourse in the profession and a greater integration of policy engagement into the professional socialisation process will enable practitioners to feel more secure in intervening in policy processes. In other words, social workers will tend to engage more in the policy process when policy issues are discussed in the discourse, when involvement in efforts to change policies is encouraged in official documents and when the tools to engage in this type of activity are provided in social work training. Similarly, when social workers have managerial roles within the organisations that employ social workers, the prevalence of these sentiments in the professional discourse will encourage them to facilitate the policy engagement of their employees.

Finally, the profession also has an impact upon opportunity. It is likely that social workers and social work organisations will choose to engage more in policy in societies in which social work is a profession that has managed to become more embedded in society over time, has a well-defined professional domain, enjoys greater legitimacy to play a policy role and thus has more opportunities to affect policy. As Sicora and Citroni (2021) note, public recognition of the importance of the profession, a monopoly over fields of practice, greater professional autonomy and a more solid academic standing apparently lead to a sense within the profession that it can, and should, encourage practitioners to engage in this type of practice. In such cases, the social work profession will have a voice in public debate and its positions and that of its members will be perceived as relevant. A word of caution is required here. Even if a professional organisation is strong and enjoys widespread support among professionals, for different reasons, it may decide to limit its participation in policy debates and refrain from encouraging its members to do so. Indeed, there are examples of social work organisations that have preferred to concentrate on more narrow professional issues rather than supporting broader policy engagement (Guidi, 2019).

People: service users and other citizens

Service users are central in defining social work's role in society (Driessens and Lyssens-Danneboom 2022). Yet, although the interface between service users and social workers is essential, it is often complex and, at times, challenging. This is due to the distinctive identities, perspectives and needs that professionals and service users bring to the table, and the implications of these in the meetings between them (Fargion, 2018; Rollins, 2020). This is, of course, the case for diverse aspects of social workers' practice. It is no less the case for their policy engagement as it is for their direct practice. As such, a fuller understanding of the context in which social workers engage in policy requires us to relate to the role that service users and, more generally, citizens play in this.

In the specific case of the policy engagement of social workers, we need to acknowledge that service users are generally the subject of the policies for which social workers advocate. The social work profession exists to address needs through the services that are provided to individuals, families and communities. While these needs are often predefined and the policies to address them are already in place, the policy engagement of social workers is generally (though, as we noted in Chapter 2, not always) about creating policies to address new needs that emerge and about changing policies that already exist because they relate inadequately to needs or have a detrimental impact on service users. The impetus for this commonly emerges from service users themselves. It is their rights that are being undermined, their needs that are not being addressed and they who face adversity, and it is they who are acutely aware of the social problems that require solutions and of the policies that need to be corrected, changed or dismantled (Sherwood-Johnson and Mackay, 2021).

Here, we focus on two aspects of the social worker–service user interface that have direct relevance for the discussion of the context in which the policy engagement of social workers takes place: first, the role that service users play in determining the issues that social workers seek to address; and, second, the understanding that service users are also change agents. Service users often serve as partners to social workers in seeking to effect policy change, inspire them to engage in policy processes and press organisations that employ social workers and policymakers to heed calls by them to change policies (Lavee and Cohen, 2019); in doing so, they influence the form that social workers' policy engagement takes.

Throughout the profession's history (Simon, 1994), service users have always played a role in defining the goals of social workers' policy interventions, and they have often been active participants in efforts to bring about policy change (Sirkis and Moskovitz, 2015). Yet, in the past, the profession typically adopted a top-down approach in its efforts to address individuals' needs and further social justice (Beresford and Croft, 2001). Although this was always less the case in community social work, it was only after the impact of radical social work in the 1970s and the adoption of the notion of user involvement in the 1980s that the contribution of clients, now referred to as 'service users', became central to social work. Parallel to these developments, some of which reflected the growing consumerism of the neoliberal era and the power of social movements, in particular, that of people with disabilities, there was a growing demand within social work that the profession take heed of individual service users and their collective voice (Beresford and Croft, 2004), and incorporate them in the diverse facets of its activity.

The impact of this growing emphasis on the role of service users in social work and the way in which they have become subjects rather than the objects of policy has been observed in teaching and training (Driessens et al, 2016), research (Cossar and Neil, 2015), programme design (Müller and Pihl-Thingvad, 2020) and practice (Krumer-Nevo, 2020). They also play a crucial role in creating the motivation for social workers to engage in policy. This can take different forms. In two studies on the policy practice of community social workers in Israel, we found that most of the policy issues that social workers sought to address were brought to their attention by members of the community (Aviv et al, 2021; Gilboa and Weiss-Gal, 2022). An additional recent example of the role of service users in identifying needs and problems and in bringing about policy change is that of urban renewal in Israel. Lavee, Cohen and Nouman (2019) discuss the ways in which residents of low-income neighbourhoods slated for urban renewal projects pushed the social workers in these communities to initiate policy change in order to safeguard the interests of the residents in the face of gentrification efforts by contractors. A joint effort by social workers and activists, among them residents of the neighbourhoods, led to changes in local policies and eventually to the addition of layers to existing policies that better related to social aspects of the urban renewal process. Examples of the participation of service users and citizens in social workers' policy efforts on a national or regional scale can be found in Spain, when social workers, service users and other citizens collaborated in an effort to prevent austerity measures in the social services (Guidi, 2020), and in the Canton of Bern in Switzerland, when social workers and others successfully mobilised to prevent cuts in social assistance.

The partnering of service users and social workers in policy engagement can also take a more structured form that is intended to overcome the inherent difficulties in efforts by social workers to translate service user knowledge into concrete policy efforts that can lead to policy change (Boone et al, 2019). The preparation of the *General Report on Poverty* in Belgium between 1992 and 1995 was an initial effort to formally incorporate people living in poverty in the formulation of government anti-poverty policies. Yet, while the consultation stage of the process did indeed bring together people living in poverty with social workers and other professionals, their impact on the solutions was limited (Degerickx et al, 2020). In the 2000s, a participatory action research project in Israel sought to achieve similar goals. It brought service users, social workers, academics and bureaucrats together in order to employ bottom-up knowledge to identify lacunae in the benefits system and consider policies to address these. The meetings were recorded and the conclusions submitted to policymakers and the general public (Krumer-Nevo and Barak, 2006).

Environments: some conclusions

Our claim in this chapter is that four environments – the welfare regime, policy and problems, the profession, and people – have an impact on social workers' policy engagement. Clearly, we still do not have sufficient cross-national data to reach definitive conclusions concerning the direct impact of some of the environments, particularly the welfare regime and policies/problems, on this type of social work practice. Nevertheless, it is quite obvious that the impact will be most potent when various environments combine. They will create the context in which the other factors incorporated in the PE conceptual framework come into play. Thus, environments will impact the opportunities that social workers have to play a policy role, the facilitation of this and their motivation to engage in policy.

Developed welfare states, in which the resources devoted to social policies are relatively significant and social workers play a major role in the provision of services, will offer a more accessible setting for the engagement of social workers in policy formulation and provide access to more diverse routes to do so. Social crises and the adoption of social policies that have a detrimental impact upon service users and undercut the services provided by social workers will afford fertile ground for the mobilisation of social workers to influence social policies. In addition, service users, either as individuals in communities or members of organisations, will bring emerging social problems or the limitations of existing policies to the attention of social workers, encouraging them to act and to become partners in policy efforts. In that sense, the welfare regime, the problems and policies, and service users will all have a major impact on the opportunity, facilitation and motivation of social workers to engage in policy.

With this, the velocity of social workers' policy activity and the forms that it takes will depend much on the status of the social work profession, the goals that the profession seeks (being narrowly professional or having a wider social justice focus) and the nature of the policy discourse within professional organisations. The impact of the profession will be on the opportunities that individual social workers and their representative organisations have to impact the policy process, the level of facilitation that will exist in the organisations that employ social workers and the social workers' motivation to impact policy. The more embedded the profession is in society, the more support its representative organisations enjoy among social workers, the greater the emphasis on policy engagement in training and, crucially, the more prominent social policy issues and a structural understanding of these are in the professional discourse, the more likely that social workers will engage in policy.

4

Opportunity

Introduction

Moving from the environments that provide a broad context in which social worker efforts to influence policies take place, this chapter focuses on the first of the three categories of factors that are affected by environments. These three factors – opportunity, facilitation and motivation – directly affect the level and the form of policy engagement by social workers in the different routes (see Figure 4.1). Here, we explore the specific institutions on the national and local levels in which policy is formulated, and the impact that these institutional settings and external events related to them have on the opportunities that social workers have to engage in policy.

We posit that efforts by social workers to affect social policy will inevitably be focused on the social policy formulation process itself and on the relevant institutions at the local, regional, national or international levels in which this takes place. The implication of this is that these policy efforts will only be possible if social workers have access to this process and to the policy institutions in which it transpires. Thus, while the emergence of new social problems, identified by the social workers themselves or by their service users, can lead to efforts by social workers to engage in policy efforts, these will only be possible if the social workers and/or their service users can have access as citizens and/or as professionals, either directly or indirectly, to the institutions in which policy is determined. Even within developed welfare states in which social workers are the implementers of services, the involvement of social workers in policy may be very limited due to a strict distinction between the policy role of elected officials or bureaucrats and the professional role of social workers or other professionals who implement services. To use the terminology we employ here: social workers' policy involvement in the various policy routes is dependent on the *opportunity* that they actually have to affect the policy process (Gal and Weiss-Gal, 2020).

The goal of this chapter, then, is to shed light on the place of institutional opportunities in shaping levels and forms of policy engagement by social workers in the civic and professional policy routes. It seeks to emphasise that a better understanding of the level and form that social workers' policy role takes requires us to consider the opportunities and limitations that enable or impede social workers' access to policy processes and arenas (Rocha et al, 2010). It will also seek to link this discussion on opportunities to both the

Figure 4.1: Opportunity and the PE conceptual framework

facets of the environments that impact it and to the two other categories of factors that impact the policy engagement of social workers, that is, facilitation and motivation.

The discussion draws upon scholarship in the fields of social work, social policy, sociology and political science in order to create a framework to underpin the discussion. We will begin by discussing the notion of opportunity structures as a conceptual foundation for a better understanding of the relevance of the policy setting for the policy engagement of social workers and then draw upon examples from various countries in order to illustrate the ways in which the form of social workers' involvement in national-level policy processes differs across nations. While most of this discussion will focus upon policy and political processes on the national level, towards the end of the chapter, we will turn the spotlight to a discussion of opportunity within the realms of urban and street-level policymaking.

Opportunity structures

A convenient point of departure for this discussion is the commonplace observation that the aim of policy activities by social workers, regardless of the policy level they focus upon, will always be to influence (or to become) formal policy actors, that is, those decision-makers who decide upon policies. These decision-makers have the formal authority to formulate policy because they hold recognised positions of power within the institutions that set policy. It is within these institutions that the policy formulation process takes place and, as such, where social workers who desire to play a role in this process must seek influence. Thus, policy involvement in democratic societies can only be undertaken if social workers as citizens and professionals have, to some degree, access to the institutions (and the policymakers within them) in which policy is discussed, formulated and decided upon. As we will see in the final section of this chapter, opportunities also emerge in cases in which formal decision-makers devolve the policymaking process to street-level professionals by enabling them to enjoy differing degrees of discretion during implementation. In doing so, they afford street-level opportunities to social workers, which enables them to become de facto policymakers.

A useful framework for conceptualising both the process through which social workers make efforts to affect policy and the context in which this generally takes place is to draw upon the discourse concerning opportunity structures. This is because for policy actors who are not an integral or formal component of the policy formulation process, exerting influence over this process generally[1] requires access to it.

The notion of opportunity structures offers a way to think about this. This notion originally emerged to enable scholars to identify the circumstances under which social movements manage to mobilise support, place matters on the public agenda, access the policy process and bring about political or policy change despite the fact that they are not an integral part of the political system (Kriesi, 2004). Based on an analysis of historical and contemporary case studies, the core conclusion of this scholarship is that the policy-related activities of these movements are dependent on a specific political context and, no less important, the rules of the game, or, in other words, the institutional context in which policy is formulated. As David Meyer and Debra Minkoff (2004: 1458) note: 'The basic premise is that exogenous factors enhance or inhibit prospects for mobilization, for particular sorts of claims to be advanced rather than others, for particular strategies of influence to be exercised, and for movements to affect mainstream institutional politics and policy.'

Although originating in the social movement discourse and often pertaining to political behaviour external to the formal policy process (such as protest activity), in recent years, the concept of opportunity structures has been applied in other fields. It has moved from mobilisation and movements, to mainstream policy-related activities and individuals. Thus, the concept has been employed to describe the factors affecting the impact of political actors on environmental policy in a small city (Stevenson and Greenberg, 2000), the integration of feminists into the political establishment in Australia (Chappell, 2002), the furthering of feminist policy in Israel (Herbst and Benjamin, 2012), the career development of politicians in the European Union (Borchet, 2011), the integration of immigrants in politics in Portugal (Oliveira and Carvalhais, 2016), the possibilities of achieving transnational justice (Orjuela, 2018), the policy advocacy efforts of non-profits (MacIndoe and Beaton, 2019), and the non-electoral political participation of individuals in a cross-national comparative perspective (Vráblíková, 2014). Common to all these diverse studies is the conclusion that 'to participate, individuals and social/political groups need open political opportunities' (Vráblíková, 2014: 271).

Returning to policy engagement by social workers, the opportunity structures approach accentuates the recognition that this is not only associated with the impact of economic and social conditions in a specific society (see Chapter 3), the readiness of their workplaces to enable such engagement (see Chapter 5), and the desire or motivation of social workers to influence policy (see Chapter 6). Rather, diverse factors also determine social workers' opportunities to access the policy formulation process and the readiness of policymakers to give them a place and voice in this process.

Jennifer Mosley (2013) skillfully employed the notion of opportunity structures to underscore the impact of the growth in government contracting and collaborative governance in the US as a structural opportunity that increased the possibilities for policy advocacy by social workers in human service non-profits. Similarly, in their efforts to create a conceptual framework for understanding social workers' participation in protests organised by marginalised groups, Håvard Aaslund and Charles Chear (2020) also draw on the idea of political opportunities.

The variables that have emerged in the wide-ranging research on opportunity structures are numerous (for a political variables, see Meyer and Minkoff, 2004: 1468). Clearly, not all of them are relevant to efforts by social work professionals to affect social welfare policy. Nevertheless, it appears that both distinctively institutional and more temporal factors can play a role in determining the accessibility of social workers to the policy process. These two types of factors are discussed in the following.

Institutions and policy engagement

A better understanding of the policy setting within which social workers seek to become policy actors and its openness to their involvement in the policy process is critical in order to explain both the degree to which social workers engage in policy and the specific ways in which this is undertaken. An initial step in better understanding the opportunity structures relevant to social workers' efforts to influence policy is to clarify what policy institutions are and why they are important.

The recognition that institutions are crucial elements in the policy process in any society (and certainly in a democratic society) has always existed in the political and policy sciences (Eisenstadt, 1968; Polsby, 1968). However, it is only in recent decades that the discourse moved from an understanding of policy institutions as a neutral site in which the policy process takes place, to the realisation that institutions in and of themselves have an impact on policy (Goodin, 1996; Pierson and Skocpol, 2002; Weingast, 2002). In an effort to underscore the ways in which these institutions actually influence the policy process, this more recent body of knowledge, termed 'neo-institutionalism', offers a definition of institutions that focuses primarily on structures, procedures and rules, and endeavours to better understand how they change and what their impact on policies is.

The point of departure for the vast body of neo-institutional literature is, put simply, that institutions matter. They matter because, as James March and Johan Olsen (2008: 4) note, political institutions 'are not simply equilibrium contracts among self-seeking, calculating individual actors or arenas for contending social forces. They are collections of structures, rules, and standard operating procedures that have a partly autonomous role in political life.' In other words, the way institutions work and the forms that they take have an independent influence on the outcomes – the policies – that emerge from them.

Central to this discourse on political institutions is the insight that these are structures, comprising rules and procedures, which have the legitimacy to engage in the policy formulation process (Blondel, 2008). More formally, an institution is defined as 'a relatively enduring collection of rules and organized practices, embedded in structures of meaning and resources that are relatively invariant in the face of turnover of individuals and relatively resilient to the idiosyncratic preferences and expectations of individuals and changing external circumstances' (March and Olsen, 2008: 1). The rules, practices and narratives that comprise an institution constrain and frame the actions within them that are undertaken by formal and informal policy actors (Lowndes and Roberts, 2013). As such, these rules and practices play a major role in determining policy processes and outcomes. Thus, for example, policy change that requires legislation will be influenced by the nature of the legislative process. This process will be affected by the veto power of parliamentary committees, the impact of parliamentary rules (such as the use of a filibuster), the structure of the parliament and whether it is unicameral or bicameral, and if its decisions require ratification by referenda or sub-national legislatures. The structure of policymaking within the state bureaucracy and the norms that govern this process can also be crucial. For example, it will depend much on whether there is an external consultation process or if the use of formal advisory committees is common. Similarly, the nature of the content of policy decisions will be influenced by the degree to which the judicial system is likely to intervene in the policy process.

The policy institutions identified in the social work literature as important arenas for policy-related activities (Haynes and Mickelson, 2009; Weiss-Gal and Gal, 2014) have all been the subject of studies adopting a neo-institutional perspective. These include the legislature (Blomgren and Rozenberg, 2012; Auel and Christiansen, 2015; Papp and Russo, 2018), the judicial system (Easterly, 2016; Lindquist, 2017), the executive branch (Madama, 2013) and local government (Davies and Trounstine, 2012). Close examination of the workings of these institutions over time reveals the factors that lead to institutional change and the ways in which the structure and internal workings of institutions at a given period in time influence the policy formulation process and the results of this process. This literature is particularly useful, therefore, in that it emphasises the impact of the rules and procedures that comprise these institutions on the policy process, on policy actors and on the ways in which they determine policy outcomes.

In the case of social workers seeking to influence policies, the neo-institutionalist discourse is enlightening, in that it underscores the role of the rules of the game in determining their participation (and that of other policy actors) in this process. As part of this discourse, scholars have explored the access of members of professional groups, particularly economists, to the policy process (Weir and Skocpol, 1985; Christiansen, 2017; Mandelkeren, 2019). Yet, this literature does not say much about the ways in which the rules that comprise the policy formulation process affect its openness to the participation of policy actors, in this case, social workers.

Clearly, the nature of the policy process within institutions will be critical if we seek to better understand the levels of social workers' policy engagement, the strategies that they employ, the modes and types of policy that they seek to further, and the policy routes that they adopt. The importance of institutions in determining the levels and strategies of the policy engagement of social workers can be illustrated in the following examples.

Lobbying is a dominant strategy through which policy change is advanced in the US. The employment of this form of political behaviour is an accepted and very common feature of policymaking institutions, both elected and appointed, within that country, from the local to the federal levels. Indeed, while lobbying is undoubtedly a facet of policy processes in other liberal democracies (Coen and Richardson, 2009; Halpin and Warhurst, 2016), it is arguably most prominent and formally entrenched in the US (Godwin et al, 2013). This reflects specific institutional facets of the pluralist US political system, not least its presidential system that undermines the role of parties, and an electoral system that necessitates members of legislatures on the state and federal levels to compete in relatively small districts and requires significant resources (Berry, 1984; Baumgartner et al, 2009). As a result, lobbying is an accepted (if often criticised) and strongly regulated component of the policymaking process (Browne, 1998; Chari et al, 2007; Schlozman, 2010). Indeed, interest groups and their lobbyists play an outsized and ever-growing role in the formulation of policy on all levels in the US.

As such, like other public interest and professional groups in the US context, within social work, lobbying or legislative advocacy are central avenues for seeking policy impact. Access for social workers to the social policy formulation process in the US requires them to adhere to the rules of the game and engage in lobbying. Indeed, much attention has been devoted to lobbying for social change in the policy engagement literature in social work in the US (Richan, 2006; Haynes and Mickelson, 2009; Taliaferro and Ruggiano, 2013; Jansson, 2018). As social workers in the US welfare state tend to be employed in non-profits (Mosley, 2013), this type of policy engagement is typically undertaken at the federal, state and local levels either by social workers engaging in policy practice on behalf of the non-profits in which they are employed or by the NASW, social work's representative professional organisation (a route that we term 'involvement by or through professional organisations') (Hartnett et al, 2005; Hoefer, 2013; Beimers, 2015). The role of the profession through its representative organisations is critical here. Indeed, the NASW devotes major resources to its lobbying effort, both by employing professional lobbyists on the federal level and by encouraging its members to play an active role in lobbying.[2] Although the lobbying often focuses on efforts to further policies that serve social workers' direct interests (such as licensing or funding issues), it also relates to policies that affect service users (such as voting rights, abortion and cash benefits).

While social workers in other welfare states also avail themselves of lobbying as a mean of furthering policy, typically by way of their representative organisations (Mendes et al, 2015), the contours of the policy process in those nations, as well as the institutional constraints and opportunities that derive from these, often lead to other forms of policy engagement. In the UK, in other countries (primarily those with similar parliamentary systems) and indeed in the European Union, formal and informal consultations with external actors comprise an integral part of the policy process and can thus provide access into the policy formulation process for social work professionals (Smith, 1982; Kerley and Starr, 2000; Fraussen et al, 2020).

Thus, for example, green papers, which are preliminary reports of government policy intentions introduced in the UK in 1967 (Silkin, 1973), offer interested parties a structured opportunity to relate to government policy discussions in their early stages and to have a potential impact on the eventual policy. While these documents may clearly have other political goals (Wiggan, 2012) and the actual impact of the organisations, communities and individuals participating in the consultation processes has been questioned (Polsby, 2001), they do offer such external actors an opportunity to join the policy process.

As such, social workers in the UK tend to participate in the consultation processes leading to green papers in the context of professional or civil society organisations, either as representatives of providers or on an individual basis. They do so particularly when the policy in question pertains directly to social workers' professional roles in social services. Here, again, it is primarily through the route of policy engagement by and through professional organisations, such as the BASW, and organisations representing the administrators of social services, such as the Association of Directors of Adult Social Services in England and Social Work Scotland, that social workers play a policy role. An interesting and extensive example of this is the role of social workers in the policy process that emerged following the death of 'Baby P' (Peter Connelly) and the undertaking of an inquiry into that tragic incident (Jones, 2014). This incident shed light on the limitations of the child protection system and, more broadly, on the needs of vulnerable children, and it led to a policy process that centred on an independent review of the child protection system headed by social work academic Eileen Munro (2011). It also led to the establishment of the Social Work Reform Board in 2010 and a process of consultation with organisations and individuals from both within social work and outside the profession concerning the reform of social work across adult and children's services (Simpson, 2013). This is a clear case of social workers engaging in a process of formulating policy that affected both service users and professionals.

In Israel, the notion of opportunity structure and its influence on policy practice by social workers is manifested in social workers' participation in legislative committees in the Knesset, the Israeli national parliament. Legislative committees in legislatures and parliaments across the world comprise a major component of the policy process, typically playing both legislative and oversight roles (Jann and Wegrich, 2007; McAllister and Stirbu, 2007; Helboe Pedersen et al, 2015). In multiparty settings, such as Israel, in which coalition governments are the norm and parliaments provide committees and their chairs with the capacity to initiate or block legislation or to engage in sufficient oversight, this is likely to be even more expected (Strøm, 1998; Kim and Loewenberg, 2005). Legislative committees in the Knesset comprise a major component in the policy process, and they have a significant degree of impact in both their legislative and their oversight roles (Friedberg and Hazan, 2009; Friedberg, 2011; Rosenthal, 2018).

A combination of factors makes the committees appealing policy arenas and creates opportunity structures for interventions into the policy process. The relative accessibility of a unicameral parliament in a small country with a highly centralised political system combines with a deliberate effort by the Knesset administration to open the deliberations of committees to non-traditional policy actors (Rubinstein and Medina, 2005). The committee meetings are broadcast and, apart from some exceptions, their deliberations are open to the public. Moreover, there is a liberal approach to the participation of non-Knesset members in the committee discussions. Knesset by-laws enable committees to invite ministers and state officials to testify before them in deliberations touching upon their fields of activity and jurisdiction. While not required specifically by law, the participation of experts and other interested parties in the deliberations of Knesset committees is also the norm, and their participation has become one of the rules of the political game. These typically include professionals, representatives of advocacy organisations and interest groups, and citizens.

Studies indicate that these institutional norms do indeed motivate Israeli social workers to participate in parliamentary committees at a level that is apparently unusual in welfare states (Gal and Weiss-Gal, 2011; Bochel and Berthier, 2020). This is a useful example of the ways in which social workers can affect policy through policy practice, academic policy involvement or professional organisations. Quantitative and qualitative analyses of the levels and forms of participation by social workers in these committees over a seven-year period (1999–2006) (Gal and Weiss-Gal, 2011) reveal that social workers participated in 14 per cent of the deliberations of parliamentary committees engaged in social policy issues. Most of the participation was in five of the committees: four permanent and one temporary. Social workers participated in over a third of all the committee meetings in three of these committees. In three other committees, social workers were present in over half of all the meetings.

Social workers employed by the state were those most likely to participate in the committee discussions (58 per cent of the social worker participants). Most were high- or intermediate-level civil servants in the Ministry of Welfare and Social Services. They included heads of departments, regional directors and inspectors. However, just over a quarter (28 per cent) of the social work participants were street-level professionals from local social welfare services. Most of the remainder represented non-profits, primarily advocacy and professional organisations.

Analyses of the role played by the social worker participants revealed that social workers tended to primarily facilitate and enrich the social policy formulation process (Weiss-Gal and Gal, 2014; Weiss-Gal and Nouman, 2016). Social workers, particularly those employed by advocacy organisations, also challenged policymakers and placed matters on the agendas of the committees. The affiliations of the social worker participants in these committees, the manner in which their participation emerged and the role that they played in the committee deliberations all shed light on why this path to engaging in policy is significant in the Israeli context and how it created opportunity structures that encouraged social workers' participation in the policy process.

An additional insight as to the way in which this opportunity structure worked is revealed in findings on who initiated social workers' participation in legislative committee meetings (Lustig-Gants and Weiss-Gal, 2015). Crucially, it was often institutional representatives that reached out to social workers rather than a case of social workers seeking to overcome barriers in order to access the policy process. Nearly half of the first appearances by social workers in the committees were responses to invitations by the committee administrator, either directly to the social worker or indirectly to the agency where they worked. Somewhat over two fifths of the first appearances were initiated by the agency and about a tenth by the social workers themselves. This is particularly the case for social workers employed by central or local government and is an example of how the existence of opportunity structures can contribute to, what we call, 'facilitation'. Thus, the possibility to participate in parliamentary committee meetings and efforts to reach out by the committees encourage the leaderships of state and local government organisations to facilitate the participation of their social employees in the policy process.

The expectation emerging from the bodies of knowledge described earlier is that opportunity structures within policymaking institutions will influence the forms that social workers' policy engagement will take. An understanding of the rules and modes of operation of policymaking institutions, particularly those determining access to these, sheds light on the policy involvement of social workers.

Problem windows and policy windows

A major critique of the neo-institutional perspective is that an emphasis on institutions is inherently conservative. In other words, stressing the impact of institutions on policy tends to overstate the capacity of these institutions to maintain the status quo and to resist efforts to introduce change in existing policies (Béland, 2009). Additional factors can, and do, provide opportunities to impact policies and affect the institutions in which social policy is formulated. Indeed, in the context of this discussion, it would be foolhardy to focus solely on the accessibility that the features of policy institutions afford social workers seeking to influence policy without considering that these institutions and their accessibility are subject to additional developments that can create opportunities for social workers and, as such, have a major impact upon the degree to which the institutions are receptive to social worker policy actors.

These developments, either external or internal to the policymaking system, can be described as temporal opportunity variables that create opportunity structures for social worker engagement in policy. We draw here on two concepts formulated by political scientist John Kingdon (2003) in his multiple streams approach to policy formulation. We employ them to describe variables that affect the context of opportunity structures for social workers seeking to impact policy.

One type of these are problem windows. These are developments in society or the emergence of social problems that open windows of opportunity because policymakers are convinced that they need to establish policies and institutions to address these problems. Policy developments following the COVID-19 pandemic are a recent example of this type of problem window (Ladi and Tsarouhas, 2020; Schmidt, 2020). As we noted in detail in Chapter 3, these problems can, in turn, also have a major impact upon the degree of openness of the policy process to social workers. Thus, in 1912, the US Congress took the unusual step of establishing the first government agency devoted to children. This reflected growing concern with the welfare and health of children living in poverty, and the risks that they faced. These concerns were underscored by research undertaken by social workers and the publication of Lewis Hine's stark photographs of child labour (Freedman, 1994), and, together with intensive lobbying efforts by social work leaders, eventually convinced Presidents Theodore Roosevelt and William Tuft of the necessity of addressing this social issue by establishing the Children's Bureau (Branco, 2019). In Israel, public concerns about poverty that resulted in widescale protest and galvanised public opinion led to the creation of windows of opportunity for the policy engagement of social workers in the early 1970s and the middle of the second decade of the 2000s. In both cases, government policymakers established commissions to formulate policies to combat policy in which social workers played a significant role, primarily because poverty was perceived as the profession's domain of expertise.

Another form that these variables can take are developments in the political arena. These are what Kingdon (2003) called 'policy windows'. Changes in the political map following elections or due to changes within legislative bodies may bring to power political forces and politicians with which social workers are aligned or affiliated, or, at the very least, who are more responsive to policy alternatives supported by social workers. An example of this is the integration of social workers in the policy process on the national, regional and local levels during the democratisation process in Spain following the end of the Francoist regime. The long-time affiliation of social workers with the Partido Socialista Obrero Español (PSOE) – the Spanish Socialist Party that formed the government in 1982 shortly after the return of democracy to Spain – led to significant involvement on the part of social workers in the formulation of social policies during the initial years of this administration. Thus, in Cataluña, social workers linked to the Socialist Party in Catalonia actively participated in the design of a proposal for public social services.

The adoption of the 1996 Social Worker's Law by Israel's parliament reflects the employment of the representative organisations route by social workers to further a policy that served their direct interest and indirectly affected service users. This piece of legislation not only offered a legal definition of the term 'social worker', but also sought to proffer a degree of protection to the profession in the face of encroachment onto its fields of activity (Doron, 2012). The law was the culmination of a long-term effort by the Israeli Social Workers Association to deflect entry by members of other professions into traditional social work domains and the employment of professionals from other fields in leadership positions in the social services (Goldstein and Rosner, 2000). Favourable political circumstances – the election of a left-leaning government and the fact that, at the time, both the minister of labour and welfare and the chair of the Parliamentary Committee on Social Welfare, Labor and Health were supportive of social work – offered the social work profession a unique window of opportunity to pass the piece of legislation.

In order to address concerns regarding leadership positions, the law granted the minister of welfare and social services discretion to determine the administrative positions protected for social workers. In 2001, a list of all managerial-level positions in local social services and virtually all the senior administrative positions in the Ministry of Welfare and Social Services was incorporated into the law (Weiss et al, 2004b), thereby ensuring that only accredited social workers could fill these positions. This decision had knock-on effects, in that it created important opportunity structures for social workers seeking to play a policy role, both within the Ministry of Welfare and Social Services and outside of it. It not only led to social workers filling most of the policymaking positions in the social welfare field, but also offered access to the policy process to additional social workers.

Personal changes in political leadership can also be a factor in the emergence of opportunity structures that facilitate social worker engagement in the policy process (Kingdon, 2003). A useful example of this is the major contribution of social work 'New Dealers' to the formulation of social policy in the US during the 1930s and 1940s (Trattner, 1984). Two of the most prominent social workers who played crucial leadership roles during the

Roosevelt administration were Frances Perkins, who served as secretary of labour between 1933 and 1945 (Burnier, 2008), and Harry Hopkins, who headed major New Deal agencies, such as the Federal Emergency Relief Administration and the Works Projects Administration (Hopkins, 1999). Both Perkins and Hopkins had been important policy actors in New York prior to their appointment to positions in the federal government. After advocating for labour legislation as head of the New York City Consumers League and serving on the New York Industrial Commission under Governor Al Smith, Perkins was appointed by the newly elected governor of New York, Franklin D. Roosevelt, to serve as the state's industrial commissioner in 1928 (Martin, 1976).

Hopkins was involved in advocacy and administration for the Association for Improving the Condition of the Poor and other charities in New York before serving as head of the Temporary Emergency Relief Administration in the state in the early years of the Depression under Roosevelt (Adams, 1977). As New York governor, Franklin D. Roosevelt was keenly aware of the capabilities of Perkins and Hopkins. Indeed, during her term of office in Albany, Perkins had grown close to the Roosevelts and often stayed at their home while at Albany, the state capital. She was also actively involved in Roosevelt's campaigns for both governor and president (Perkins, 1946). Although Hopkins was much less personally acquainted with Roosevelt during this period, he had also actively campaigned on Roosevelt's behalf. Perkins, by contrast, knew Hopkins well and admired his work. Following his election as president, Roosevelt recruited Perkins and Hopkins (at Perkins' suggestion) to his new administration. While New Deal policies were often criticised by social workers at the time, the terms in office of Perkins and Hopkins not only led to the adoption of significant social policies, but also had a knock-on effect and created opportunities for additional social workers to hold key positions in the Roosevelt administration and have a direct influence on policymaking (Fox Schwartz, 1973).

Opportunity at the local level

Opportunities that provide access to policy for social workers exist not only on the national level, but, we contend, also on the local level, primarily within the decision-making bodies that engage in policy formulation within local government. Exploring the impact of opportunity on the local level offers exciting insights into the policy role of social workers. One obvious facet of this is the access afforded to social workers who hold political office on the local level and, as a result, become formal policymakers. As we noted in Chapter 2, the literature indicates that this civic route is one that is opted for by social workers in different countries.

More generally, opportunities on the local level can be understood by employing similar theoretical tools to those used to identify opportunities on the national level to an analysis of policymaking within local government. Efforts by scholars to incorporate neo-institutionalism into studies on local-level politics and governance have been central to the study of urban politics in recent decades (Davies and Trounstine, 2012). Particularly useful in this context is the way in which Vivien Lowndes, Lawrence Pratchett and Gerry Stoker (2006) draw upon the term 'rules-in-use' (coined by Elinor Ostrom [1999]) to describe how access to the policy process in local government is determined: 'These are the specific combination of formal and informal institutions that influences participation in a locality, through shaping the behaviour of politicians, public managers, community leaders and citizens themselves' (Lowndes et al, 2006: 542).

One fruitful avenue in our quest to uncover the role of opportunity in the policy engagement of social workers can be found in studies that focus on policy entrepreneurs, that is, those individuals or small groups of social workers who engage in long-term processes to bring about policy change. While most social workers engaged in policy will not be policy entrepreneurs, these cases offer rich insights that have relevance to other social workers seeking to impact local policies.

The burgeoning research on local policy entrepreneurs, particularly social workers, who engage in policy practice within the local authorities in which they are employed underscores the importance of local-level opportunity structures for the policy practice of social workers. It shows how social work professionals who are highly motivated to further policy change and have the tenacity and commitment to engage in drawn-out struggles can succeed in achieving policy goals (Cohen, 2021; Zhang et al, 2021). Given the fact that they often lack the political power or formal status usually associated with policy formulation, a key quality of social work policy entrepreneurs is their capacity to understand the bureaucratic context and the needs of actors within it, their talent to work with others to achieve their goals, and, crucially, their ability to identify opportunities to further their agenda (Frisch-Aviram et al, 2018).

The impact of opportunities emerged in case studies looking at the activities of social worker policy entrepreneurs in different policy fields in Israel (urban renewal, employment services for lone parents and social services for refugees). We found that these social workers did indeed manage to bring about the adoption of new policies in three different local authorities. Although these policy formulation efforts took a long time and entailed much effort by the social workers, they ultimately succeeded in gaining the explicit agreement of the mayors in each of the municipalities to adopt the policy changes they advocated. The social workers in each of the cases enjoyed the readiness of management to facilitate their policy engagement.

The social workers all availed themselves of opportunities to participate in local government policy arenas, beyond the confines of the social services in which they were employed, in order to further their policy goals. This was enabled by: the relatively lax and informal rules-in-use determining access to decision-makers and to decision-making forums for employees within the local authorities; the less-than-rigid hierarchical structure of urban government; the capacity of committee chairs within the city council to invite relevant parties to their deliberations; and the readiness of elected and non-elected officials to meet formally and informally with either social workers employed by the local authority or the services users with whom they worked.

Social workers can also impact local opportunities and not only be impacted by them. The policy practice described earlier was a long process (between three and ten years in these cases). Gaining access to relevant arenas and thus availing themselves of the opportunities to participate in policy formulation processes entailed lengthy struggles and turf battles on the part of the social workers that necessitated processes of softening up opposition within the local bureaucracies. One reason for the initial lack of accessibility derived from disagreement over the role of social workers in domains and in policy processes not directly and obviously linked to the provision of social services. Thus, for example, social workers in Israel seeking to incorporate social considerations into urban renewal processes were initially rebuffed because this was perceived as the domain of urban planners. The refusal to incorporate social workers into these arenas was often embedded in a conflict over the place of social considerations in processes generally considered the domain of other professionals (Aviv et al, 2021). Framing the policy goals as being congruous with those of local government was a tactic employed by the social workers to help overcome this opposition, manipulate the rules and create local opportunity structures for them.

This strategy entailing the exploitation of the opportunity structures that existed to gain access to the institutions that determined policy or, in lieu of this, the creation of new forums to contribute to this process was often employed by the social workers. They exploited the existing 'rules-in-use' to enable them to participate in the formulation of policy. One way to do this was to establish close working relationships with other local professional groups within the corridors of power and, through these ties, to gain access to the policy process in an unfamiliar domain. Thus, in a struggle to ensure the integration of social concerns in urban renewal planning processes, social workers managed to convince the committee chair of the local Planning Committee to invite them to make their case in a discussion on urban renewal in the committee. Utilising this opportunity to participate in a relevant policy formulation arena, the head of social services expressed her concern about the limited ability of low-income populations to cope with the complex processes engendered by urban renewal. She made the case for the incorporation of social aspects into planning processes. The response by the committee members was positive, and it was decided that the committee chair would convene a round table to consider improving the process. In another case, which concerned the establishment of employment services for lone parents by a municipality, the social workers succeeded in establishing an employment round table that brought together local government and employers to discuss employment options for women in the local economy. In this case, the social workers managed to create policymaking institutions to which they had access. Another strategy for participation was to seek direct formal or informal access to decision-makers. Thus, social workers endeavoured, and often managed, to meet the leading municipal officials, directors-general or mayors of the cities, or to raise the problems and policy options in meetings with local elected officials.

Temporal opportunity factors also play a role in enabling social worker policy entrepreneurs on the local level to bring about policy change. Thus, changes in administration due to electoral results create political windows of opportunity. In a case concerning efforts by social workers to establish social services for non-Israeli migrant workers in a large Israeli city, initial efforts to convince the incumbent mayor to adopt this policy were unsuccessful. With new city elections about to take place, the director of the social service administration submitted a list of proposals for local social policies towards migrant workers to the two most prominent mayoral candidates in the upcoming elections. He then invited each of the two mayoral candidates to his office in order to press for the formulation of municipal policy regarding these workers. Both of them agreed to the policy proposal. Indeed, following the election of one of them to the post of mayor, he delivered on his promise and the municipality initiated the establishment of the service, the first of its kind in the country (Aviv et al, 2021).

Opportunity at the street level

Opportunity also plays a role in explaining another policy route of social workers: street-level policy engagement. Here, we refer to policy decisions taken by street-level social workers and, in particular, those who serve in managerial roles. Unlike the policy practice efforts of social work policy entrepreneurs that tend to focus on the introduction of new policies within the formal institutions of local or national government and can be seen as layering, the effort here is to reformulate on the ground those national policies that determine the working of the social services in which social workers are employed and to adapt them to professional work within the confines of those social services. These are therefore the sorts of policy changes that can be described as conversion. As we noted in Chapter 2, street-level social workers impact policy on the ground when they decide to adapt policies to the characteristics of their service users or to their needs and work situation. Here, social workers are not seeking to direct access policy institutions, nor are they necessarily seeking to bring about formal changes in policies; instead, they are utilising the degree of freedom granted to them, consciously or inadvertently, by formal policymakers to formulate (or sometimes reformulate) policy. This is a facet of professional discretion.

Despite initial assumptions that the adoption of NPM principles would lead to stronger top-down control of policy implementation and to the dramatic curtailment of discretion, research over the last two decades has shown these to be wrong (Evans and Harris, 2004; Ellis, 2011). Indeed, discretion has been the subject of much scholarly interest in recent years, and this has moved beyond the narrow boundaries of professional decisions regarding individuals and the implementation of existing policies. Alongside evidence of the continuation of discretion, the impetus for much of the renewed interest in discretion has been the discourse on the role of street-level bureaucrats initiated by Lipsky (2010), in which discretion played a central role, and on subsequent efforts to develop this theory in diverse disciplines among the policy science, public administration and social work fields (Nothdurfter and Hermans, 2018).

The discretion discourse has developed in different directions of late, but of particular interest to our discussion is the growing understanding that discretion is an 'inherent feature of public policy' (Hupe and Hill, 2020: 255) and should be examined as such. In that sense, formal state policies often create opportunity structures for social workers within social services to formulate policies on the ground because integral to the formal policy are explicit avenues for managers and professionals to employ discretion in their implementation of the policy. However, these policy frameworks also unintentionally create opportunity structures for policymaking on the ground because formal state policies are vague and ambiguous. Given existing resources and contexts, the policies may often be impractical, and because regulation is lax, this offers much leeway to change them (Brodkin, 1997).

These street-level policy efforts, then, are about, what Stephanie Baker Collins (2016) describes as, utilising 'space in the rules' and 'space outside the rules'. They are conscious efforts by social workers to translate, adapt and reformulate existing state policies, and, in doing so, to become policy actors in their own right in their own backyard. These efforts take place in a specific institutional context, in which social workers have the capacity, either formally or informally, to engage in policy formulation within the social service in which they are employed, and they do so. These are policy processes that take place within this context, specifically affect the workings of these organisations and their service users, and are relatively unaffected by external actors, even those within local government.

Studies on the ways in which managers in social services formulate policy on the ground by making use of their discretion reflects this notion of opportunity. This is particularly the case for social workers in managerial positions. In his pioneering case studies on the discretion of senior and local managers in social services in England, Tony Evans (2013, 2016b) noted that senior managers do indeed act as policymakers in adapting policies and in encouraging or enabling local managers and practitioners to adopt impact attitudes to policy. While these studies alert us to the policymaking role of management in social services, it is noteworthy that in the English case, the senior managers are not social workers, their policy efforts tend to be unofficial and they occur despite apparent efforts by national and local policymakers to limit their discretion.

In three studies undertaken in the Israeli context, the policy impact of social workers in managerial roles is made explicit. In that country, statutory requirements ensure that all managerial posts in social services are held by social workers, thus making it an interesting case to explore how social workers affect policy as managers.

In a study of directors of social services (alongside managers in education and policing), Drorit Gassner and Anat Goffen (2018) afford us an insight into the ways in which these directors seek to influence policy so as to better serve the needs of their service users. Of particular interest are efforts to undertake the conversion of policies. These can take the form of transforming policy directives into work plans prior to their implementation or introducing changes ranging from minor adaptions to major modifications during the direct delivery of services. An example of the transformation of policies is when social services facilitated the participation of children in afterschool programmes even when their parents failed to pay the mandatory minimal fee (Gassner and Goffen, 2018: 560). Adapting policies is reflected in the example of the director of a local social service who was aware that women who had suffered from domestic violence filed complaints at the police station but avoided approaching social services for fear of losing custody of their children and therefore began providing social services at police stations rather than at social services departments (Gassner and Goffen, 2018: 561). In each of these cases, social workers in managerial positions had an opportunity to address the specific needs of their service users. They took advantage of the lax regulation of their services by the state and the local government to make significant changes in the ways in which formal state policies were implemented in the social service that they led.

In a study that focused specifically on the policy role that social workers serving as directors of social services in Israel played in the reformulation of policy on emergency material assistance, Anat Sery and Idit Weiss-Gal (2021) identified the diverse fields and issues in which they formulated policies. These focused on the service user groups prioritised, the eligibility conditions for receipt of assistance, what and how assistance was provided, and the levels of material support given. Some of the directors in the study sought to adhere closely to the Ministry of Welfare and Social Services directives regarding this assistance (which is primarily funded and ostensibly regulated by the ministry), but most of them adopted departmental policies that amended, sometimes dramatically, state policies. Given the wide gaps between the formal goal of the policy (to address the emergency needs of service users), the level of funding and the perceived unique needs of the communities served by local social services, most of the directors felt obliged to adapt the policies. Explicit recognition of the role of professional discretion in state policy on emergency assistance, the ambiguity and a lack of coherence in the policy directives, and weak regulation by national and local government created the opportunity structures that enabled social workers serving as directors of social services to make policy in this case.

Finally, it emerges that it is not only directors of social services in Israel who use their discretion as an opportunity to affect policy, but also team managers. In a study that explored the policy decisions of team managers in social worker teams in local social services, Tzadiki and Weiss-Gal (2021) report that when torn between budgetary constraints and the needs of their service users, the team managers often became de facto street-level policymakers. Dealing with vague policy directives, they made decisions as to how the teams that they led could best implement policies pertaining to the provision of both psychosocial services and material support.

Opportunities: some conclusions

Opportunity refers to the accessibility of diverse levels of the policy formulation process to social workers. Across the world, social workers engage in policy formulation, though this tends to take different forms and levels in diverse countries. The claim in this chapter is that the varying capacity to do so across nations is not only a result of differences in the social, economic or professional environment in which social workers work (as described in Chapter 3). Nor is it only a result of personal motivation and the nature of the workplace of social workers in the various countries (factors discussed in the following chapters). Rather, it is also linked to the national-, local- and street-level opportunity structures and temporal opportunities that enable social workers to enter arenas in which social welfare policy is formulated or to influence it on the ground.

These opportunity structures are created due to the specific forms taken by the institutions in which policy is formulated and, in particular, the rules, norms and structures that determine access to them. As examples described here show, these opportunities are also influenced by environmental factors (for example, social problems) and temporal developments within the policy process (see Figure 4.1).

In sum, in order to better understand the levels and forms of social workers' policy involvement, we must examine not only environmental factors (the welfare regimes in which social workers operate or the characteristics of the social work profession in their country), individual motivational factors (what social workers want to do) and organisational factors (what their organisations enable them to do), but also the opportunity factors that determine the options that exist for them in the policy process. The chapter has sought to explain why this is so and has provided case examples from the US, Spain, the UK and Israel of social workers in positions ranging from the street level to the highest political echelons. We have also seen how social workers utilise opportunities to influence policies and create opportunities for their policy engagement.

5

Facilitation

Introduction

Most social workers are employed in organisations. This seemingly trivial observation has considerable relevance to an understanding of the engagement of social workers in policy and is central to the discussion on, what we term, 'facilitation'. Unless they are self-employed, the actual engagement of social workers in diverse policy routes will depend to a large extent on the degree to which their place of occupation, specifically, the organisational context that has a predominant impact upon them, is willing to facilitate their policy engagement (see Figure 5.1). As such, the focus of this chapter is on the impact of the organisational context in which social workers undertake their professional work on their policy engagement as citizens and professionals.

An initial example of the impact of facilitation can be found in the research on the factors associated with at least one of the policy routes: policy practice. It is very clear in showing that one of the most important factors linked to this type of practice is the support that social workers get from their workplace (McLaughlin, 2009; Lustig-Gants and Weiss-Gal, 2015; Gewirtz-Meydan et al, 2016: Weiss-Gal, 2017a; Nouman et al, 2019; Weiss-Gal and Gal, 2020; Gilboa and Weiss-Gal, 2022). The findings on the engagement of hospital social workers in policy practice illustrate this well. Data from different countries (Canada, Israel and the US) and covering social workers in hospitals in diverse sectors (state, local and non-profit) reveal that support for involvement in policy-related activities offered by the hospital itself or, more strongly, by the specific department in which the social workers work is crucial in encouraging engagement in policy-related activities aimed at influencing the hospital's policies and those of other organisations or state bodies (Herbert and Levin, 1996; Jansson et al, 2016; Sommerfeld and Weiss-Gal, 2018). Organisational support for policy engagement in a hospital setting can facilitate not only the policy practice of social workers, but also that of an additional helping profession, specifically, nurses (Bar Yosef et al, 2020).

Organisational support is not only relevant to explaining policy practice; it can also encourage social workers to engage in additional policy routes. It can take the form of support for the voluntary political participation of social workers (Douglas, 2008). An example of this is the support (albeit discreet) that some social workers in Israel received from their organisations

Figure 5.1: Facilitation and the PE conceptual framework

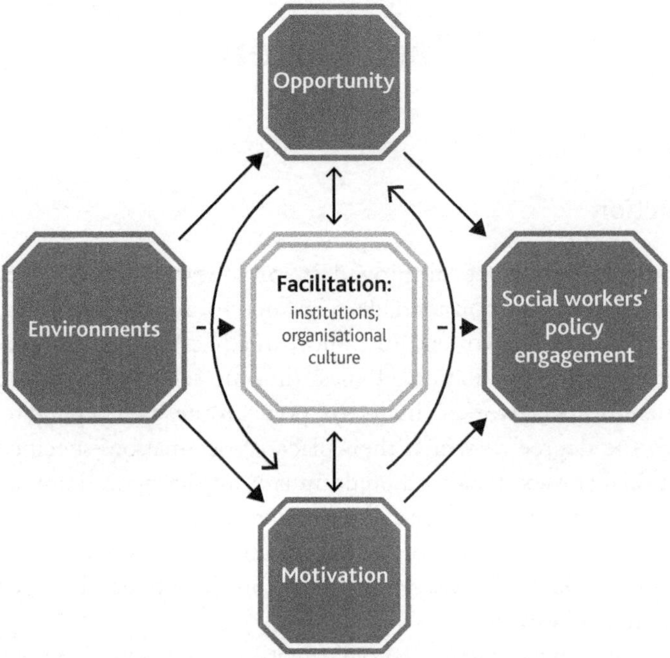

during the 2011 mass social protests (Makaros and Moshe Grodofsky, 2016). It is also relevant to explaining the decision of social workers to engage in other policy routes, among them, running for elected office (Haynes and Mickelson, 2009; Binder and Weiss-Gal, 2021) and academic policy engagement (Gal and Weiss-Gal, 2017).

Later in this chapter, we will show that the divergence between types of organisations that employ social workers is important (these range from public entities, such as local social services or state institutions, through non-profit service providers and advocacy organisations, to for-profit corporations).[1] Yet, at this stage, regardless of the type of organisation, the very fact that an individual social worker's decision as to whether and how to engage in a policy-related activity will often be taken in a workplace setting is of critical importance to explaining policy engagement by social workers. In other words, social workers' engagement in policy will be facilitated if the dominant values and modes of practice in their immediate work environment, that is, 'the organisational culture', allow or encourage them to engage in this type of practice and provide them with the resources, facilities and support necessary to do so. By way of contrast, if this is not forthcoming, the options for social workers to engage in most of the policy routes, in particular, policy practice, will be extremely limited.

The goal of this chapter is to explore the impact of social workers' workplace, that is, the organisation in which they are employed, on their policy engagement. As can be seen in Table 5.1 at the end of the chapter, the evidence on the impact of organisation on the engagement of social workers in policy processes is robust, and it has emerged in studies undertaken over a relatively long time span and in different national and organisational contexts. While the level of this impact varies and the form that this takes differs, it is significant. The ways in which this impact is operationalised diverge in this body of work (some of it our own), and it encompasses: the goals of the organisation; the job descriptions of the social workers; the degree to which the agency leadership actively supports the policy engagement of social workers; and the tangible encouragement for this. It can also include the sector to which the agency belongs. Yet, it all serves to underscore that organisations are important when we seek to understand why and how social workers engage in policy as citizens and professionals. A more difficult task is to identify in this literature why this is so. Indeed, it is relatively rare to find full-throated, theoretically embedded explanations for the facilitating role of organisations with regard to the policy engagement of social workers.

Organisations as institutions

In order to better understand the ways in which organisations impact policy engagement, we draw here on theoretical knowledge on organisations and on the findings of studies on the facilitating role of organisations on the policy engagement of social workers. These will enable us to identify conditions under which social workers in organisations engage in policymaking and the factors that impact the form that this will take.

A useful point of departure for this analysis is to explore the creative ways in which the notions of institutions and institutionalisation have been employed within the organisational literature over recent decades (Buchanen, 2020). While sharing in common with other institutional approaches the fundamental assumption that institutions matter, the ways in which scholars in the organisational field set themselves apart from scholars in other disciplines that focus on institutions is enlightening and relevant to a better understanding of policymaking by social workers.

This approach to the study of organisations originally emerged from the same neo-institutional framework employed in Chapter 4 to explain the ways in which institutional norms affect the access of social workers to the policymaking process and offer them the opportunity to be part of the game. However, the goal there was to better understand how policy is determined within policymaking institutions and, more specifically, what this means for social workers' access to these policymaking arenas or processes, as well as the forms that social workers' policy engagement takes as a result of this access. Here, the questions that the institutionalist perspective enables us to answer are different and reflect the impact of this theory on organisational studies in recent decades. The focus moves from the external institutions in which policy is made, and that social workers seek to access in order to affect policy, to the organisations in which social workers are employed. The central question is: how does the way in which organisations relate to policymaking affect the policy-related behaviour of social workers within these organisations?

A focus on institutions that emerged in the 1970s within the organisational sciences is often attributed to two path-breaking articles. In the first of these, John Meyer and Brian Rowan (1977) contended that in contrast to the then-prevailing belief that the structure of organisations primarily reflects the demands of control and coordination within them, in fact, the structures, policies and practices within organisations are often a reflection of institutional rules that exist in the context in which the organisations operate. These institutional rules, termed 'myths' by the authors, refer to assumptions regarding the desired positions, policies, programmes and procedures of modern organisations. These myths are supported, and at times enforced, by public opinion or that of important constituents, by knowledge that is created in educational systems, or by requirements that are enshrined in laws. By formally adopting these myths concerning how they ought to be run, organisations seek legitimacy within society.

In a second path-breaking piece, Paul DiMaggio and Walter Powell (1983) took this approach one step further. They observed that, over time, structural change within organisations is less driven by competition or by a need for efficiency; rather, they undergo a process of homogenisation, becoming more similar to other organisations in their field. DiMaggio and Powell describe this as institutional isomorphism, and it occurs because organisations seek political power and institutional legitimacy as a means to achieve their goals. In order to achieve this, organisations structure themselves in ways that concur with the demands or expectations of their relevant environments, be they the state, competing organisations or professionals that the organisations depend upon.

The years since have seen the emergence of organisational institutionalism. A common theme in this body of work is the understanding that 'social norms and shared expectations are key sources of organizations' structures, actions and outcomes' (David et al, 2019: 1).

The original, and enduring, focus of this body of knowledge has been on the ways in which the opportunities that organisations have to impact policy and the resulting interface between organisations and external factors, such as the state and other organisations, affect the ways in which organisations operate and structure themselves (Scott, 2008). Alongside this, the concept of institutionalisation has also been increasingly employed to better describe processes within organisations, their effects on individuals and the role of members of the organisations in interpreting and translating these processes. Scholars have advocated moving beyond a monolithic perspective of organisations and have emphasised the need to explore different analytical levels within organisations, as well as the ways in which ideas, norms and practices are translated across, between and within them (Drori et al, 2020). A focus on public sector organisations has led to the observation that both formal texts and processes of socialisation, sometimes described as normative institutionalism, are employed by managerial levels to convey desirable values and practices to employees within bureaucracies (Olsson, 2020). At the same time, there is also evidence of the agency of staff members within bureaucratic organisations with regard to practices and processes within them (Powell and Rerup, 2017; Smets et al, 2017).

Crucial to any effort to understand the impact of organisations on the policy efforts of social workers employed by these organisations is the notion of organisational culture. Typically focusing on assumptions, values and artefacts (that is, physical representations that take the form of rituals, slogans and traditions), organisational culture seeks to encompass facets of the symbolic and cognitive aspects of organisational life (Kondra and Hirst, 2009). Organisational culture can be defined as a set of shared mental assumptions that guide interpretation and action in organisations by defining appropriate behaviour for various situations (Ravasi and Schultz, 2006).

The notion of organisational culture has been employed as a means through which to better understand the behaviour of employees of organisations in various situations and in relationship to diverse processes of change within the organisation or its environment (Parker and Bradley, 2000; Schein, 2010). Not surprisingly, these also include social welfare organisations in which social workers are employed (Kwon and Guo, 2017; Julien-Chinn and Lietz, 2019). Over the last decade, the role of symbols and systems of meaning has been of growing interest among organisational institutionalists, thus bringing culture and organisational culture to the fore (Aten et al, 2012; Zilber, 2012). There is recognition in this literature that the process by which values and practices are instituted within organisations is through discourses, in other words, by way of texts (be they written or expressed orally) that define the actions that are required or acceptable (Philips et al, 2004). In turn, these will affect the way members of the organisation think, feel and behave (Schein, 2010).

A key insight within the organisational culture discourse is that leadership within organisations can play a major role in determining the contours of the organisational culture and changes in that culture over time. This is a key claim in the work of Edgan Schein (2010) and has been explored, and underscored, in organisations providing social services and employing professional social workers. Michael Shier and Femida Handy (2016) show how executive leaders in non-profits seek to instil a commitment to social change among employees through the organisational culture of their agencies, while Rosemary Vito (2020) emphasises the role of the directors of child welfare agencies in Canada in creating organisational cultures that can further the effectiveness of their services.

Up until this point, by drawing upon the insights of organisational institutionalism, we have highlighted how the behaviour of organisations can be affected by the opportunities that they have to influence policies relevant to them and how this impacts what occurs within the organisations themselves. Organisational culture describes the efforts by the organisation as a whole (or its components) and its different leadership levels to guide the behaviour of employees in fulfilling their roles in various situations. Thus, in seeking to better understand the facilitating function of organisations vis-a-vis social workers' policy engagement, we need to understand how the organisations' role in the policy process is reflected in those facets of its organisational culture that are relevant to its social work employees' efforts to impact policy. Fitted with an organisational institutionalist lens, and with the help of research undertaken on the policy engagement of social workers, we can now explore the degree to which different types of organisations in which social workers are likely to be employed as professionals facilitate the engagement in policymaking of their social worker employees.

Social workers in organisations

Advocacy organisations

With regard to the social work–social policy nexus, the most obvious type of organisation to explore is that which engages in advocacy. Advocacy organisations are non-profit organisations whose primary focus is making public claims and pursuing related social change. In their review of advocacy organisations in the US, Kenneth Andrews and Bob Edwards (2004) add that these will tend to conflict with the social, cultural, political or economic interests or values of other constituencies and groups. Following the accelerated growth of such organisations in the US since the 1960s, advocacy organisations have emerged in other countries as well, and some, like Amnesty International, operate on the international level. Given that their primary goal is to affect policy (as opposed to the provision of services), advocacy organisations devote major efforts and diverse strategies to effectively participating in the policy formulation process, particularly by placing issues on the agenda or criticising existing policies and offering alternatives to them (Gen and Wright, 2013). Due to their often-limited resources and the contentious nature of the objectives that they seek, these organisations will be more likely to go beyond 'politics as usual' and revert to unconventional action when they seek to draw attention to issues that would not be addressed otherwise (Prakash and Gugerty, 2010).

Social workers are employed by advocacy organisations that engage in policy processes ranging from the community to the national and international levels (McNutt, 2011). Not surprisingly, this is more prevalent in those organisations that focus on social justice and rights issues, or on the population groups that are most likely to be served by social workers. Indeed, the employment of social workers in advocacy organisations will commonly follow their experience as case or community workers in the field dealing with these issues or social groups. Often, social workers hold leadership positions in these organisations. Whitney M. Young Jr is a useful example of this. He trained as a social worker in the US after his demobilisation in the wake of the Second World War. Following his field training, Young moved up the ranks of the Urban League, an advocacy organisation for black people, from the role of the industrial relations secretary of the St. Paul branch of the organisation to eventually leading the Urban League nationally between 1961 and his death in 1971. As executive director of the Urban League during a decade of dramatic transformation in civil rights in the US, Young adopted diverse strategies to further civil and social rights for black people, ranging from participation in protest activities and joining coalitions, to informal meetings with the country's political leaders, among them, President Lyndon B. Johnson (Weiss, 1990).

As policy engagement is the *raison d'être* of advocacy organisations, it is hardly surprising that the facilitation of policy engagement by social workers in these organisations is widespread and is reflected in the organisational culture created within them. This leads to greater involvement of social workers employed by advocacy organisations in various stages of the policymaking process. Indeed, social workers employed on different levels within these organisations will be encouraged to engage in policy in order to achieve the organisation's goals. This will take the form of not only policy practice and direct on-the-job engagement in the policy process, but also voluntary political participation through social action. Evidence of the policy engagement of social workers employed by advocacy organisations emerged in our study of the participation of social workers in legislative advocacy in parliamentary committees in Israel (Gal and Weiss-Gal, 2011). We found that 8 per cent of the social workers who participated in these meetings were employed by advocacy organisations, even though they comprise only a very small fraction of the social work workforce. Moreover, over a fifth (22 per cent) of the 27 social workers who participated frequently in committee meetings over the seven-year period studied were employed by advocacy organisations (Gal and Weiss-Gal, 2011). Indeed, the social worker who participated most in parliamentary committee deliberations was the executive director of a major advocacy organisation for children's rights. Not only were social workers employed by advocacy organisations more likely to engage in legislative advocacy in parliamentary committees, but an examination of the inputs of social workers in these committees also revealed that social workers in advocacy organisations engaged more in challenging existing policies and placing matters on the agenda than did social workers employed by local or central government (Weiss-Gal and Gal, 2014).

Social workers in non-profit social service providers

Non-profit social service providers are the major employers of social workers in many countries. Indeed, social workers have leadership, administrative and rank-and-file roles in these organisations. In the US, for example, a third of the entire social work workforce are employed by non-profit service providers (Salsberg et al, 2017). Similarly, the impact of both the subsidiarity principle in the provision of social services in many European countries and outsourcing trends in other countries leads to a prominent role for non-profits in the employment of social workers. How do these organisations relate to advocacy, and do they facilitate the engagement of their social work (and other) employees in policymaking? Here, the answer is more complex than in the case of advocacy organisations, but the evidence is greater.

An initial response to this question is that non-profits in general (Lu, 2018), and non-profit social service providers more specifically, do indeed engage in advocacy alongside their prime service provision role. Quantitative and case studies in different countries provide clear evidence of this (Donaldson, 2007; Schmid et al, 2008; Mosley, 2010; Verschuere and De Corte, 2015; Fyall and Allard, 2017; Clear et al, 2018). However, less clear is the extent to which these organisations engage in policy-related activities and the amount of resources they devote to this type of advocacy (Kimberlin, 2010; Feldman et al, 2017), which depends much on how advocacy is measured. After surveying the literature, Michal Almog-Bar and Hillel Schmid (2014: 17) conclude that 'political advocacy is ... marginal and limited in scope'.

While there is a clear expectation in the social work literature that the non-profits providing social services also engage in advocacy on behalf of their clients (Hasenfeld, 2015; Hoefer, 2019b), institutional theory offers a useful explanation regarding both the complexities entailed in doing so and the form that the engagement of non-profit social service organisations takes (Garrow and Hasenfeld, 2014). Non-profit social service providers tend to be extraordinarily dependent on the state for resources in order to provide effective services efficiently (Lu, 2015). In order to safeguard their continued existence and growth, these organisations need to ensure that the state or local government regard the services as important and the funding required as a justifiable budgetary outlay. As such, organisations are required to adopt diverse strategies in order to maintain support by decision-makers. This is the case not only for non-profits' internal structures and practices, but also for their interface with relevant policymakers on different levels of government, who have potential impact on policy formulation, regulation or funding. In particular, the leadership of the organisations will typically seek to adhere to the policymaking norms and participate in the policymaking forums that the government employs in this process (Mosley, 2011). Yet, it is not only the continuing support by the state that concerns non-profit service providers; they will also be motived by the needs of clients and the expectations of other stakeholders, as well as the social work professionals that often comprise much of the leadership and the staff of the organisations (Mellinger and Kolomer, 2013). These demands will often relate not only to what services the organisations provide and how this is undertaken, but also to the positions that they adopt on broader policy issues that are perceived to be integral to their agenda. Addressing these demands will sometimes require adopting different, more conflictual, tactics in the public arena. In other words, and to employ the insights of organisational institutionalists, the quest for resources and legitimacy from the state and for legitimacy from relevant environments is critical in understanding the impetus to engage in policy formulation by non-profit social service organisations (Almog-Bar and Schmid, 2014).

The range of policy-related activities that the leaderships of non-profit social service providers can, and do, engage in or encourage their social work employees to undertake are wider than those of advocacy organisations. These can range from the adversarial to the collaborative, and they will clearly often depend on the goal of the activities, the arena in which the organisation is active, the populations it serves, the resources that it has and the context in which they are undertaken (Fyall and Allard, 2017; Cai et al, 2021). Indeed, the forms of policy engagement that non-profit social service providers adopt, the issues that they address and the positions that they take will inevitably create difficult challenges for the leaderships of these organisations as they seek to ensure their legitimacy from the government, their service users and the professionals that comprise the backbone of the organisations – the social workers that they employ.

Finding an acceptable balance between these, sometimes competing, pressures is not simple.

Nevertheless, research indicates that it is typically 'insider' forms of advocacy that non-profit social service providers prefer over 'outsider' types of policy-related activities and that they will tend to shy away from 'biting the hand that feeds them' (Schmid et al, 2008). The leaderships of these organisations largely seek to promote their policy agenda through informal or formal meetings with policymakers, rather than the more public and conflictual tactics intended to generate public support and exert overt pressure on policymakers that are common in the case of organisations that focus solely on advocacy. Non-profit social service providers will opt primarily for elite collaboration with elected officials and administrators in government over confrontation, recruiting clients and supporters for protest activities, or employing the media, though these means will sometimes be employed in situations when other avenues are ineffectual or the goal is to strengthen support in the community or among professionals or to affect government decision-makers indirectly (Donaldson, 2007; Almog-Bar, 2018). Nevertheless, the preference is for, what the leadership of a non-profit organisation in Australia described as, 'advocacy with gloves on' (quoted in Onyx et al, 2010: 43). This was put bluntly by an executive director of a non-profit working with the homeless in the US:

> Marches, we're beyond marches, whoever is still doing marches is lost somewhere in the 60s. It's a sound bite, people see the march, and things go back to where they were. Come on, get a grip, but if it makes the people who march feel good, fine. So now, what do we do to bring it into reality? Set up a series of crucial meetings with crucial players that either stand in the way, or that help in getting it done. (Quoted in Mosley, 2011: 856)

The ways in which non-profits providing social services relate to their policy role is reflected in the policy-related activities not only of the top leadership of these organisations, but also of their street-level social work employees. The second facet of institutional theory – that which focuses on the ways in which institutional processes affect the organisational culture with the organisation – is a useful way to think about this and shows how both a readiness to engage in policymaking and a preference for insider engagement trickle down to front-line social workers and can facilitate their policy engagement. Existing data indicate that street-level social workers in non-profits undertake policy activities that can be defined as voluntary political participation and policy practice. In one of the earliest studies on the subject, Linda Cherrey Reeser and Irwin Epstein (1990) found that street-level social workers employed in non-profits engaged in different types of policy-related activities than either public employees or private practitioners. They were more likely to engage in voluntary political participation, such as protest activities, contributing money to election campaigns or participating in political rallies, than public employees. A total of 91 per cent of the respondents reported high levels of engagement in non-conflictual policy-related activities over the previous year, such as visiting public officials and giving public testimony. Using the same measures in a small-scale Canadian study a few years later, Donna Hardina (1995) found that just over two thirds of the social workers employed in non-profits engaged in non-conflictual activities, while only 21.4 per cent engaged in more activist protest activities.

In a study of social workers employed in Israeli non-profit social service providers that also included advocacy as one of their organisational goals (Gewirtz-Meydan et al, 2016), we asked social workers if they had engaged in 29 different types of policy practice activities during their career. The findings showed that on a scale of 0 to 1, the average level of engagement in policy practice was 0.43. A large proportion of social workers (86 per cent) engaged in bringing a need or a policy problem to the attention of colleagues. A total of 76 per cent were involved in getting feedback from service users about the social worker's own organisation in order to affect its policies, and 71 per cent brought a social problem to the attention of policymakers. Informing service users about a policy problem or limitation and motivating them to act in order to create policy change was an activity undertaken by 66 per cent of the social workers who participated in the study. Also common was enhancing the awareness of people in the community of policy problems that affect them (65 per cent). By contrast, only a minority engaged in: writing a blog or posting a comment on a website about a policy problem (both 17 per cent); appealing to the courts with regard to a policy issue (16 per cent); participating in a policy-related committee (13 per cent); and writing a letter to the editor of a newspaper on a policy-related issue (11 per cent). We concluded from this that the social workers preferred working with colleagues and service users, and bringing policy problems to their attention, rather than engaging in more direct and formal activities, such as participating in policy-related committees, or in more 'public' interventions, such as writing about a policy problem in the media.

Social workers in central and local government

The discussion of the role of facilitation within the government is complex because the government bureaucracy is not only the organisation in which social workers are employed, but also where policies are often formulated. Social workers can be found at all levels of government, and the way in which these two functions overlap differs much between the levels of government and the formal role of social workers on the different levels.

Social workers who hold high-level positions in the government are involved in policy formulation as an integral part of their jobs (Egeberg, 2002). In this case, the issue of facilitation is negligible. These social workers engage in policy practice in their informal meetings with elected officials who head the offices in which they work and in the legislature. They formulate policies by suggesting policy recommendations to the politicians, by serving as members of committees and teams engaged in discussing the implementation of policies, by drafting directives to street-level bureaucrats and regulating the work of these bureaucrats, and, of course, by playing a key role in determining the ways in which government resources are distributed. In our research in Israel, we observed social workers serving as senior officials in the Ministry of Welfare and Social Services participating in commissions determining policies to combat poverty and the role of local social services (Gal and Weiss-Gal, 2020). In a study of social workers' participation in parliamentary committee meetings, we found that 30 per cent of the social workers present in these meetings were from the government sector, most of them senior officials in that ministry (Gal and Weiss-Gal, 2011). This proportion rose to just over half when the focus was on parliamentary committees dealing with financial issues (Weiss-Gal and Nouman, 2016).

Although social workers can be high-level officials or may be direct practitioners in various institutions or services provided under the auspices of federal or provincial authorities, they are much more likely to be employees of local government social services. The fact that these social workers also engage in policy practice is less obvious, and issues of facilitation require our attention. Apart from motivational factors, which will be discussed at length in Chapter 6, the decisions by street-level social workers employed by local government to engage in on-the-job policy practice will typically be influenced by the organisational culture of their workplace. This is hinted at in an early study on social workers' policy practice (termed 'advocacy' there). In the study, Mark Ezell (1994) found that social workers working in local social services who said that advocacy was part of their job or one of their agency's primary functions were likely to do much more advocacy than those who felt otherwise.

Various factors will contribute to constructing the facets of the organisational culture relevant to policy engagement in local social services. As state employees within local government agencies, the organisational culture of street-level social workers will inevitably be institutionalised as a result of efforts by the state through its political or bureaucratic organs to define the goals of its agencies and the roles and behaviour of the public employees within them. While the specific goals of different agencies will differ, the state will seek to create a degree of uniformity in the behaviour of civil servants, to enhance their commitment to the public good and democratic governance, to ensure vertical accountability, and to maintain hierarchical policy formulation processes. Sometimes described as a 'public service ethos' (Pratchett and Wingfield, 1996), the assumption is that public employees should also adhere to values traditionally associated with accountability, integrity, impartiality, organisational citizenship behaviour and a commitment to the public interest (Rayner et al, 2011). In recent decades, the aggressive introduction of NPM principles – a policy change adopted in many welfare states (and one of the environments alluded to in Chapter 3) – has affected the organisational culture of social workers through its institutionalisation in the state bureaucracies in which they are employed. The introduction of NPM has led to efforts to instil additional, and sometimes contending, values and norms to the existing public service ethos within public administrations, among them, welfare state institutions. These include principles such as cost-efficiency, competition, instrumental rationality, transparency and consumer choice (Welbourne, 2011; Spolander et al, 2014).

Efforts to instil principles and values into the organisational culture of state institutions take various forms. One is legislation pertaining to the definition of the role of public employees in democratic societies. In the US, the Hatch Act relates specifically to the political engagement of federal public employees. In addition to related legislation adopted on the state level, the Hatch Act seeks to circumvent partisan political activities by public employees and has been interpreted as limiting advocacy activities by social workers employed by federal and local government in the US (Rocha et al, 2010). Efforts to forge a common organisational culture can also be promoted through formal government decisions and documents detailing their implementation. In the UK, a series of government reform initiatives that draw on NPM thinking were launched over the last three decades, attempting to radically restructure and narrowly focus the role of social work and the tasks of social workers in the community (Diaz and Hill, 2019). These initiatives have permeated to the local government level, thus limiting the space for on-the-job policy engagement in the UK (Simpson, 2013). In Italy, by contrast, an effort to institutionalise the idea of the participation of social workers employed by the state and their service users in the planning of social services was sought through the adoption of national legislation in 2000. Silvia Fargion (2018) found that the law's incorporation took different forms in the organisational culture of local social services across the country, and in some cases, it empowered social workers and led to their engagement in policy formulation.

Other formal documents – such as codes of ethics for civil servants (Gilman, 2005), mission statements, documents detailing standard operating procedures and job descriptions (Weiss-Gal and Levin, 2010; Pató, 2017), directives published by the regulatory bodies within public administration, and training programmes intended to facilitate the effective dissemination of these – are also efforts to construct a unitary organisational culture within public bureaucracies and socialise employees into the values and norms that comprise it. These can impact the organisational culture that will determine the readiness of social workers' relevant organisational context to support their policy engagement. In the Israeli case, recommendations by a committee for reform of local social services led to the formal incorporation of policy practice into the definition of the tasks of these services and the inclusion of policy practice into the Ministry of Welfare and Social Services' training programmes (Ministry of Welfare and Social Services, 2010). Facilitation in this case will inevitably depend on the way in which the organisational culture in social workers' social service agency interpret and implement this recommendation.

The organisational culture within local social services is not only affected by the institutionalisation of general bureaucratic norms and practices or the impact of professional values; rather, this culture within social services also reflects the specific perceptions of local government. This system is far from monolithic and local social services tend to enjoy a degree of freedom (which differs significantly across and within nations), and the organisational culture within them will show this (Lowndes, 2005; John, 2014). The readiness of the leadership of local government to accept efforts by social workers to influence policies within the local government system or beyond will be reflected in the organisational culture of the local authority and its component agencies, and will clearly have an impact on social workers' policy-related activities. At times, it appears, the expectations of managers of social services and the attitudes of high-level officials within local government to the policy involvement of social workers will be perceived to be conflicting, which will create dilemmas for social workers' policy practice. This is how a family caseworker related to this tension in the study by Nouman, Levin and Lavee (2019: 9):

> I'm not a young social worker but want to believe that I can do my work in a neutral manner, without the pressure of the dual loyalty dilemma. I believe that, if the need arises, and I have to jeopardize my job in order to engage in the policy arena, the Ministry of Social Affairs and Social Services supervisory division and my managers in the organization will be there for me and will know how to help me avoid trouble.

There is much cross-national divergence in the degree to which the organisational culture in local social services does indeed facilitate policy practice engagement by social workers. In our cross-national study on policy practice (Gal and Weiss-Gal, 2013), we found that while social workers in local government agencies in Israel and Spain were able to engage in policy practice, in other countries (particularly the US, Sweden, England and Russia), this was much less the case. When the majority of social workers in a particular country are public servants who face major limitations on policy-related activities within the framework of their workplace, this leads social workers seeking to affect policy to refrain from engaging in this type of practice while on the job and to opt to act through professional organisations or as citizens rather than as professionals. Similarly, a strongly hierarchical bureaucracy and the dominance of the political leadership over professionals will make it extremely difficult for social workers who are state employees to engage directly in policy practice. A useful example of the impact of these on the readiness of social workers to engage in policy practice is that of Sweden, in which nearly all social workers are local government employees and the dominant form is that of a workforce focused exclusively on dealing with the direct needs of individuals and families (Thoren and Salonen, 2013). Research on local social welfare services in that country underscores the predominance of local politicians and managers in decisions regarding policy issues, as well as the very limited influence of social workers on these decisions (Johansson, 2012).

While top-down formal and informal documents and messages from within the public service and local government will contribute to making the organisational culture in the local social services in which social workers are employed and thus influence the degree and form of their policy engagement, the local leadership of social services clearly plays a key role in interpreting organisational texts and forging the organisational culture within local agencies (Evans, 2016b). Indeed, it is to be expected that the leadership of the units in local social services in which social workers are employed will have a marked impact on the contours of the immediate organisational context in which social workers operate and on the way in which engagement in policy by social workers is perceived in that context.

This will particularly be the case in nations in which the principle of a hierarchical policy formulation process within public service is not always followed and the dominance of political decision-makers is not strictly enforced. Indeed, apart from vertical organisational inputs, studies indicate that the attitude of managers in local social services to the policy engagement of street-level social workers (and the way in which this is reflected in the organisational culture in these local agencies) will be impacted by an additional source: the horizontal impact of the social work profession, also identified in Chapter 3 as one of the environmental factors affecting social workers' policy engagement. When the managers of these services are social workers, core values of the profession and expectations regarding the roles that social workers should play, the types of interventions that they should adopt and the goals they should seek are likely to be reflected in the local organisational culture. Managers of these services are keenly aware of the discourse within the profession and appear to seek to align themselves with this.

Evidence of the impact of local social services on the policy practice of social workers employed by them can be found in a number of studies (Lustig-Gants and Weiss-Gal, 2015; Boehm et al, 2018; Lavi et al, 2019; Weiss-Gal and Gal, 2020). In all of these, there is clear evidence that the organisational culture within social services in local government is a key factor in determining the level and form of policy engagement by social workers. Thus, in a study on social workers' response to social problems created by urban renewal, Einat Lavee, Nissim Cohen and Hani Nouman (2019) found that a supportive organisational environment in local social services was critical in increasing efforts to influence local policy in this field. Support by the leadership of local social services for the policy practice of social workers also emerged in a study on their participation in parliamentary committees in the Israeli parliament. It found that this participation was often an initiative of social services in local government (Lustig-Gants and Weiss-Gal, 2015). Finally, in a study of the policy practice of community social workers employed by local social services, we found that organisational support was a major factor in explaining the level of policy engagement (Weiss-Gal and Gal, 2020).

Exploring the attitudes of social service managers in Israel, where policy practice has attained prominence in the professional discourse in recent years, Ayelet Makaros, Nehami Baum and Sivan Levy (2020) found that managers generally adopted supportive attitudes towards policy practice. While they were keenly aware of the practical obstacles faced by social workers seeking to engage in policy practice and were split over whether it was them or their employees who should lead in policy-related activities, they did seek to integrate these perceptions into the organisational culture of their agencies. One of them put it as follows: 'The message is that every social worker will do both casework and policy practice. It doesn't matter if they work with teenage girls, elderly people, young families, or violence. Everyone will engage in casework and be actively involved in policy change' (Makaros et al, 2020: 156). In another study in Israel that focused on the policy practice role of social workers, the support by managers for engagement in policy and the obstacles faced by street-level social workers in doing so are displayed in the following quote from an interview with a caseworker in the elderly field:

> I've never been trained in the policy field, and I don't think it is taught at university today, but since the new urban policy is harmful to my clients and *as my managers* and my clients expect it of me, I understand

that I need to learn about this area and act within it. (Nouman et al, 2019: 9, emphasis added)

Facilitation: some conclusions

We began this chapter by noting that the fact that social workers tend to engage in their professional role in the context of organisations is not trivial when we seek to understand their involvement in policymaking. Indeed, the basic claim of the chapter is that the level and form of social workers' policy engagement will be strongly influenced by the support that they receive for this in their place of employment. We called this 'facilitation'.

An organisational institutionalist perspective helps understand why this is so for social workers employed in diverse sectors and on various levels within organisations. This perspective directs us to study both the impact of the policy context on the behaviour of organisations in that environment and the way in which this has a direct effect on the behaviour of employees in organisations. Thus, as we can see in Figure 5.1, facilitation directly affects the engagement of social workers in policy, but it is impacted by the opportunities that organisations employing social workers have to access policymaking and by some of the environments discussed in Chapter 3, among them the social work profession, service users and the structure of welfare state institutions.

Organisational culture is the way in which organisations inform employees of how they are expected to act, and this is also the case with regard to the policy arena. In particular, we have found that social workers will engage in policy practice when the organisational culture is more supportive of social workers' policy engagement and they are aware of this. In the chapter, we explored the ways by which this occurs in different types of organisations in which social workers are employed (advocacy organisations, non-profit service providers and the public administration). The findings reported in the chapter indicate that this will occur when: explicit support for policy engagement within the organisation is greater (vertically); political control is weaker; and professional accountability is stronger. In the case of local social services, we underscored the role of the leadership of these services and the factors that influence this.

Table 5.1: A summary of research on the role of organisations in social workers' policy engagement

Author(s) (date of publication)	Country	Research methodology	Number of respondents (of whom social workers)	Policy engagement variable	Organisational variable(s)	Impact of organisational variable(s)
Reeser and Epstein (1990)	US	Quantitative	1969: 682 1986: 1020 (1702)	Institutionalised social actions and non-institutionalised social actions (protest activities)	Agency auspices	Public employees were least involved in both types of activities; private practitioners were not less involved.
Ezell (1992)	US	Quantitative	339 administrators 'predominantly employed by non-profits' (339)	On-the-job advocacy	Administrators as compared to street level	Administrators devote significantly more time to advocacy on their jobs than micro-practitioners.
Ezell (1994)	US	Quantitative	353 (353)	On-the-job advocacy	Agency auspices Agency functions Job description	State and non-profit employees more than self-employed and for-profit. Most social workers who said that advocacy was one of their agency's primary functions did more job-related advocacy than those who felt otherwise. More than 50 per cent of those with advocacy as part of their job engaged in five or more hours of advocacy per week.

Table 5.1: A summary of research on the role of organisations in social workers' policy engagement (continued)

Author(s) (date of publication)	Country	Research methodology	Number of respondents (of whom social workers)	Policy engagement variable	Organisational variable(s)	Impact of organisational variable(s)
Hardina (1995)	Canada	Quantitative	89 (69 active social workers)	Class advocacy and Institutionalised social actions (legislative advocacy)	Agency auspices	Significantly higher proportion of social workers employed in private practice engaged in class advocacy than non-profit or state employees; no significant differences regarding legislative advocacy.
Herbert and Levin (1996)	Canada	Quantitative	457 (457 social workers in 96 hospitals)	On-the-job advocacy	Organisational support for internal or external advocacy	Some 66 per cent of respondents reported that their department encouraged involvement in internal advocacy (x = 2.4), while 64 per cent reported encouragement for external advocacy (X = 2.2). Most respondents (56 and 58 per cent, respectively) reported that the hospital's attitude towards internal advocacy and external advocacy was either neutral or discouraging.
Lustig-Gants and Weiss-Gal (2015)	Israel	Quantitative	190 (95 participants in parliamentary committee discussions and 95 in comparison group)	Testimony practice in parliamentary committees	Who initiated the initial testimony? What were the reasons for the testimony?	Local government and non-profit agencies were a major source of the initiative to participate in the legislative committee deliberations.

(continued)

Table 5.1: A summary of research on the role of organisations in social workers' policy engagement (continued)

Author(s) (date of publication)	Country	Research methodology	Number of respondents (of whom social workers)	Policy engagement variable	Organisational variable(s)	Impact of organisational variable(s)
Gewirtz-Meydan et al (2016)	Israel	Quantitative	106 (106 social workers in nonprofits)	Policy practice	Organisational support for involvement in policy practice	One of the strongest associations emerged between organisational support for policy practice and level of policy practice involvement.
Jansson et al (2016)	US	Quantitative	295 (94 hospital social workers)	Policy advocacy	Tangible job supports Organisational receptivity	Health professionals who perceive the organisational climate as being receptive to policy advocacy engagement, as well as those who reported receiving high levels of tangible supports to engage in policy advocacy, were more likely to engage in policy advocacy.
Boehm et al (2018)	Israel	Quantitative	165 (165)	Political involvement (Verba et al, 1995)	Management support for political involvement	Management support helped explain the political involvement of social workers ($t = 4.016^{**}$).
Lavee et al (2019)	Israel	Qualitative	101 (18 interviews and two focus groups, with 15 in each)	Influencing policy design		A supportive organisational environment proved to be the third force in increasing street-level bureaucrats' engagement in practices aimed at changing the design of policy or to act in ways that reinforced the state's responsibility for its citizens.

Table 5.1: A summary of research on the role of organisations in social workers' policy engagement (continued)

Author(s) (date of publication)	Country	Research methodology	Number of respondents (of whom social workers)	Policy engagement variable	Organisational variable(s)	Impact of organisational variable(s)
Sommerfeld and Weiss-Gal (2018)	Israel	Quantitative	109 (109 hospital social workers)	Policy practice	Tangible organisational support for policy practice engagement	Organisational support for policy practice contributed to the explained variance of community social workers' engagement in policy ($R^2(\%) = .04$).
Nouman et al (2019)	Israel	Qualitative	63 (23 interviews and three focus groups)	Engagement in policy practice	Expectations of the welfare service management	Social workers can overcome barriers and facilitate their involvement in the policy arena; highlights policymakers' role in shaping social workers' modes of operation.
Weiss-Gal and Gal (2020)	Israel	Quantitative	106 (106 community social workers)	Policy practice	Organisational support for policy practice engagement	Organisational support for policy practice contributed most of the explained variance of community social workers' engagement in policy ($R^2(\%) = 14$).
Weiss-Gal et al (2020)	Israel	Quantitative	621 (621)	Policy practice	Organisational support for policy practice engagement	Social workers in non-profits engaged in policy-related behaviour more so than their colleagues employed in hospitals or as direct practitioners in local social services. The role social workers undertake as professionals in their work setting in policy processes is primarily internal, indirect and informal. This style of policy engagement can be linked to both organisational constraints and individual factors.

6

Motivation

Introduction

Social workers are individuals with agency (Jeffery, 2011). In their role as either professionals or private citizens, the decision by social workers to engage in policy change or its formulation will inevitably be influenced by their *motivation* to do so. After having discussed the environments that provide the context in which this decision is taken, the opportunities that affect it and the organisational culture that facilitates it, in this chapter, we move to the micro level, that is, to *motivation*. This includes a sense of efficacy and a wide range of individual perceptions, attitudes, knowledge, values, skills, traits, identities (for example, gender and ethnicity) and job-related characteristics that directly affect the engagement of social workers in policymaking.

As such, the final component of the PE conceptual framework discussed in this book is the motivation of individual social workers to engage in policy. Clearly, even when social workers have opportunities to participate in the policy process as professionals or as private citizens, some will choose not to do so, while others will take active steps to enter the fray. As citizens, the decision to become engaged in the policy process can vary from the most passive mode of participation – voting or contributing to a party or candidate – to much more active participation, such as volunteering to campaign for a specific candidate or running for election and holding political office. As professionals, even if they can join professional organisations that seek to recruit them or if their workplaces enable them to participate in the policy process, there are those social workers who will show an interest in this type of intervention and others who will not or will be reluctant to do so. The same will be the case for social work academics, even though they have a relatively wide degree of autonomy to engage in policy. We claim that the decision to affect policy on all these levels is ultimately very much dependent on the desire, willingness and readiness of an individual to do so.

Here, we explore diverse factors that define the motivation of individual social workers to engage in policy-related activities. By drawing upon data from studies undertaken by us and others, and on a number of theories from political science, public administration and psychology, we will claim that motivation is a relatively broad umbrella category that comprises diverse facets and variables that impact social workers' policy engagement, as presented in Figure 6.1.

Figure 6.1: Motivation and the PE conceptual framework

We will begin by looking at what the CVM tells us about various motivational factors that impact social workers' engagement in different policy routes. The discussion will then seek to explore the role of underlying values and professional attitudes in social workers' policy motivation. Here, aside from empirical insights, we also examine the relevance of public service motivation (PSM) research for understanding social workers' motivation to engage in policy in their workplace. We will then look at, what we term, 'institution-based motivation', which refers to factors linked to social workers' role in the workplace. The chapter will conclude with a discussion of the role of personality traits and two identities – specifically, gender and ethnicity – in motivating social workers to engage in policy.

Civic voluntarism

The approach most often employed to identify individual-level factors that contribute to social workers' engagement in voluntary political participation, in running for office and in policy practice is the CVM that was formulated in the 1990s by Sidney Verba, Kay Lehman Schlozman and Henry E. Brady (1995). In its original formulation, this model underscored the importance of resources, psychological engagement with politics and recruitment to politics in explaining voluntary political participation in the US. More recently, the authors (Schlozman et al, 2018) added an individual's commitment to specific issues to the components of the model.

Extremely popular in the political participation literature (Klofstad, 2016), this model has offered strong evidence of the impact of access to resources, such as money, time, education and adult civic skills, on the readiness of individuals to engage in very diverse types of voluntary political activities. In addition, it has shown that an interest in politics, knowledge concerning politics, identification with a political party and a sense of efficacy when engaging in political activities all contribute to explaining voluntary political participation. Finally, people are more likely to engage in politics if they are recruited by an organisation or someone in their social circles to do so, and if they believe that their participation can further a specific policy issue close to their heart (Nygård and Jakobsson, 2013; Kirbiš et al, 2017; Baber, 2020).

In their efforts to explain the policy engagement of social workers, scholars have also drawn upon facets of the CVM (for a useful summary of studies undertaken in the US, see McClendon et al, 2020). Much of this work has focused on the voluntary political engagement of social workers, which is the form of policy engagement that corresponds to the type of behaviour that the model originally sought to explain (Hoefer, 2021a). In an early effort to adopt the CVM, David Hamilton and David Fauri (2001) found that social workers' political engagement was best explained by their membership in professional organisations that served as a recruitment network and their sense of political efficacy, a facet of psychological engagement with politics. A few years later, Jennifer Ritter (2008) confirmed these results by showing that a psychological engagement with politics and belonging to a recruitment network (in this case, the NASW) were critical in predicting the political activity of social workers. Sunny Harris Rome and Susan Hoechstetter (2010) also emphasised psychological engagement with politics in their large-scale study on the political participation of social workers. They found that self-efficacy, that is, the sense that social workers can have an impact on politics, is an important predictor of political engagement. In a recent article comparing the political participation of Swiss and US social workers, Jason Ostrander, Tobias Kindler and Janelle Bryan (2021) showed that belonging to a recruitment network, either a professional association or a trade union, was associated with greater political participation. A comparable result emerged in a study of the political activism of social work students (Swank, 2012). It also found that belonging to an activist network was a major predictor of activism. What emerges from this body of work is that social workers with a sense that they can have an impact on politics, as well as those that have been part of an organisation involved in policy processes and that recruits its members to engage in different forms of political participation, are much more likely to participate in voluntary political activities. These include voting, participating in marches or demonstrations, and active involvement in a political campaign.

Similarly, studies on the willingness of social workers to run for elected office have also drawn, explicitly or implicitly, on the CVM and its assumptions. Based on their findings from a national survey of social workers who had either run for public office or had been elected, Shannon Lane and Nancy Humphreys (2011) found that access to resources (money and time), possessing civic skills (in particular, through their social work training) and recruitment to politics by friends or organisations characterised those social workers who sought political office. Writing about Swiss social workers holding elected office, Kathrin Amann and Tobias Kindler (2021) underscore the impact of mobilisation networks – associations, professional organisations and trade unions – as crucial to social workers' motivation to stand in elections. In a study of social worker politicians in the UK, Hefin Gwilym (2017) emphasises the psychological engagement of the social workers in politics from early life and throughout their social work career as crucial. A study of the factors identified by social workers elected to the Alberta legislative assembly in Canada as influencing their decision to run also notes the role of professional and political networks as crucial in encouraging their political participation. Alongside these, the social workers also emphasised the impact of their families and the values and knowledge that they gained from their social work education and professional work (McLaughlin et al, 2019). Two studies reporting on the efforts by the Campaign School for Social Workers in the US to encourage more social workers to run for political offices (Ostrander et al, 2017; Lane et al, 2018) found three factors associated with the readiness of participants in the programme to seek election for political positions: greater access to information on politics; political efficacy; and explicit efforts to recruit them for political office.

In the social work academic discourse, the CVM has been employed even more broadly in order to understand policy-related activities that are farther removed from the political participation goals of the original study by Verba and his colleagues (Hoefer, 2019a; Nouman, 2020). One example of this is a recent effort to employ the CVM to explain why social workers engage in, what we termed in Chapter 2, 'policy involvement by, and through, professional organisations'. In this case, it was support for political activism of the NASW chapter in Texas (Hoefer et al, 2019).

Another policy route explained by this model is policy practice. In research on the policy practice of social workers in non-profit human service organisations (Gewirtz-Meydan et al, 2016), community social workers in local social services (Weiss-Gal and Gal, 2020), hospital social workers (Sommerfeld and Weiss-Gal, 2018) and social work participants in parliamentary committees (Lustig-Gants and Weiss-Gal, 2015), we found the CVM useful in identifying motivational factors that contributed to explaining the engagement of social workers in policy-related activities. Personal resources were significantly associated with this, specifically, the extent to which individuals believed that they had the skills to engage in policy practice. The CVM component of psychological engagement in politics – an interest in politics and the sense that a politician would be likely to listen to what the social workers had to say – also helped explain engagement in policy practice. Finally, as implied in the model, membership in a professional network was shown to be a factor linked to social workers' policy practice.

The evidence of the contribution of the notion of civic voluntarism to explaining various routes to policymaking by social workers is strong, yet it has its limitations. The model is valuable, in that it underscores the ways in which some resources contribute to a better understanding of social workers' policy engagement, in particular: policy practice skills; a psychological engagement in politics, with an emphasis on individual social workers' sense that engagement by them can have an impact; and membership in professional networks that encourage social workers to actively engage in policy processes. The studies that focus on what social workers do as citizens in the political arena, either as voters or as candidates for office, and draw upon the CVM as an explanatory model are most convincing. This is not surprising given the affinity of these types of policy engagement with the original goals of the CVM studies.

Nevertheless, even in these studies, the findings sometimes stray from the CVM. Thus, while Verba and his colleagues note that families play a role in determining the resources that are associated with engagement in political activities, the emphasis in their work is primarily on the role of family income. Yet, in studies on social workers standing for election, the emphasis moves from fiscal resources to the degree to which political issues were present in their families when growing up and the values that were imparted to them by their parents, which were identified as crucial factors in the decision to enter politics (Greco, 2020; Binder and Weiss-Gal, 2021). Similarly, the ways in which environmental factors, the impact of social work values or the impact of work with service users contributed to the decision to run for election and indeed to the issues that these social workers focused upon while in office moves the discussion beyond the

CVM. These factors, which are specific to social work, are obviously not addressed in the model.

The limitations of the CVM are more obvious when it is employed to explain other forms of social workers' policy engagement. This is particularly true of on-the-job policy practice. In these cases, the fact that the policy engagement by professionals takes place in the context of an organisation and is not dependent solely on the motivation of the social workers obviously requires us to consider facilitating factors and the interface between an individual social worker's desire to influence policy and the readiness of the workplace to enable this. Similarly, as we explain later, the role that a social worker holds in the organisation, particularly if it offers opportunity for (or indeed requires) policy-related activities, can clearly be a motivating factor that enhances engagement in this type of activity. As such, in studies on policy practice, CVM factors tend to be employed alongside organisational factors.

Yet, the limitations of the civic voluntarism approach in explaining social workers' policy engagement go beyond those identified so far. There are strengths and weaknesses in this approach. It identifies factors that help overcome obstacles that limit an individual's capacity to influence their surroundings by participating in the political/policy process. It also underscores the resources that some individuals have to do so and the relevance of the support from family, friends and networks in this endeavour. However, the CVM does little to reveal the underlying values and professional attitudes, as well as the individual features and internal personality characteristics, that motivate individuals to seek to actively impact policy processes. These are important if we are to better understand what inspires social workers to engage in some form of policymaking.

Our work and that of colleagues in other countries on the policy engagement of social work academics accentuates these strengths and weaknesses (Gal and Weiss-Gal, 2017). On the one hand, a cross-national analysis of the engagement of social work academics in policy in 12 countries confirmed that policy-related resources, which is a factor reflecting relevant civic skills, correlated with policy engagement in all but one of the nations (Portugal). However, we also found that perceptions, in particular, the sense that social work academics have a policy role and that academia has a social role, were also significantly correlated with policy engagement. In a qualitative study on social work academics in Israel who frequently engaged in policy-related activities (Weiss-Gal and Gal, 2019a), we found that they drew legitimacy for their actions from inner sources of ideology, personality and values. Crucially, they felt that their efforts to influence policy reflected an obligation of social work academics, and they all identified with social work's social justice goals.

Personal values and professional attitudes

Personal values and professional attitudes appear to be a major component of the motivation of social workers to engage in policy-related activities. These will inevitably reflect not only the life experiences of social workers and their upbringing, but also the professional socialisation processes that they underwent and that were identified in Chapter 3 as one of the environments that indirectly affect policy engagement. Similar to social workers who run for elected office and social work academics who engage in policy practice, social workers in organisations who choose to undertake policy-related activities and those who engage in street-level policy change also tend to explain their policy engagement by referring to their personal values and professional attitudes. This was reflected in a study of social workers in the US, in which Mark Ezell (1994) found that personal values and a sense of professional responsibility were how social workers justified their engagement in advocacy activity. In an Australian study based on a focus group of social workers in managerial positions, Philip Mendes (2007) found that in addition to their personal background and their experiences as social workers in the field, their commitment to social justice and human rights played a key role in promoting the involvement of social workers in social justice activism.

In research focusing specifically on social workers' policy practice, core personal values and professional attitudes that draw upon these values were found to play a role in explaining this type of practice, as they have also been found to do both in the political domain more generally (Schwartz et al, 2010) and with regard to other types of social work practice (Tartakovsky, 2016). Studies have linked attitudes towards the place of policy practice in social work to the actual engagement in policy practice (Lavee and Cohen, 2019; Nouman et al, 2019). For example, a study that focused on community social workers engaged in policy practice on the local level in Israel (Gilboa and Weiss-Gal, 2022) indicated that most of them perceived policy practice to be an integral component of social workers' role in general, and that of community social workers in particular. They regarded engagement in policy practice as a professional requisite. This role perception was anchored in their understanding that policy change was crucial to enhancing a community's quality of life and addressing its problems.

More underlying personal values and professional attitudes also play a role in determining social workers' engagement in policy practice (Gilboa and Weiss-Gal, 2022). In a study based on an Israeli sample of 411 social workers (Weiss-Gal and Gal, 2008), we found that beliefs concerning social justice played a major role in the social workers' perceptions of, and involvement in, policy practice. More specifically, the more progressive the social workers' socio-economic orientation and the more inclined they were to attribute poverty to social and structural factors, the more support they expressed for policy practice and the more they actually engaged in it. In addition: the more the workers viewed the government as responsible for social welfare, the greater their support was for policy practice; the greater their opposition to the view that cash benefits have negative effects on their recipients, the more willing they were to pay for social welfare services; and the greater their support for universal services, the more they actually engaged in policy practice. The strongest associations were between the view that poverty is rooted in social or structural causes, on the one hand, and both support for and engagement in policy practice, on the other. A structural understanding of community problems also played a role in explaining the policy practice of community social workers (Gilboa and Weiss-Gal, 2022).

The place of underlying values and professional attitudes has also emerged with regard to street-level policy engagement (Evans and Harris, 2004; Gofen, 2014; Gassner and Gofen, 2018; Schiettecat et al, 2018; Tzadiki and Weiss-Gal, 2021). In a recent study, Anat Sery and Idit Weiss-Gal (2021) showed that senior managers' impact on the reconstruction of emergency material assistance on the ground in social services in Israel could be attributed to professional attitudes towards the place of material assistance in social services and its perceived impact on family function, perceptions of poverty and people living in poverty.

PSM

Motivation theory offers another useful way to think about how beliefs and values energise, direct and sustain the behaviour of individuals. It focuses upon the internal and external factors that impel or induce action on the part of individuals (Locke and Latham, 2004). Within this wide body of knowledge, PSM research examines the unique motivations of public employees (Perry et al, 2010) and has been the subject of much scholarly interest over the last two decades, particularly in the public administration discourse (Perry and Vandenabeele, 2015). This is because it focuses on explaining the altruistic behaviour of individuals seeking to 'serve the interests of a community of people, a state, a nation, or humankind' (Rainey and Steinbauer, 1999: 23).

PSM is comprised of four sub-dimensions: 'compassion' is seen as a sense of sympathy for the suffering of others; 'commitment to the public interest' relates to an aspiration to further the common good; 'self-sacrifice' describes a willingness to prefer service to others over tangible personal rewards; and 'attraction to politics and policymaking' depicts a preference for serving the public interest by influencing politics and making a difference in policy processes (Anderfuhren-Biget, 2012). More generally, PSM has been described as 'the belief, values and attitudes that go beyond self-interest and organizational interest, that concern the interest of a larger political entity and that motivate individuals to act accordingly whenever appropriate' (Vandenabeele, 2007: 547). Research employing PSM and its components has typically focused on public employees and sought to explain their job satisfaction, their choice of occupation or employment, and their individual or organisational performance (Ritz et al, 2016). Not surprisingly, perhaps, social workers have also been the subject of some of this research (Bangcheng, 2009; Kjeldesen, 2013; Roh et al, 2016).

One of the interesting directions that research on PSM has taken over the last decade is to examine its impact on the political and policy-related behaviour of individuals. In this research, the effort has been to determine if PSM and its components can be associated with various types of voluntary political engagement and a willingness to engage in prosocial behaviour. In a study of civic attitudes among Australians, Jeannette Taylor (2010) found that high PSM was found to be associated with engagement in non-electoral political activities, such as signing a petition, participating in a demonstration, contacting a political or public servant to express a view, and a readiness to try to do something alone, or with others, about a law considered unjust or harmful. Adrian Ritz (2015) employed two of the components of PSM – 'attraction to politics and policymaking' and 'commitment to the public interest' – to study the types of policy behaviour of local councillors in Switzerland. His findings indicate that the attraction to politics component of PSM explains some of the behaviour of elected local officials. A recent study (Ritz et al, 2020) of public employees in two Swiss state agencies also found that PSM was associated with voting behaviour and signing petitions (though not membership in a political organisation).

This research into the impact of PSM is obviously particularly pertinent to our efforts to better understand why social workers employed in state social services are motivated to choose to engage in policy practice. A study undertaken on a sample of 143 social workers in Israel, most of whom were caseworkers, offers support for this way of thinking about motivation and the engagement of social workers in policy. It focused on the link between PSM, willingness to engage in policy practice and actual engagement in this type of practice (Melzer, 2017). The study found a positive and statistically significant relationship between all four components of PSM and the degree of willingness to engage in policy practice on the part of the social workers. The strongest associations were between 'attraction to politics and policymaking' and 'self-sacrifice'. It also found positive and statistically significant relationships between attraction to politics and policymaking, willingness to engage in policy practice and actual engagement in policy practice.

Institution-based motivation

Moving from resources, skills, perceptions and values, institution-based motivation refers to two additional components of motivation. These focus on the association between social workers' motivation to engage in policy and, first, the formal expectations of the roles that social workers have within the organisations in which they are employed, particularly when these are managerial roles, and, second, the experience that they have gained throughout their career within this context. Studies on the motivation to engage in policy among social workers holding managerial positions offer enlightening evidence of these two motivational components. Individual social workers in managerial or administrative positions are more likely to engage in the policy process within their own organisation or beyond if this is part of the formal and informal expectations of those in these positions and if they have more opportunities for participation in policy processes, both in the organisation and beyond. In this sense, the claim is that the motivation of social workers will reflect the type of facilitating organisational dynamics described in Chapter 5, whereby the policy engagement of social workers (in this case, social work managers) will be encouraged by the organisation in which they are employed to do so. Here, we complement the impact of a more general organisational culture by noting that the motivation of social work managers to engage in policy will also be enhanced if they sense that their managerial role affords them access to policymaking processes within their own organisations and to decision-making forums in their policy environment, or if they have high levels of discretion over the way policies are interpreted and implemented by their staff. Finally, the motivation of social workers in managerial positions will be greater because they possess more knowledge on policy and its consequences, and because they tend to adopt a more structural understanding of individual problems or have a stronger self-efficacy to act as policy actors.

Research has found that this is the case for social work managers, even for social workers whose authority is limited to directing the activities of a small number of social workers. Beginning with Irwin Epstein's pioneering study on advocacy activities among social workers in Michigan in 1978, a number of studies have found that social workers holding administrative positions engage more in policy activities as citizens or professionals than do street-level social workers (Epstein, 1981). In another early study, Mark Ezell (1992) sought to challenge the assumption that social work administrators are necessarily a conservative force in social welfare by exploring their engagement in policy. Indeed, he found that they devoted more time to advocacy and were more politically active than other social workers. On the basis of these findings, he concluded that social workers holding managerial positions were more change oriented than their street-level caseworker colleagues.

More recently, this finding was consolidated in research in different countries which found that social workers in managerial positions in different social services tend to believe that they should engage in policy-related activities (Makaros et al, 2020) and do, in fact, engage in on-the-job policy practice (Lai, 2004; Lustig-Gants and Weiss-Gal, 2015; Sommerfeld and Weiss-Gal, 2018; Weiss-Gal and Gal, 2020) and in voluntary political participation (Douglas, 2008). The authors of these studies generally attribute these findings to the fact that managers have more opportunities, greater expectations and more knowledge and self-efficacy.

While the association between role and policy engagement is clearly identifiable in these studies, and a formal managerial position undoubtably motivates social workers and offers them the authority and resources to play a policy role, it is less obvious whether this is not largely a consequence of individuals with prior motivation to influence policy being in a position to do so. Put differently, it may be that the motivation to play a policy role already existed among these social workers prior to their appointment to the managerial position and the post simply provided them with more opportunities to engage in policy.

The answer to the question as to when the motivation to engage in policy among social work managers began is not clear, and we lack any convincing empirical basis in this regard. Nevertheless, there are indications that the motivation for policy engagement of social workers who reach managerial positions later in their career may also be linked to the career experience that they have and to their standing within the organisation. This finding has relevance, then, not only for social workers in managerial positions, but also for all social workers. More specifically, we do know that seniority and tenured position have been found to be associated with greater involvement in policy practice among social workers (Douglas, 2008; Lustig-Gants and Weiss-Gal, 2015; Weiss-Gal and Nouman, 2016; Weiss-Gal and Gal, 2020) and nurses (Bar Yosef et al, 2020). This association was also found with regard to voluntary political participation (Abo El Nasr, 1991; Ezell 1993; Douglas, 2008; Harris Rome and Hoechstetter, 2010). These findings imply that longer job experience and greater employment security lead to both greater knowledge about the impact of policies, as well as the advantages and limitations of them, and a sense of confidence and efficacy regarding involvement in policy formulation. We also assume that the more secure social workers feel in their job and the higher their status among colleagues and superiors, the more likely they are to seek to impact policies and take the potential risks associated with this.

Personality traits

Alongside the facets of motivation discussed earlier, there is also some initial evidence that underlying personality traits can determine the motivation of social workers to engage in policy. Developments in political science and a pioneering study in social work suggest that this may be a fruitful avenue to explore. In recent years, political scientists have explored the link between personality traits and political participation, and revealed that these traits can contribute significantly to a better understanding of diverse forms of political participation, in particular, voting behaviour, campaign participation and protest activity. This impact can take direct or indirect form and it differs across national contexts, apparently reflecting distinctive institutional configurations (Gerber et al, 2011; Chang et al, 2020). In these studies, scholars have typically employed the Big Five personality factors: openness to experience; conscientiousness; extroversion; emotional stability; and agreeableness (Mondak and Halperin, 2008).

A compelling initial effort to employ this body of knowledge in the study of social workers' policy engagement was undertaken by Talia Meital Schwartz-Tayri (2020). In a study on the willingness of social work students in Israel to engage in policy practice, Schwartz-Tayri combined predictors drawn from both the civic voluntarism literature and studies linking the Big Five personality traits to political participation in order to explain this readiness. Her research model explained 49 per cent of the variance in students' willingness to engage in policy practice, leading Schwartz-Tayri to conclude that predictors from both the CVM and personality traits should be bound together to better understand the dynamics of this type of activity. Of the Big Five personality traits examined in the study, openness to experience, conscientiousness and extroversion were all, directly or indirectly, significantly associated with willingness to engage in policy practice. She suggests that openness to experience may lead to a willingness among social work students to explore new professional practices in the future and find creative ways to deal with social problems linked to unjust social policies. Schwartz-Tayri asserts that conscientiousness may induce future social workers to acquire political skills and knowledge that enables them to advocate for others. She also contends that extrovert students will be more likely to seek the political skills that will enable them to engage in policy practice.

The place of gender and ethnicity

Finally, the discussion on motivation cannot ignore two sources of some of the beliefs, values and personality traits that lead social workers to engage in policy activities: their gender and their ethnicity. Our claim here, then, is that gender and ethnicity influence the different facets of social workers' motivation to engage in any of the policy routes and so need to be considered when seeking a better understanding of their policy motivation. However, while gender appears to have an adverse effect on the motivation of women to engage in, at least, some forms of policy engagement, belonging to a minority ethnic group seems to motivate involvement by social workers in policy.

Across the world, the majority of social workers are women. This clearly requires us to explore the impact of gender on policy engagement given the knowledge that we have on the historically more limited participation of women in the policy process. Scholars have intensively discussed the link between gender and political participation, especially when seeking to understand the often small number of women in political offices and among candidates who run for elected office (Lawless et al, 2014). While in the past, studies on voluntary political participation indicated that women participated less than men, this gender gap has virtually disappeared in democratic societies (Kittilson, 2019), and the focus of contemporary studies is primarily on gender gaps in various forms of political activity and the degree to which women run for elected office and ultimately serve as policymakers. The findings in most countries show that women are under-represented in national parliaments and that men tend to engage more than women in political activities, such as direct contact, collective actions and membership in political organisations (Hughs and Paxton, 2019).

Various explanations have been offered for this enduring gender gap in political and policy arenas. These focus on both supply-side and demand-side theories, which inevitably overlap to a certain degree (Paxton et al, 2007). Supply-side explanations focus on: structural factors, such as the gendered division of labour in the home and the time restraints that many mothers have; lingering cultural attitudes, particularly those grounded in religion that view politics as unsuitable for women; and the features of the political system that, in effect, limit female political participation due to candidate selection processes and the amount of funds required to run for office.

Alongside these, a useful approach to explaining female under-representation in the political arena, and one that is particularly relevant to the issue of motivation, is to think about demand-side theories, in particular, about the link between gender and political ambition (Lawless, 2015). The claim here is that differences in the way men and women perceive their own traits and assess their suitability for elected office are more likely to discourage women than men from running for political office. Not only does traditional gender socialisation assign specific tasks within the family to women and create difficulties for them in balancing home and work (and political activity), but 'whereas men are taught to be confident, assertive, and self-promoting, cultural attitudes toward women as political leaders continue to suggest that these characteristics are inappropriate or undesirable in women' (Lawless, 2015: 354). As such, women are less motivated to seek political office than men.

Within social work, women have always played a major role in the profession as a whole (Stotzer and Tropman, 2006). Many of the social workers identified with policy formulation and change on the community, local and national levels are women. These efforts have spanned diverse policy routes and have taken place both within formal policymaking arenas and in the work of advocacy organisations and social movements. Nevertheless, the adverse impact of gender on policy engagement appears to remain potent within the profession. The relatively limited number of female social workers running for political office reflects this. In a study on MSW students, Meehan (2018) found that while female students expressed an interest in running for local political office, they also doubted their qualifications to do so significantly more so than their male contemporaries. This sense of self-doubt regarding political participation also emerged from the findings of a study of 23 clinical social workers in the US (Ostrander et al, 2019), which revealed that female social workers described themselves as unqualified and/or unknowledgeable in the political arena and had low levels of political ambition. Many of them also described the challenges of achieving a work–life balance that only left a limited amount of time for political engagement.

Findings reflecting the impact of gender on other policy routes also provide some insights into a gender gap that still exists. In a quantitative study on the engagement of Israeli social workers in policy practice (Weiss-Gal and Gal, 2008), we found that men reported being significantly more involved in policy practice than women. Similarly, in a study of social workers' participation in parliamentary committees, we found that the proportion of male social worker participants was higher than their proportion in the profession as a whole, as was their readiness to actively participate in the committee deliberations (Gal and Weiss-Gal, 2011). In a study that focused specifically on the meetings of parliamentary committees dealing with financial issues, it emerged that among the social workers who attended, 60 per cent were women, while among those who actually spoke, only 48 per cent were women (Weiss-Gal and Nouman, 2016). In research undertaken in South Korea examining the attitudes towards, and engagement in, policy advocacy activities by the top executives of social work organisations, men in these positions were found to be more likely to attribute importance to these policy activities and to engagement in them than were women (Shin, 2020).

In addition to gender, the role of ethnicity in affecting the policy engagement of social workers is important because, in many societies, members of minority ethnic groups are excluded populations that suffer disproportionally from discrimination, inequality and poverty. Thus, not only have they been the subject of social work interventions in these societies, but the social work profession has tended to draw members of these minority ethnic groups to its ranks (Salsberg et al, 2020). Indeed, within the social work discourse in recent years, there has been growing recognition of the need to incorporate ethnicity and race into the ways in which we think about the profession, its practitioners and its service users. In particular, scholars writing from a critical perspective have drawn upon theoretical models in other disciplines to reflect on the importance of taking race and ethnicity into account when addressing social problems within minority ethnic communities (Graham, 2007; Kolivoski et al, 2014; Kiehne, 2016; Einbinder, 2020). In this literature, the impact of ethnic affiliation as a source of motivation for social workers has been underscored (Wainwright, 2009; Bent-Goodley et al, 2017). This is also the case for their policy-related behaviour (Nouman and Azaiza, 2021a).

Research within political science on the link between ethnic identity and political participation has revealed that ethnic identity has an impact on the level and the form of political behaviour. Although this diverges much across nations and ethnic groups, the impact of ethnicity on politics is clearly evident and consistent in studies across Western democracies. Broadly speaking, members of minority ethnic groups tend to be less active in politics, to vote less and to engage more in contentious or protest activities in order to express their policy demands (Just, 2017). Why this is so has been the subject of much conjecture. In an effort to compare the different models relating to this, Jan E. Leighley and Arnold Vedlitz (1999) tested these quantitatively for various ethnic groups in Texas. Their conclusion was that socio-economic status, psychological resources and social connectedness best explain the political participation of members of ethnic groups. In other words, members of minority ethnic groups who are poorer, less socially mobile and discriminated against, have less interest in politics and a lesser sense that they can impact the political system, and have weaker ties to their community participate less in politics.

Given that ethnicity can impact the political behaviour of individuals from minority ethnic groups, the question arises as to whether this is the case for social workers as well. The indications are that, in contrast to gender, membership in minority ethnic groups tends to increase a readiness to engage in policy among social workers. The data on the political engagement of social workers from minority ethnic groups is scarce, often dated and primarily focused on black social workers in the US. These findings indicate that while ethnicity does appear to play a motivational role in social workers' policy engagement, in contrast to the data on the political participation of minority ethnic groups in general, social workers from minority ethnic groups tend to be more engaged in policy than both other members of their ethnic group and indeed other social workers.

Historical accounts of policy engagement by social workers reveal that individual black social workers played a key policy role within the profession (Carlton-LaNey, 1994; Sheppard and Pritzker, 2021). The data on social workers running for political office in the US show that they are more likely to be people of colour than are other candidates (Lane and Humphreys, 2011). Findings from studies on the voluntary political participation of social workers indicate that black social workers are the most politically active (Ezell, 1993; Wolk, 1981). In their study of the policy engagement of street-level social workers in the 1960s and 1980s in the US, Linda Cherrey Reeser and Irwin Epstein (1990) found that black social workers had a relatively high level of political activism compared to their non-black colleagues. Insights into the forms of policy engagement adopted by black social workers can be found in a study undertaken by Tricia Bent-Goodley (2003), in which she found that working with interest groups was the most common type of policy activity that the respondents engaged in, followed by voter registration. A quarter of the participants engaged in rallying activities, and most of their policy activity was on the local level. Her conclusion from the findings was that black social workers diverge from the norm in social work in their tendency to engage less in consensus-building approaches than in conflict-oriented approaches.

Data on the policy engagement of social workers from the Arab minority in Israel also indicate that they are more politically active than their Jewish counterparts. In an early study, we found that Arab social workers were significantly more involved in policy practice than Jewish social workers (Weiss-Gal and Gal, 2008). In a recent study on the political engagement of social workers and their efforts to encourage service users to do so, Neveen Ali-Saleh Darawshy, Amnon Boehm and Esther Boehm-Tabib (2021) also found that Arab social workers were more politically active than Jewish social workers. The types of activity were diverse and tended to focus on local political activities, though it is not clear if these were undertaken as civilians or professionals engaging in policy practice in the context of their job. A similar finding emerged in our study on the participation of social workers in parliamentary committees in the Israeli parliament (Gal and Weiss-Gal, 2011). It emerged that the proportion of Arab social workers participating in the committees (10 per cent of the social workers) was double that of their representation in the profession (4.3 per cent).

Drawing on the findings of a study on the engagement of Israeli-Arab social workers in policy practice, Nouman and Azaiza (2021b) sought to conceptualise the link between the motivation of social workers to engage in policy and their belonging to a minority ethnic group. They identified three components of this: the degree to which individuals identify with the minority ethnic group and regard its social status as deprived and discriminated against by the majority ethnic group; the degree to which, as individuals, they have a sense of being victims of discrimination; and their affiliation with ethnic recruitment networks.

Motivation: some conclusions

This chapter has explored various facets of the motivation of individual social workers to engage in different routes to impact policy. The basic claim here is that in addition to the impact of environments, access to the policymaking process and the effect of organisational culture, social workers' motivation to engage in policy is an important determinant of their actual policy engagement. There are diverse components that comprise this umbrella category of social workers' motivation to engage in policy, though these may overlap and will often impact, augment or even undermine one another.

In order to identify the facets of social workers' motivation to engage in policy, we have drawn on theoretical models and the findings of research undertaken within social work and other disciplines. The most common approach to policy motivation in the social work discourse is the CVM, which focuses on three facets of motivation: personal resources (including policy skills); psychological engagement in politics; and belonging to recruitment networks. This model was useful in explaining social workers' engagement in the civil policy routes, such as voluntary political participation (for example, voting, participating in political campaigns) and running for office, and their engagement in the professional routes, especially policy practice, academic policy involvement and policy engagement through professional organisations.

In addition, we underscored the role of values, attitudes and perceptions in understanding why social workers decide to engage in policy. Here, we drew upon empirical findings of studies on social workers' willingness to engage in policy practice and found the PSM approach to be a useful framework for looking at this, particularly as it underscores the impact of socialisation on this, in particular, professional socialisation.

Alongside these facets of motivation, we note that the institutional context in which professional work is undertaken also impacts social workers' willingness to engage in policy. Here, we refer to their managerial role within an organisation and the experience and status that they have attained during their career. Additional insights into the policy motivation of social workers can be found in the literature on the links between personal traits and political engagement. Finally, this discussion of the motivation of social workers to engage in policy cannot ignore the impact of gender and or ethnicity on this. Drawing on explanations that relate to the gendered contexts of female social workers, as well as the traits and assumptions that emerge from these, helps explain why female social workers are more reluctant to run for political office or engage actively in policy practice. By contrast, social workers belonging to minority ethnic groups appear to more motivated to engage in policy-related activities, and this appears to be related to the sense that they personally, and the ethnic group to which they belong collectively, suffer from discrimination.

Explaining the policy engagement of social workers and beyond

Introduction

The premise upon which this book is based is that the social work profession explicitly seeks to address the life challenges and improve the well-being of individuals, families and communities, and to promote social change and development, social cohesion, and the empowerment and liberation of people (IFSW, 2014). Social policies can, and do, have major relevance for these core aspirations of the profession because they affect those contexts in which people exist and that have a major impact upon their lives and their well-being.

Within social work discourse, engagement in policy is no longer seen as limited to a small number of exemplary social work leaders who engage primarily in policy, to community social workers who integrate policy change with organising communities or to radical social workers. Rather, efforts to impact policy are now perceived by many scholars, practitioners and social work professional organisations to be a part of what all social workers should and can do, regardless of the welfare sector they belong to, the field in which they practice, the service user group with whom they work or the practice method that dominates their professional activities. In addition to the other professional efforts that they undertake to promote well-being, to solve problems or to enhance the human rights of their service users, social workers are urged to engage in policy-related activities, either as professionals or as citizens. In other words, the current discourse takes for granted that policy formulation is not the sole domain of formal policymakers or of other professionals who set policies that social workers implement. Rather, social workers can be party to the social policy formulation process as implementers, policy practitioners, academics, active citizens or elected politicians.

Findings from diverse types of studies and rich anecdotal knowledge from across the globe, which we have presented in this book, indicate that social workers do indeed engage in social policy formulation and change. Although, overall, the engagement of social workers is apparently limited in at least some of the policy routes (for example, policy practice, holding elected office and so on), it appears to be much more common than in the past and is generating significant attention in practice and in the professional and academic arenas. Certainly, there can be little doubt now that social workers no longer just passively implement social policies without having any input into, voice in or impact on them. Whether on the ground or in an array of formal and informal policy arenas, as professionals or as citizens, or directly or indirectly, they advance policies and impact their design. This policy engagement: takes diverse forms and include various tactics; takes place at different stages of the policy process; occurs in arenas ranging from the organisation in which social workers are employed to an array of local and national policy arenas; relates to diverse modes and types of policies; and follows distinctive policy routes.

As we described in Chapter 1, in recent years, the discourse around the policy engagement of social workers has been transformed and has taken new and exciting directions. Scholars have adopted more theoretically grounded approaches and rigorous, though diverse, research methodologies in their studies, and these have explored different organisational perspectives and aspects of social workers' policy engagement. These efforts provide us with innovative ways for understanding social workers' policy engagement, and they have revealed new forms of this type of practice. The insights that emerge from this cutting-edge scholarship obviously have major relevance to the ways in which scholars, professional leaders, social workers in the field and service users understand the profession and what its practitioners can, and are expected to, do.

This book's contribution to the vibrant discourse on the policy engagement of social workers is our response to a simple but, we believe, important question: what explains why, how and when social workers engage in policy? The straightforward answer to this is that social workers will seek to influence social policies that relate to problems that affect their service users and/or that directly or indirectly affect the social workers themselves. Social workers' decisions as to if, when and how to impact policies will depend on their willingness to engage in policy and the degree to which they sense that they have a viable option to do so. A more precise response required us to create a conceptual framework that not only is firmly embedded in the field of knowledge that is social work, but also draws upon theoretical and empirical insights from diverse disciplines. The wealth of research on the policy engagement of social workers that has been created over recent decades has provided the empirical foundation for the formulation of the PE conceptual framework, which is the focus of the chapters of this book.

Our interest in this issue has developed over recent years. From an original focus on what explains policy practice (Gal and Weiss-Gal, 2015), this book presents subsequent efforts to think of the policy engagement of social workers in a broader way that encompasses additional policy routes. In addition, it reflects an explicit acknowledgement of the impact of the environments that create the context within which social workers' policy engagement takes place and the contribution of these environments to explaining this activity. In this final chapter, we summarise the conclusions that we have reached and discuss the implications of these.

The components of the PE conceptual framework revisited

As can be seen in Figure 7.1, the four categories of factors that comprise the PE conceptual framework are *environments, opportunity, facilitation* and *motivation*. These four categories of factors explain the level of social workers' policy engagement in six policy routes and the ways in which they operate in each of them.

Environments are the wider contexts in which social workers' policy activities take place and that have an indirect impact on their actual engagement in policy. As can be seen in Figure 7.1, the impact on the policy engagement of social workers of the four environments identified here – welfare regime, problems/policies, the profession and people (service users and other citizens) – will be mediated by the other three categories of factors in the framework.

First, the structuring of the welfare state, the role of social work in it and the status of the profession in society will impact the levels and the ways in which the policy process is accessible to the impact of social workers or, in other words, the *opportunities* that social workers have to affect the policy formulation process. Second, *environments* also affect *facilitation*. Through the introduction of governance reforms that, to some extent, limit the agency of social workers (for example, NPM) or, alternately, the prevalence of social workers fulfilling managerial positions in social service organisations and these managers' affinity to a professional discourse that promotes policy engagement, *environments* affect the degree to which social services enable or restrict social workers' engagement in policy (*facilitation*). Finally, the nature and severity of the social problems that affect service users, the policies that determine the functioning of welfare state services, the ways in which the social work profession relates to policy engagement, and the degree to which service users demand that social workers act to address a lack of policy or its limitations will affect social workers' *motivation* – in other words, their attitudes towards policy change, their political efficacy or their willingness to engage in policy processes – which then affects their policy engagement through different routes.

Opportunity refers to factors that determine the access that social workers have to the social policy formulation process. Central to the discussion on *opportunity* is the understanding that the institutions in which policies are made have rules, norms and processes that effectively regulate access to them, and these will determine not only the level of engagement, but also when and how social workers participate in the policy formulation process. We described these as opportunity structures. These rules, norms and processes

Figure 7.1: The PE conceptual framework

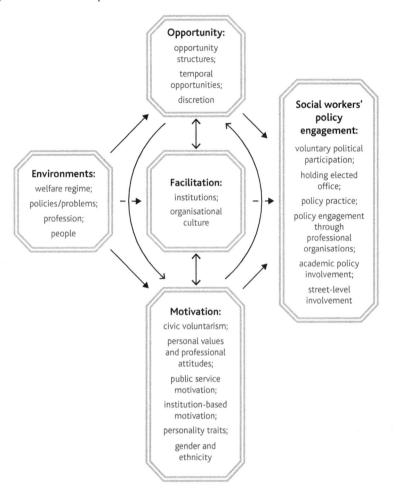

are not the same across countries and over time, and they lead to differences in the form and level of social workers' engagement in policy. Social workers in the US will tend to employ lobbying as a key tool to influence policymaking in that country, participation in the UK can take the form of structured consultations through policy tools such as green papers, while social workers in Israel are frequently to be found in policy discussions taking place in parliamentary committees. Divergences in opportunity are also the case for policymaking on the local level, where the participation of social workers in policymaking will often be determined by the specific formal and informal rules that determine policymaking within local authorities and by the degree to which the policymaking process is open to street-level bureaucrats, among them, social workers.

Access to policymaking institutions by social workers will also be influenced by windows of opportunity that can open due to political events. Examples of these are the rise to power of political figures or political parties that incorporate social workers in decision-making, such as the ascent of the Socialist Party in post-Franco Spain and the election of Franklin D. Roosevelt as President of the US. This access can also occur due to the opening of problem windows, such as the sense that social workers have the unique knowledge required to address pressing social problems, as was the case for dealing with poverty in Israel. Finally, *opportunity* can take the form of discretion on the street level. Evidence from different countries indicates that when social policies offer discretion in their implementation, either formally or informally, this provides social work professionals with the scope to change policies during this policy stage.

Facilitation focuses upon what happens within the workplace and on the degree to which this context enables social workers to engage in policy. As most social workers are employed in organisations, the way in which organisational contexts relate to the policy engagement of their employees and how this is reflected in organisational cultures are crucial in understanding when and how social workers engage in policy. Our discussion of this category began with the insight that the behaviour of organisations in the policy arena is defined by the options that they have to do so and the resulting interface between organisations and externalities, such as the actions, values and expectations of the state, other organisations, professionals and the general public. This interface not only determines the ways in which organisations act in policy arenas, but crucially also impacts the structures and expectations of the organisation, as well as the policy-related behaviour of their employees. As such, the organisational culture relevant to social workers and the way in which it relates to their policy engagement will reflect the organisation's expectations of social workers. However, the organisational culture will also be influenced by the attitudes of the social workers (*motivation*), in addition to the effect of external influences, such as those of the profession and service users.

The data on the impact of organisations on the policy engagement of social worker employees is robust, though the nature of this clearly varies across different types of organisations and contexts. Thus, studies indicate that the types of activities undertaken to further policy by social worker employees in advocacy organisations differ from those in non-profit service providers or from those employed in the state sector. Within the state bureaucracy, the policy-related expectations of social workers employed in high-level administrative positions are very different from those employed in local social services.

Motivation consists of diverse micro-level factors that affect the individual social worker's engagement in policy. Drawing on studies undertaken within social work that reflect knowledge from public administration, political science and psychology, the category incorporates a wide range of factors, including values, attitudes towards social work aims and strategies, perceptions of political self-efficacy, and also more fundamental personality traits and identities.

A key model that has informed much of the research on the motivation of social workers to engage in policy is the CVM, which underscores such components as psychological engagement in politics, a sense of political efficacy and membership in professional networks that encourage social workers to engage actively in policy processes. This is particularly useful in understanding the willingness of social workers to engage in efforts to affect policy as citizens, either through voluntary political activity or by running for elected office. A second model that has relevance to the policy engagement of social workers draws upon motivation theory, and it is the PSM model that has sought to explain the decision by individuals to become civil servants. In particular, the 'attraction to politics and policymaking' component of this model has been found to be associated with the policy engagement of social workers. In addition, research has identified other personal values and professional attitudes that are associated with social workers' level of policy engagement. The motivational factors also include, what we described as, 'institution-based motivation', which relates to the role that individual social workers have within an organisation, their employment status and their experience within the workplace. Recent work has also linked personality traits to social workers' willingness to engage in policy. Finally, research has shown that both the gender and the ethnic identity of individuals can impact social workers' motivation to engage in different types of policy activity.

The interrelation between opportunity, facilitation and motivation

As can be seen in Figure 7.1, not only do the environments have an impact on the three other categories, as we illustrated earlier; rather, these categories also impact one another in different ways. *Opportunity* impacts *facilitation* and *motivation* because access to the institutions and processes in which policies are set or the capacity to change policies after they have been formally adopted (*opportunity*) will be likely to determine how, and if, organisations are willing to enable the engagement of their employees in policy (*facilitation*) and the willingness of social workers in these organisations to engage in policy (*motivation*). This impact is seen when: social service agencies in the US enable their social work employees to give testimony in legislative deliberations on social welfare issues; social service providers in Switzerland respond to outreach by government officials by encouraging their employees to participate in informal consultations on the implementation of social welfare legislation; and social service managers in Israel enable social work members of their teams to respond to invitations by parliamentary committees to provide relevant insights from the field in their deliberations. Alongside the impact of *opportunity* on *facilitation*, in all of these cases, the willingness of social worker employees in these organisations to participate in these processes because they believe that these arenas are accessible to them and they can actually have an impact on the policy process reflects the impact of *opportunity* on *motivation*. The readiness of social workers to participate in mass demonstrations in Spain during the Great Recession, either as citizens or as professionals, also reflects this. Not only were the social workers encouraged by their professional organisation to participate in these demonstrations, but, critically, they also believed that these actions could have an impact on the political discourse and on policy decisions.

Moving to opportunities created by discretion, if policy processes offer the social work managers of social services or the heads of street-level teams in these services the opportunity to interpret, and indeed to change, policy during its implementation and they decide to do so, this will again be a case of *opportunity* impacting *motivation*. If these interventions are undertaken with the tacit or explicit support of their superiors within the organisation, this will obviously show the impact of *opportunity* on *facilitation*.

The existence of an organisational culture that enables social worker employees to participate in policy processes (*facilitation*) can also often serve as a means through which to encourage them to do so. In other words, it will impact their *motivation* to engage in the policy process. This will certainly be the case if organisations, or specific units within these, not only enable this, but also offer concrete support for this type of activity. This is obvious in the case of social work academics who are encouraged by their universities to engage in the policy process as part of the university furthering its social impact goals. In other organisations, the support can take the form of the inclusion of policy activities in the role definition of employees (described as institutional motivation in Chapter 6) and explicit inclusion of policy practice in the goals of the agency and its social workers. It can also be reflected in in-house policy practice training and formal recognition of policy achievements. In these cases, social workers will perceive of policy engagement as something that not only is desirable, but also enjoys legitimacy within the context of their workplace. Crucial to this type of organisational support is the sense that street-level social workers engaged in policy activities within local government or beyond know that their managers support their actions and will provide them with backing if needed, which emerged in studies undertaken in Israel.

Yet, *facilitation* can also create *opportunity*. In cases in which organisations encourage their social worker employees to seek to create new forums in which they participate and can influence local policy, or when universities encourage their social work faculty members to push for the creation of advisory bodies that can have an input into the policy process, the opportunities are created by the organisations that employ social workers.

Finally, *motivation* is not only a function of opportunity and facilitation, as we mentioned earlier; rather, it also creates *opportunity* and *facilitation*. The impact of *motivation* on *opportunity* typically occurs when social workers act purposely to create or enhance their access to the policy process. This occurs when social workers on the local or national level decide to act to create, and introduce changes into, policymaking institutions so that they can be party to the policy formulation process. This can take the form of creating new decision-making committees at the local level, as we saw in the case of local policy entrepreneurs in Israel, but it can also be a consequence of the incorporation of social workers into the work of national-level policy forums, which we saw in the introduction of a new social welfare policy in Italy. The impact of social workers' *motivation* on *facilitation* can also take the form of social worker employees, sometimes in response to the demands of service users, seeking to influence their employers to enable them to engage in policy practice, to participate in the activities of their representative organisations or even to run for political office. In these cases, we can witness the importance of the social workers' agency in changing the contexts that enable them to fulfil their professional obligation and duty to impact policy.

Moving beyond

Clearly, our ambitious efforts to explain the wide expanse of social workers' policy engagement are dependent upon the empirical evidence that exists. While our own work and that of other colleagues offer support for many of the elements of the PE conceptual framework and hopefully provide a solid infrastructure for an understanding of social workers' policy activities, much still remains to be explored and substantiated in future research.

A research agenda

There are at least four fields of research that a potential research agenda based on the PE conceptual framework could explore. First, there is a need to identify additional components in each of the elements of the conceptual framework. Culture and religion are virtually unexplored, but potentially important, *environments* that may have an impact of the policy engagement of social workers. Similarly, there are conceivably personality traits and values not yet studied that can be essential sources of *motivation*. Moreover, we can only assume that there are additional policy routes that exist, which further studies in different contexts and settings will help us to identify.

Second, the interaction within each component is also important. Thus, for example, more work is required to better understand the link between some of the *environments*, among them, the form that welfare regimes take and the nature of social problems, and social workers' policy engagement. Moreover, although we have incorporated diverse facets of *motivation* to engage in policy in the framework, we do not yet have a sufficient understanding of all the links between them. We can assume that there is an association between political socialisation in the family, attitudes towards the political system, political efficacy and a willingness to engage in policy but understanding the nature of this association requires additional research.

Third, the interaction between the various components of the four categories of the PE conceptual framework still remains a challenge. The links among the four categories and between them and the policy routes leaves much to be studied. Thus, for example, we would like to better understand how professional socialisation (*environments*) affects the perceptions of policy involvement, the values and the political efficacy of social work students and social workers to engage in different routes (*motivation*), as well as what the exact dynamics are of the choices that social workers make when deciding which policy route to choose. Similarly, the role of service users in shaping both *facilitation* and *motivation* requires more research. This could look at their role in motivating social workers and professional organisations to engage in policy, but it could also enable us to think more about the impact of service users on the internal dynamics of social welfare organisations and, more intriguingly, on the opportunities that social workers have to impact policy.

Lastly, we need to culturally validate the model. Much of the data on the PE conceptual framework is based upon studies in established welfare states and liberal democracies. However, social work exists across the globe, and social workers seek to impact policy in very diverse societies. Initial findings from such countries as China, India, South Africa and Ethiopia show this. Additional studies from these settings and others across the world will undoubtedly shed new light on the framework and provide useful insights regarding its relevance and usefulness. Studies in these countries will inevitably enrich the framework, add to its components and make it more relevant to social work practice across the world.

Implications for social work education and practice

Hopefully, despite the theoretical focus of this book, its insights will also be useful to social work educators and practitioners. The findings of studies described in this book and our own experience as social work educators offer support for the notion that teaching policy engagement can be useful in the process of creating *motivation* to engage in policy. More specifically, it can provide future and current social workers with the values, knowledge, skills, tools, sense of efficacy, psychological involvement in politics and perceptions with regard to policy engagement that are crucial to their engagement in the policy process. There are myriad ways to achieve this, either explicitly or implicitly. These include designated courses on policy engagement, incorporating policy-relevant subjects into existing courses, including assignments that require policy engagement or simulate it in diverse courses, and facilitating students' interaction with social workers engaged in policy. Similarly, promoting policy engagement within field training will offer students hands-on opportunities for policy practice and may also have an indirect knock-on effect on the social workers with whom they have contact. Less explicit efforts within social work education can also further this agenda. Faculty can impact students' appreciation of the possibilities for policy engagement by serving as role models and bringing their experiences to the classroom. Organising public events within schools that focus on the relevance of policy, holding student debates on policy issues and highlighting the policy role of alumni can all contribute to students' sense that they can and should play a policy role.

The findings can also help educators, and, through them, their students, to better understand the role of *environments*, *opportunity* and *facilitation* in the policy engagement of social workers and how social workers seeking to influence policy can affect these. In particular, the 'discovery' of the salience of opportunity structures for social workers seeking to influence social policy should lead us to rethink the current emphasis in social work training. Effective policy practice training needs to provide students with a solid understanding of the relevant policy environment in which they seek to engage and the degree to which social workers have the agency to create new opportunities through which to impact policy. In the same vein, social work education should also explain and illustrate to students and social workers that they can impact *facilitation*. Motivated social workers can act to encourage and demand their organisations to support their policy engagement in diverse ways.

The PE conceptual framework also has potential implications for the practice of social workers in the field. *Opportunity*, and its contribution to efforts to affect policy, can encourage social work professional organisations to seek to create the opportunities necessary for them and their members to influence policymakers. These can include ensuring access to existing policymaking arenas or creating new sites in which social workers can play a policy role. Hopefully, individual social workers will become more aware of the structural and temporal opportunities that enable them to access the policy process. Knowledge on the impact of the *facilitation* role of organisations and their leadership in encouraging social workers to engage in policy can lead administrators in these organisations to offer material or symbolic incentives to their employees to engage in policy or to provide them with the tools needed to do so effectively. In-work courses on advocacy are an example of this. As for *motivation*, individual social workers can take from the book evidence of their potential to impact policy, ideas as to how this can be undertaken and the importance of a better understanding of the role of their managers and their own knowledge on the policy process in enabling this to succeed.

In sum, in the preceding chapters of this book, we hope that we have succeeded in offering the reader a convincing conceptual framework for understanding the engagement of social workers in policy. The goal has been to enlighten scholars and professionals who care about social work and about what it can contribute to people, communities and societies. By drawing on cutting-edge thinking and data in social work and in related fields of knowledge, we believe that this framework will be able to move the social work discourse on policy forward. All this should contribute to a better and more effective social work profession that will improve the well-being of service users and advance social justice.

Notes

Chapter 2

[1] We are grateful to Tobias Kindler for his input into the description of this struggle.

[2] See: www.socialworkers.org/Advocacy/Political-Action-for-Candidate-Election-PACE/
Why-Social-Workers-Should-Run-for-Office#:~:text=Social%20workers%20run%20
for%20public,leadership%20to%20improve%20their%20communities

[3] See: www.socialworkfuture.org

[4] See: http://cqrcengage.com/socialworkers/

Chapter 4

[1] Clearly, there are situations in which the impact is indirect, through external means, though this would most likely be in more extreme cases.

[2] See: www.socialworkers.org/Advocacy

Chapter 5

[1] Due to a lack of data, we will not discuss the engagement of social workers in for-profit corporations in this chapter.

References

Aaslund, H. and Chear, C. (2020) 'Marginalised groups protest against social welfare and public health: conceptualising the challenge for social workers', *European Journal of Social Work*, 23(6): 1032–43.

Abo El Nasr, M.M. (1991) 'Social work practice and local politics in Egypt', *International Social Work*, 34(1): 7–25.

Abramovitz, M. and Hopkins, T. (1983) 'Reaganomics and the welfare state', *Journal of Sociology & Social Welfare*, 10(4): 563–78.

Adams, H.H. (1977) *Harry Hopkins: A Biography*, New York: Putnam's Sons.

Adams, R. (2002) *Social Policy for Social Work*, Basingstoke: Palgrave.

Ahonen, P., Hyyryläinen, E. and Salminen, A. (2006) 'Looking for governance configurations of European welfare states', *Journal of European Social Policy*, 16(2): 173–84.

Allen, H., Garfinkel, I. and Waldfogel, J. (2018) 'Social policy research in social work in the twenty-first century: the state of scholarship and the professions, what is promising, and what needs to be done', *Social Service Review*, 92(4): 504–47.

Almgren, G., Kemp, S.P. and Eisinger, A. (2000) 'The legacy of Hull House and the Children's Bureau in the American mortality transition', *Social Service Review*, 74(1): 1–27.

Almog-Bar, M. (2018) 'Insider status and outsider tactics: advocacy tactics of human service nonprofits in the age of New Public Governance', *Nonprofit Policy Forum*, 8(4): 411–28.

Almog-Bar, M. and Schmid, H. (2014) 'Advocacy activities of nonprofit human service organizations: a critical review', *Nonprofit and Voluntary Sector Quarterly*, 43(1): 11–35.

Almog-Bar, M., Weiss-Gal, I. and Gal, J. (2015) 'Bringing public policy into policy practice', *Journal of Social Work*, 15(4): 390–408.

Amann, K. and Kindler, T. (2021) 'Social workers in politics – a qualitative analysis of factors influencing social workers' decision to run for political office', *European Journal of Social Work*, DOI: 10.1080/13691457.2021.1977254

Anderfuhren-Biget, S. (2012) 'Profiles of public service-motivated civil servants: evidence from a multicultural country', *International Journal of Public Administration*, 35(1): 5–18.

Anderson, D.K. and Harris, B.M. (2005) 'Teaching social welfare policy: a comparison of two pedagogical approaches', *Journal of Social Work Education*, 41(3): 511–25.

Andrews, K.T. and Edwards, B. (2004) 'Advocacy organizations in the U.S. political process', *Annual Review of Sociology*, 30: 479–506.

Arlotti, M. and Aguilar-Hendrickson, M. (2018) 'The vicious layering of multilevel governance in Southern Europe: the case of elderly care in Italy and Spain', *Social Policy & Administration*, 52(3): 646–61.

Aronson, J. and Smith, K. (2010) 'Managing restructured social services: expanding the social?', *British Journal of Social Work*, 40(2): 530–47.

Aten, K., Howard-Grenville, J. and Ventresca, M.J. (2012) 'Organizational culture and institutional theory: a conversation at the border', *Journal of Management Inquiry*, 21(1): 78–83.

Auel, K. and Christiansen, T. (2015) 'After Lisbon: national parliaments in the European Union', *West European Politics*, 38(2): 261–81.

Aviv, I., Gal, J. and Weiss-Gal, I. (2021) 'Social workers as street-level policy entrepreneurs', *Public Administration*, 99(3): 454–68.

Baber, H. (2020) 'Intentions to participate in political crowdfunding – from the perspective of civic voluntarism model and theory of planned behavior', *Technology in Society*, 63(2020): 101435.

Bailey, R. and Brake, M. (eds) (1975) *Radical Social Work*, London: Edward Arnold.

Baker Collins, S. (2016) 'The space in the rules: bureaucratic discretion in the administration of Ontario Works', *Social Policy and Society*, 15(2): 221–35.

Bangcheng, L. (2009) 'Evidence of public service motivation of social workers in China', *International Review of Administrative Sciences*, 75(2): 349–66.

Banks, S. (2012) *Ethics and Values in Social Work* (4th edn), Basingstoke: Palgrave Macmillan.

Bar-Nir, D. and Gal, J. (2011) 'Who has the power? The role of NPOs in local authorities', *Voluntas*, 22(1): 1–25.

Barretti, M. (2004) 'What do we know about the professional socialization of our students?', *Journal of Social Work Education*, 40(2): 255–83.

Bar Yosef, A., Weiss-Gal, I. and Kagan, I. (2020) 'Predictors of hospital-based registered nurses' engagement in on-the-job policy activities', *Research in Nursing & Health*, 43(5): 489–98.

Bastagli, F., Coady, D. and Gupta, S. (2012) *Income Inequality and Fiscal Policy*, IMF Staff Discussion Note 12/08, Washington, DC: International Monetary Fund.

BASW (British Association of Social Workers) (2019) 'The code of ethics of social work'. Available at: https://basw.co.uk/system/files/resources/basw_code_of_ethics_-_2021.pdf

Baumgartner, F.R., Berry, J.M., Hojnacki, M., Kimball, D.C. and Leech, B.L. (2009) *Lobbying and Policy Change: Who Wins, Who Loses, and Why*, Chicago: University of Chicago Press.

Baynesagn, A.H. (2020) 'Being visible in the policy process: the experience of the school of social work at Addis Ababa University', *British Journal of Social Work*, 50(8): 2389–404.

Beimers, D. (2015) 'NASW involvement in legislative advocacy', *Journal of Policy Practice*, 14(3–4): 256–74.

Béland, D. (2009) 'Ideas, institutions, and policy change', *Journal of European Public Policy*, 16(5): 701–18.

Béland, D. and Powell, M. (2015) 'Continuity and change in social policy', *Social Policy & Administration*, 50(2): 129–47.

Béland, D., Cantillon, B., Hick, R. and Moreira, A. (2021) 'Social policy in the face of a global pandemic: policy responses to the COVID-19 crisis', *Social Policy & Administration*, 55(2): 249–60.

Beltran, S.J., Miller, V.J. and Hamler, T. (2022) 'Social workers' impact on policy through regulations: a case study of the U.S. Long-Term Care Ombudsman Program', *Journal of Social Work,* , 22(2): 539–55.

Bent-Goodley, T. (2003) 'The role of African-American social workers in social policy', in T. Bent-Goodley (ed) *African-American Social Workers and Social Policy*, Binghamton, NY: Haworth Press, pp 1–17.

Bent-Goodley, T. (2015) 'A call for social work activism', *Social Work*, 60(2): 101–3.

Bent-Goodley, T., Snell, C.L. and Carlton-LaNey, I. (2017) 'Black perspectives and social work practice', *Journal of Human Behavior in the Social Environment*, 27(1–2): 27–35.

Beresford, P. and Croft, S. (2001) 'Service users' knowledges and the social construction of social work', *Journal of Social Work*, 1(3): 295–316.

Beresford, P. and Croft, S. (2004) 'Service users and practitioners reunited: the key component for social work reform', *British Journal of Social Work*, 34(1): 53–68.

Bernklau Halvor, C.D. (2016) 'Increasing social work students' political interest and efficacy', *Journal of Policy Practice*, 15(4): 289–313.

Berry, J.M. (1984) *The Interest Group Society*, Boston: Little, Brown.

Bifulco, L. and Centemeri, L. (2006) 'Governance and participation in local welfare: the case of the Italian Piani di Zona', *Social Policy & Administration*, 42(3): 211–27.

Binder, N. and Weiss-Gal, I. (2021) 'Social workers as local politicians in Israel', *British Journal of Social Work*, https://doi.org/10.1093/bjsw/bcab219.

Birkland, T.A. (2020) *An Introduction to the Policy Process: Theories, Concepts, and Models of Public Policy Making* (5th edn) , London: Routledge.

Blomgren, M. and Rozenberg, O. (2012) 'Legislative roles and legislative studies: the neo-institutionalist turning point?', in M. Blomgren and O. Rozenberg (eds) *Parliamentary Roles in Modern Legislatures*, Abingdon: Routledge, pp 8–36.

Blondel, J. (2008) 'About institutions, mainly, but not exclusively, political', in R.A.W. Rhodes, S.A. Binder and B.A. Rockman (eds) *The Oxford Handbook of Political Institutions*, Oxford: Oxford University Press, pp 716–30.

Bochel, H. and Berthier, A. (2020) 'A place at the table? Parliamentary committees, witnesses and the scrutiny of government actions and legislations', *Social Policy and Society*, 19(1): 1–17.

Bode, I. (2006) 'Disorganized welfare mixes: voluntary agencies and new governance regimes in Western Europe', *Journal of European Social Policy*, 16(4): 346–59.

Boehm, A., Darawshy, N.A.S. and Boehm-Tabib, E. (2018) 'Social workers and politics: direct political involvement and encouragement of client involvement in politics', *Journal of Sociology & Social Welfare*, 45(2): 3–24.

Bonoli, G., Natili, M. and Trein, P. (2019) 'A federalist's dilemma: trade-offs between social legitimacy and budget responsibility in multi-tiered welfare states', *Journal of European Social Policy*, 29(1): 56–69.

Boone, K., Roets, G. and Roose, R. (2019) 'Learning to play chess: how to make sense of a politics of representation with people in poverty', *Social Policy & Administration*, 53(7): 1030–44.

Borchert, J. (2011) 'Individual ambition and institutional opportunity: A conceptual approach to political careers in multi-level systems', *Regional and Federal Studies*, 21(2): 117–40.

Branco, F. (2019) 'Social reform in the US: lessons from the Progressive Era', in U. Klammer, S. Lieber and S. Leitner (eds) *Social Work and the Making of Social Policy*, Bristol: Policy Press, pp 71–87.

Brierton Granruth, L., Kindle, P.A., Burford, M.L., Delavega, E., Johnson, D.H., Peterson, S. and Caplan M.A. (2018) 'Changing social work students' perceptions of the role of government in a policy class', *Journal of Social Work Education*, 54(10): 110–21.

Briskman, L. (2020) 'The people's inquiry into detention: social work activism for asylum seeker rights', *Journal of Sociology*, 56(1): 100–14.

Brodkin, E.Z. (1997) 'Inside the welfare contract: discretion and accountability in state welfare administration', *Social Service Review*, 71(1): 1–33.

Broers, D.R. (2018) 'Identifying factors that predict policy practice among social workers', unpublished PhD dissertation, Walden University.

Brown, M.E., Livermore, M. and Ball, A. (2015) 'Social work advocacy: professional self-interest and social justice', *Journal of Sociology & Social Welfare*, 17(3): 45–63.

Browne, W.P. (1998) *Groups, Interests, and U.S. Public Policy*, Washington, DC: Georgetown University Press.

Bruch, S.K., Meyers, M.K. and Gornick, J.C. (2018) 'The consequences of decentralization: inequality in safety net provision in the post-welfare reform era', *Social Service Review*, 92(1): 3–35.

Buchanan, S. (2020) 'Corraling organizational institutionalism', *Journal of Management Inquiry*, 29(3): 251–3.

Burnier, D. (2008) 'Erased history: Frances Perkins and the emergence of care-centered public administration', *Administration and Society*, 40(4): 403–22.

Butler, S.S. and Coleman, P.A. (1997) 'Raising our voices: a macro practice assignment', *Journal of Teaching in Social Work*, 15(2): 63–80.

Cai, T., Lei, J. and Chen, Y. (2021) 'Depoliticised or repoliticised policy practice? The role of non-governmental social work organisations in policy-making in China', *British Journal of Social Work*, https://doi.org/10.1093/bjsw/bcab172

Capano, G. (2018) 'Reconceptualizing layering – from mode of institutional change to mode of institutional design: types and outputs', *Public Administration*, 97(3): 590–604.

Carlton-LaNey, I.B. (ed) (1994) 'Special issue on the legacy of African-American leadership in social welfare', *Journal of Sociology & Social Welfare*, 21.

Carson, E., Chung, D. and Evans, T. (2015) 'Complexities of discretion in social services in the third sector', *European Journal of Social Work*, 18(2): 167–84.

Chandler, S.K. (2009) 'Working hard, living poor: social work and the Movement for Livable Wages', *Journal of Community Practice*, 17(1–2): 170–83.

Chang, Y.-B., Weng, D.L.-C. and Wang, C.-H. (2020) 'Personality traits and the propensity to protest: a cross-national analysis', *Asian Journal of Political Science*, 29(1): 22–41.

Chappell, L. (2002) 'The "femocrat" strategy: expanding the repertoire of feminist activists', *Parliamentary Affairs*, 55(1): 85–98.

Chari, R., Murphy, G. and Hogan, J. (2007) 'Regulating lobbyists: a comparative analysis of the United States, Canada, Germany and the European Union', *Political Quarterly*, 78(3): 422–38.

Christensen, J. (2017) *The Power of Economists within the State*, Stanford: Stanford University Press.

Chui, E. and Gray, M. (2004) 'The political activities of social workers in the context of changing roles and political transition in Hong Kong', *International Journal of Social Welfare*, 13(2): 170–80.

Clear, A., Paull, M. and Holloway, D. (2018) 'Nonprofit advocacy tactics: thinking inside the box?', *Voluntas*, 29(4): 857–69.

Coen, D. and Richardson, J. (eds) (2009) *Lobbying the European Union: Institutions, Actors, and Issues*, Oxford: Oxford University Press.

Cohen, M. (2017) *Julia Lathrop: Social Service and Progressive Government*, Boulder: Westview Press.

Cohen, N. (2021) *Policy Entrepreneurship at the Street Level*, Cambridge: Cambridge University Press.

Colby, I.C., Dulmus, C.N. and Sowers, K.M. (eds) (2013) *Social Work and Social Policy: Advancing the Principles of Economic and Social Justice*, Hoboken, NJ: John Wiley & Sons.

Collins, M.E., Dixon, Z. and Zimmerman, T. (2022) 'Building policy practice into foundation field placement: experiences and outcomes', *Social Work Education*, 41(1): 105–18.

Combs-Orme, T. (1988) 'Infant mortality and social work: legacy of success', *Social Service Review*, 62)1): 83–102.

Corte, J. & Roose, R. (2020) 'Social work as a policy actor: understanding social policy as an open-ended democratic practice', *European Journal of Social Work*, 23(2): 227–238.

Cossar, J. and Neil, E. (2015) 'Service user involvement in social work in research: learning from an adoption research project', *British Journal of Social Work*, 45(1): 225–40.

Craig, G. (2002) 'Poverty, social work and social justice', *British Journal of Social Work*, 32(6): 669–82.

CSWE (Council on Social Work Education) (2015) *Educational Policy and Accreditation Standards*, Alexandria, VA: Council of Social Work Education.

Cummins, L.K., Byers, K.V. and Pedrick, L.E. (2011) *Policy Practice for Social Workers: New Strategies for a New Era*, Upper Saddle River, NJ: Allyn and Bacon.

Darawshy, N.A.S., Boehm, A. and Boehm-Tabib, E. (2021) 'Political involvement of social workers in majority and minority groups: comparison of Palestinians-Israelis and Jewish-Israelis', *British Journal of Social Work*, 52(3): 909–27.

David, R.J., Tolbert, P.S. and Boghossian, J. (2019) 'Institutional theory in organizational studies', *Oxford Research Encyclopedia of Business and Management*, 23 December. Available at: https://doi.org/10.1093/acref ore/9780190224851.013.158

Davies, J.S. and Trounstine, J. (2012) 'Urban politics and the New Institutionalism', in K. Mossberger, S.E. Clarke and P. John (eds) *The Oxford Handbook of Urban Politics*, New York: Oxford University Press, pp 51–70.

De Corte, J. and Roose, R. (2020) 'Social work as a policy actor: understanding social policy as an open-ended democratic practice', *European Journal of Social Work*, 23(2): 227–38.

De Corte, J., Verschuere, B. and De Bie, M. (2017) 'The political role of social work: grasping the momentum of working through interorganizational networks in Belgium', *Journal of Social Service Research*, 43(3): 404–15.

Degerickx, H., Van Gorp, A., De Wilde, L. and Roets, G. (2020) 'Giving voice to people in poverty in Belgian social policy making since the 1990s: a window of opportunity for a political demarche?', *Belgisch Tijdschrift voor Nieuwste Geschiedenis*, 3–4: 74–96.

D'Emilione, M., Assunta Giuliano, G., Raciti, P. and Vivaldi Vera, P. (2019) 'The voices of Italian social workers: from a pilot anti-poverty intervention to a national policy', in U. Klammer, S. Lieber and S. Leitner (eds) *Social Work and the Making of Social Policy*, Bristol: Policy Press, pp 53–68.

Denney, D. (1998) *Social Policy and Social Work*, Oxford: Oxford University Press.

D'Eon, M.I. (2017) 'Police enforcement of cannabis possession laws in Canada: changes in implementation by street-level bureaucrats', unpublished thesis, University of Saskatchewan, Canada.

Diaz, C. and Hill, L. (2019) 'A critical evaluation of the extent to which the reform and modernisation agenda has impacted on the professionalisation of social work in England', *Child Care in Practice*, 26(3): 272–84.

Dickens, J. (2010) *Social Work and Social Policy*, London: Routledge.

Dickinson, J.C. (2007) 'A survey of social policy placements in BSW education', *Journal of Policy Practice*, 6(1): 47–63.

DiMaggio, P.J. and Powell, W.W. (1983) 'The iron cage revisited: institutional isomorphism and collective rationality in organizational fields', *American Sociological Review*, 48(2): 147–60.

Dolgoff, R.L. (1981) 'Clinicians as social policy makers', *Social Casework*, 62: 284–92.

Domanski, M.D. (1998) 'Prototypes of social work political participation: an empirical model', *Social Work*, 43(2): 156–67.

Dominelli, L. (2002) *Anti-oppressive Social Work Theory and Practice*, Houndmills: Palgrave Macmillan.

Donaldson, L. (2007) 'Advocacy by nonprofit human service agencies: organizational factors as correlates to advocacy behavior', *Journal of Community Practice*, 15(3): 139–58.

Doron, I. (2012) 'Social workers and the law in Israel', in M. Hovav, E. Lewental and J. Katan (eds) *Social Work in Israel*, Tel Aviv: HaKibbutz Hameuchad, pp 68–89 (in Hebrew).

Douglas, L. (2008) 'Political involvement of social workers', unpublished MA thesis, Dalhousie University, Canada.

Driessens, K. and Lyssens-Danneboom, V. (2022) 'Involving service users in research and education: is this structural social work?, in K Driessens and V. Lyssens-Danneboom (eds) *Involving Service Users in Social Work Education, Research and Policy*, Bristol: Policy Press.

Driessens, K., McLaughlin, H. and van Doorn, L. (2016) 'The meaningful involvement of service users in social work education: examples from Belgium and the Netherlands', *Social Work Education*, 35(7): 739–51.

Droppa, D.C. (2007) 'Developing student competence in policy practice through policy projects in human service organizations', *The Journal of Baccalaureate Social Work*, 12(2): 83–97.

Drori, G.S., Walgenbach, P. and Höllerer, M.A. (2020) 'Organizational institutionalism: analysis across levels and domains', in R.A. Scott and M.C. Buchmann (eds) *Emerging Trends in the Social and Behavioral Sciences*, Wiley Online Library. Available at: https://researchgate.net/publication/339770284_Drori_Walgenbach_and_Hollerer_Emerging_Trends_in_Organizational_Institutionalism_ORGANIZATIONAL_INSTITUTIONALISM_ANALYSIS_ACROSS_LEVELS_AND_DOMAINS

Dudziak, S. and Coates, J. (2004) 'Social worker participation in policy practice and political activity', *Canadian Review of Social Policy*, 54: 79–96.

Easterly, B. (2016) 'Judicial responsiveness to valence issues: an event history analysis of the initial sex offender registration and notification (SORN) laws', *Law and Policy*, 38(1): 4–23.

Egeberg, M. (2002) 'The impact of bureaucratic structure on policy making', *Public Administration*, 77(1): 155–70.

Einbinder, S.D. (2020) 'Reflections on importing critical race theory into social work: the state of social work literature and students' voice', *Journal of Social Work Education*, 56(2): 327–40.

Eisenstadt, S.N. (1968) 'Social institutions', in D.A. Sills (ed) *International Encyclopedia of the Social Sciences* (vol 14), New York: Macmillan, pp 409–21.

Ellis, K. (2007) 'Direct payments and social work practice: the significance of "street-level bureaucracy" in determining eligibility', *British Journal of Social Work*, 37(3): 405–22.

Ellis, K. (2011) '"Street-level bureaucracy" revisited: the changing face of frontline discretion in adult social care in England', *Social Policy & Administration*, 45(3): 221–44.

Elmaliach-Mankita, H., Weiss-Gal, I. and Gal, J. (2019) 'Preparing social workers to affect policy: the parliament as a venue for training', *Social Work Education*, 38(4): 530–43.

Epstein, I. (1981) 'Advocates on advocacy: an exploratory study', *Social Work Research and Abstracts*, 17(2): 5–12.

Esping-Andersen, G. (1990) *The Three Worlds of Welfare Capitalism*, Cambridge: Polity Press.

Evans, M., Marsh, D. and Stoker, G. (2013) 'Understanding localism', *Policy Studies*, 34(4): 401–7.

Evans, T. (2013) 'Organisational rules and discretion in adult social work', *British Journal of Social Work*, 43(4): 739–58.

Evans, T. (2016a) 'Introduction: policy and social work', in T. Evans and F. Keating (eds) *Policy and Social Work Practice*, Los Angeles: Sage, pp 1–10.

Evans, T. (2016b) 'Street-level bureaucracy, management and the corrupted world of service', *European Journal of Social Work*, 19(5): 602–15.

Evans, T. (2020) 'Street-level bureaucrats: discretion and compliance in policy implementation', *Oxford Research Encyclopaedia of Politics*, 27 October. Available at: https://doi.org/10.1093/acrefore/9780190228637.013.1422

Evans, T. and Harris, J. (2004) 'Street-level bureaucracy, social work and the (exaggerated) death of discretion', *British Journal of Social Work*, 34(6): 871–95.

Ezell, M. (1992) 'Administrators as advocates', *Administration in Social Work*, 15(4): 1–18.

Ezell, M. (1993) 'The political activity of social workers: a post-Reagan update', *Journal of Sociology & Social Welfare*, 20(4): 81–97.

Ezell, M. (1994) 'Advocacy practice of social workers', *Families in Society*, 75(1): 36–46.

Ezell, M. (2001) *Advocacy in the Human Services*, Belmont, CA: Brooks/Cole.

Fargion, S. (2018) 'Social work promoting participation: reflections on policy practice in Italy', *European Journal of Social Work*, 21(4): 559–71.

Felderhoff, B.J., Hoefer, R. and Watson, L.D. (2016) 'Living up to the code's exhortations? Social workers' political knowledge sources, expectations and behavior', *Social Work*, 61(1): 29–35.

Feldman, G. (2019) 'Making the connection between theories of policy change and policy practice: a new conceptualization', *British Journal of Social Work*, 50(4): 1–18.

Feldman, G. (2021) 'Disruptive social work: forms, possibilities and tensions', *British Journal of Social Work*, 52(2): 759–75

Feldman, G., Strier, R. and Koreh, M. (2017) 'Liquid advocacy: social welfare advocacy in neoliberal times', *International Journal of Social Welfare*, 26(3): 254–62.

Ferguson, I. and Lavalette, M. (2007) '"Dreaming a great dream": prospects for a new, radical social work', *Canadian Social Work Review*, 24(1): 57–68.

Ferguson, I. and Smith, L. (2012) 'Education for change: student placements in campaigning organisations and social movements in South Africa', *British Journal of Social Work*, 42(5): 974–94.

Ferguson, I. and Woodward, R. (2009) *Radical Social Work in Practice: Making a Difference*, Bristol: Policy Press.

Ferguson, I., Ioakimidis, V. and Lavalette, M. (2018) *Global Social Work in a Political Context: Radical Perspectives*, Bristol: Policy Press.

Ferragina, E. and Seeleib-Kaiser, M. (2011) 'Welfare regime debate: past, present, futures?', *Policy & Politics*, 39(4): 583–611.

Figueira-McDonough, J. (1993) 'Policy practice: the neglected side of social work intervention', *Social Work*, 38(2): 179–88.

Fox Schwartz, B. (1973) 'Social workers and New Deal politicians in conflict: California's Branion-Williams case, 1933–1934', *Pacific Historical Review*, 42(1): 53–73.

Fraser, N. (1995) 'From redistribution to recognition? Dilemmas of justice in a "post-socialist" age', *New Left Review*, 212: 68–93.

Fraussen, B., Albareda, A. and Braun, C. (2020) 'Conceptualizing consultation approaches: identifying combinations of consultation tools and analyzing their implications for stakeholder diversity', *Policy Science*, 53(3): 473–93.

Freedman, R. (1994) *Kids at Work: Lewis Hine and the Crusade against Child Labor*, New York: Clarion Books.

Friedberg, C. (2011) 'From a top-down to a bottom-up approach to legislative oversight', *The Journal of Legislative Studies*, 17(4): 525–44.

Friedberg, C. and Hazan, R.Y. (2009) 'Israel's prolonged war against terror: from executive domination to executive–legislative dialogue', *The Journal of Legislative Studies*, 15(2–3): 257–76.

Frisch-Aviram, N., Cohen, N. and Beeri, I. (2018) 'Low-level bureaucrats, local government regimes and policy entrepreneurship', *Policy Sciences*, 51: 39–57.

Fruend, A., Cohen, A., Blit-Cohen, I. and Dahan, N. (2017) 'Professional socialization and commitment to the profession in social work students: a longitudinal study exploring the effect of attitudes, perception of the profession, teaching, training, and supervision', *Journal of Social Work*, 17(6): 635–58.

Fyall, R. and Allard, S.W. (2017) 'Nonprofits and political activity: a joint consideration of the political activities, programs and organizational characteristics of social service nonprofits', *Human Service Organizations: Management, Leadership & Governance*, 41(3): 275–300.

Gal, J. (2010) 'Is there an extended family of Mediterranean welfare states?', *Journal of European Social Policy*, 20(4): 283–300.

Gal, J. and Madhala-Brik, S. (2016) 'Implementation of the Elalouf Committee recommendations: the state of affairs', Taub Center for Social Policy Studies in Israel, November. Available at: https://tau bcenter.org.il/en/research/implementation-of-the-elalouf-committee-recommendations/

Gal, J. and Weiss-Gal, I. (2011) 'Social policy formulation and the role of professionals: the involvement of social workers in parliamentary committees in Israel', *Health and Social Care in the Community*, 19(2): 158–67.

Gal, J. and Weiss-Gal, I. (eds) (2013) *Social Workers Affecting Social Policy: An International Perspective*, Bristol: Policy Press.

Gal, J. and Weiss-Gal, I. (2015) 'The "why" and the "how" of policy practice: an eight-country comparison', *British Journal of Social Work*, 45(4): 1083–101.

Gal, J. and Weiss-Gal, I. (eds) (2017) *Where Academia and Policy Meet: A Cross-National Perspective on the Involvement of Social Work Academics in Social Policy*, Bristol: Policy Press.

Gal, J. and Weiss-Gal, I. (2020) 'Social workers and the policy process: when does opportunity knock?', *Journal of Policy Practice and Research*, 1(1): 6–22.

Gal, J., Köngeter, S. and Vicary, S. (eds) (2021) *The Settlement House Movement Revisited*, Bristol: Policy Press.

Garrett, P.M. and Bertotti, T.F. (2017) 'Social work and the politics of "austerity": Ireland and Italy', *European Journal of Social Work*, 20(1): 29–41.

Garrow, E.E. and Hasenfeld, Y. (2014) 'Institutional logics, moral frames, and advocacy: explaining the purpose of advocacy among non-profit human service organizations', *Nonprofit and Voluntary Sector Quarterly*, 43(1): 80–98.

Gassner, D. and Goffen, A. (2018) 'Street-level management: a clientele-agent perspective on implementation', *Journal of Public Administration Research and Theory*, 28(4): 551–68.

Gen, S. and Wright, A.C. (2013) 'Policy advocacy organizations: a framework linking theory and practice', *Journal of Policy Practice*, 12(3): 163–93.

Gerber, A.S., Huber, G.A., Doherty, D., Dowling, C.M., Raso, C. and Ha, S.E. (2011) 'Personality traits and participation in political processes', *The Journal of Politics*, 73(3): 692–706.

Gewirtz-Meydan, A., Weiss-Gal, I. and Gal, J. (2016) 'Social workers' policy practice in nonprofit human service organizations in Israel', *British Journal of Social Work*, 46(7): 1890–908.

Gibelman, M. and Schervish, P.H. (1997) *Who We Are: A Second Look*, Washington, DC: NASW Press.

Gilboa, C. and Weiss-Gal, I. (2022) 'Change from within: community social workers as local policy actors', *British Journal of Social Work*, 43(1): 19–36.

Gilman, S.C. (2005) 'Ethics codes and codes of conduct as tools for promoting an ethical and professional public service: comparative successes and lessons', paper prepared for the Poverty Reduction and Economic Management Network, World Bank, USA.

Gjersøe, H.M., Leseth, A. and Vilhena, S. (2020) 'Frontline implementation of welfare conditionality in Norway: a maternalistic practice', *Social Policy & Administration*, 54: 491–504.

Godwin, K., Ainsworth, S.H. and Godwin, E. (2013) *Lobbying and Policymaking: The Public Pursuit of Private Interests*, Los Angeles: CQ Press.

Gofen, A. (2014) 'Mind the gap: dimensions and influence of street-level divergence', *Journal of Public Administration Research and Theory*, 24(2): 473–93.

Goldstein, S. and Rosner, I. (2000) *Social Workers Law in Practice*, Tel Aviv: Ramot (in Hebrew).

Goodin, R.E. (ed) (1996) *The Theory of Institutional Design*, Cambridge: Cambridge University Press.

Gough, I. and Wood, G. (2004) *Insecurity and Welfare Regimes in Asia, Africa and Latin America: Social Policy in Development Contexts*, Cambridge: Cambridge University Press.

Graham, M. (2007) *Black Issues in Social Work and Social Care*, Bristol: Policy Press.

Gray, M., van Rooyen, C.C., Rennie, G. and Gaha, J. (2002) 'The political participation of social workers: a comparative study', *International Journal of Social Welfare*, 11(2): 99–110.

Greco, C. (2020) '"I've got to run again": experiences of social workers seeking municipal office in Ontario', unpublished thesis, Laurier University.

Green, L. and Clarke, K. (2016) *Social Policy for Social Work: Placing Social Work in its Wider Context*, Cambridge: Polity Press.

Greenslade, L., McAuliffe, D. and Chenoweth, L.F. (2015) 'Social workers' experiences of covert workplace activism', *Australian Social Work*, 68(4): 422–37.

Greve, B. (2017) 'Introduction: evaluation as an instrument in social policy', in B. Greve (ed) *Handbook of Social Policy Evaluation*, Cheltenham: Edward Elgar Publishing, pp 1–12.

Grinstein-Weiss, M., Pinto, O., Kondratjeva, O., Roll, S.P., Bufe, S., Barkali, N. and Gottlieb, D. (2019) 'Enrollment and participation in a universal child savings program: evidence from the rollout of Israel's national program', *Children and Youth Services Review*, 101: 225–38.

Guidi, R. (2019) 'Social workers' collective policy practice in times of austerity: Italy and Spain compared', in U. Klammer, S. Lieber and S. Leitner (eds) *Social Work and the Making of Social Policy*, Bristol: Policy Press, pp 105–20.

Guidi, R. (2020) 'Social justice, first? The policy action of South European social workers' professional organisations in the shadow of austerity', *European Journal of Social Work*, 23(6): 1044–56.

Gutiérrez, L.M. and Gant, L.M. (2018) 'Community practice in social work: Reflections on its first century and directions for the future', *Social Service Review*, 92(4): 617–46.

Guy, A. (2011) 'Vocational choice and attitudes toward welfare policy: students at the beginning and at the end of their undergraduate studies', *British Journal of Social Work*, 41(7): 1321–39.

Gwilym, H. (2017) 'The political identity of social workers in neoliberal times', *Critical and Radical Social Work*, 5(1): 59–74.

Hacker, J.S. (2004) 'Privatizing risk without privatizing the welfare state: the hidden politics of social policy retrenchment in the United States', *American Political Science Review*, 98(2): 243–60.

Hall, P.A. (1993) 'Policy paradigms, social learning and the state: the case of economic policymaking in Britain', *Comparative Politics*, 25(3): 275–96.

Halpin, D. and Warhurst, J. (2016) 'Commercial lobbying in Australia: exploring the Australian lobby register', *Australian Journal of Public Administration*, 75(1): 100–11.

Hämäläinen, J. (2014) 'Comparative research in social work: methodological considerations using the "diachronic–synchronic" distinction in linguistics', *European Journal of Social Work*, 17(2): 192–205.

Hamilton, D. and Fauri, D. (2001) 'Social workers' political participation: strengthening the political confidence of social work students', *Journal of Social Work Education*, 37(2): 321–32.

Hardina, D. (1995) 'Do Canadian social workers practice advocacy?', *Journal of Community Practice*, 2(3): 97–121.

Hardy, I. and Woodcock, S. (2014) 'Inclusive education policies: discourses of difference, diversity and deficit', *International Journal of Inclusive Education*, 19(2): 141–64.

Hare, I. (2004) 'Defining social work for the 21st century: the International Federation of Social Workers' revised definition of social work', *International Social Work*, 47(3): 407–24.

Harris Rome, S. and Hoechstetter, S. (2010) 'Social work and civic engagement: the political participation of professional social workers', *Journal of Sociology & Social Welfare*, 37(3): 107–29.

Hartnett, H., Harding, S. and Scanlon, E. (2005) 'NASW chapters: directors' perceptions of factors which impede and encourage active member participation', *Journal of Community Practice*, 13(4): 69–83.

Hasenfeld, Y. (2015) 'What exactly is human services management?', *Human Service Organizations: Management, Leadership & Governance*, 39(1): 1–5.

Haynes, K.S. and Mickelson, J.S. (1992) 'Social work and the Reagan era: challenges to the profession', *Journal of Sociology & Social Welfare*, 19(1): 169–83.

Haynes, K.S. and Mickelson, J.S. (2009) *Affecting Change: Social Workers in the Political Arena* (7th edn), Boston: Allyn and Bacon.

Healy, L.M. (2012) 'The history of the development of social work', in L.M. Healy and R.J. Link (eds) *Handbook of International Social Work: Human Rights, Development, and the Global Profession*, New York: Oxford University Press, pp 55–62.

Heffernan, W.J. (1964) 'Political activity and social work executives', *Social Work* 9(2): 18–23.

Heidemann, G., Fertig, R., Jansson, B. and Kim, H. (2011) 'Practicing policy, pursuing change and promoting social justice: a policy instructional approach', *Journal of Social Work Education*, 47(1): 37–52.

Helboe Pedersen, H., Halpin, D. and Rasmussen, A. (2015) 'Who gives evidence to parliamentary committees? A comparative investigation of parliamentary committees and their constituencies', *Journal of Legislative Studies*, 21(3): 408–27.

Herbert, M. and Levin, R. (1996) 'The advocacy role of social work in hospital social work', *Social Work in Health Care*, 22(3): 71–83.

Herbert, M.D. and Mould, J.W. (1992) 'The advocacy role in public child welfare', *Child Welfare Journal*, 71(2): 114–30.

Herbst, A. and Benjamin, O. (2012) 'It was a Zionist act: feminist politics of a single-mother policy votes in Israel', *Women's Study International Forum*, 35(1): 29–37.

Hill, M. and Hupe, P. (2006) 'Analysing policy processes as multiple governance: accountability in social policy', *Policy & Politics*, 34(3): 557–73.

Hoefer, R. (2013) 'Social workers affecting social policy in the US', in J. Gal and I. Weiss-Gal (eds) *Social Workers Affecting Social Policy: An International Perspective*, Bristol: Policy Press, pp 161–82.

Hoefer, R. (2019a) *Advocacy Practice for Social Justice* (4th edn), New York: Oxford University Press.

Hoefer, R. (2019b) 'Modest challenges for the fields of human service administration and social policy research and practice', *Human Service Organizations: Management, Leadership & Governance*, 43(4): 278–89.

Hoefer, R. (2021a) 'Applications of theory to social policy: civic engagement theory', *Journal of Policy Practice & Research*, 2: 67–70.

Hoefer, R. (2021b) 'The surprising usefulness of the policy stages framework', *Journal of Policy Practice & Research*, 2: 141–5.

Hoefer, R., Felderhoff, B.J. and Watson, L. (2019) 'Do social workers support NASW's political activism: evidence from Texas', *Journal of Sociology & Social Welfare*, 46(1): 3–16.

Hopkins, J. (1999) 'The road not taken: Harry Hopkins and New Deal work relief', *Presidential Studies Quarterly*, 29(2): 306–16.

Hughes, M.M. and Paxton, P. (2019) 'The political representation of women over time', in S. Franceschet, M.L. Krook and N. Tan (eds) *The Palgrave Handbook of Women's Political Rights*, London: Palgrave MacMillan, pp 33–51.

Hupe, P. and Hill, M. (2006) 'The three action levels of governance: re-framing the policy process beyond the stages model', in B.G. Peters and J. Pierre (eds) *Handbook of Public Policy*, London: Sage, pp 13–30.

Hupe, P. and Hill, M. (2020) 'Discretion in the policy process', in T. Evans and P. Hupe (eds) *Discretion and the Quest for Controlled Freedom* , Cham: Palgrave Macmillan, pp 237–58.

Hustinx, L., Verschuere, B. and De Corte, J. (2014) 'Organisational hybridity in a post-corporatist welfare mix: the case of the third sector in Belgium', *Journal of Social Policy*, 43(2): 391–411.

IFSW (International Federation of Social Work) (2014) 'Global definition of social work', 6 August. Available at: https://ifsw.org/global-definition-of-social-work

IFSW (2021) 'Coalition of health and social work international professions formed to advocate for global equitable access for vaccine and to increase health and social protection workforce', 4 March. Available at: https://www.ifsw.org/coalition-of-health-and-social-work-international-professions-formed-to-advocate-for-global-equitable-access-for-vaccine-and-to-increase-health-and-social-protection-workforce/

Ioakimidis, V. and Trimikliniotis, N. (2020) 'Making sense of social work's troubled past: professional identity, collective memory and the quest for historical justice', *British Journal of Social Work*, 50(6): 1890–908.

Ioakimidis, V., Santos, C.C. and Herrero, I.M. (2014) 'Reconceptualizing social work in times of crisis: an examination of the cases of Greece, Spain and Portugal', *International Social Work*, 57(4): 285–300.

Jann, W. and Wegrich, K. (2007) 'Theories of the policy cycle', in F. Fischer, G.J. Miller and M.S. Sidney (eds) *Handbook of Public Policy Analysis: Theory, Politics, and Methods*, Boca Raton: CRC Press, pp 43–62.

Jansson, B.S. (1984) *Theory and Practice of Social Welfare Policy: Analysis, Process, and Current Issues*, Belmont, CA: Wadsworth.

Jansson, B.S. (2018) *Becoming an Effective Policy Advocate: From Policy Practice to Social Justice* (5th edn), Belmont, CA: Brooks/Cole.

Jansson, B.S., Nyamathi, A., Heidemann, G., Bird, M., Ward, C.R., Brown-Saltzman, K., Duan, L. and Kaplan, C. (2016) 'Predicting levels of policy advocacy engagement among acute-care health professionals', *Policy, Politics, & Nursing Practice*, 17(1): 43–55.

Jaswal, S. and Kshetrimayum, M. (2020) 'Social work and the changing context: engagement in policymaking', *British Journal of Social Work*, 50(8): 2253–60.

Jeffery, L. (2011) *Understanding Agency: Social Welfare and Change*, Bristol: Policy Press.

Johansson, H. and Panican, A. (2016) 'A move towards the local? The relevance of a local welfare system approach', in H. Johansson and A. Panican (eds) *Combating Poverty in Local Welfare Systems*, London: Palgrave Macmillan, pp 1–28.

Johansson, S. (2012) 'Who runs the mill? The distribution of power in Swedish social service agencies', *European Journal of Social Work*, 15(5): 679–95.

John, P. (2014) 'The great survivor: the persistence and resilience of English local government', *Local Government Studies*, 40(5): 687–704.

Jones, C., Ferguson, I., Lavalette, M. and Penketh, L. (2007 [2004]) 'Manifesto for a new engaged practice' ['The social work manifesto'], in M. Lavalette and I. Ferguson (eds) *International Social Work and the Radical Tradition*, Birmingham: Venture Press.

Jones, D.N. and Truell, R. (2012) 'The global agenda for social work and social development: a place to link together and be effective in a globalized world', *International Social Work*, 55: 454–72.

Jones, R. (2014) *The Story of Baby P: Setting the Record Straight*, Bristol: Policy Press.

Jordan, B. (1990) *Social Work in an Unjust Society*, New York: Harvester Wheatsheaf.

Julian-Chinn, F.J. and Lietz, C.A. (2019) 'Building learning cultures in the child welfare workforce', *Children and Youth Service Review*, 99: 360–5.

Just, A. (2017) 'Race, ethnicity, and political behavior', *Oxford Research Encyclopedia of Politics*, 25 January. Available at: https://doi.org/10.1093/acrefore/9780190228637.013.238

Kam, P.K. (2014) 'Back to the "social" of social work: reviving the social work profession's contribution to the promotion of social justice', *International Social Work*, 57(6): 723–40.

Karagkounis, V. (2017) 'Social work in Greece in the time of austerity: challenges and prospects', *European Journal of Social Work*, 20(5): 651–65.

Karger, H.J. and Hernández, M.T. (2004) 'The decline of the public intellectual in social work', *Journal of Sociology & Social Welfare*, 31(3): 51–68.

Kaufman, R. (2004) 'Successful university–community partnership to change public policy: preconditions and processes', *Journal of Community Practice*, 12(3–4): 163–80.

Kaufman, R. (2019) 'Panthers in the establishment: the involvement of Jerusalem municipality social workers in social justice campaigns and in protest movements, 1965–1985', in J. Gal and R. Holler (eds) *Justice Instead of Charity*, Sde Boker: The Ben-Gurion Research Institute, pp 366–94 (in Hebrew).

Kerley, B. and Starr, G. (2000) 'Public consultation: adding value or impeding policy?', *Agenda: A Journal of Policy Analysis and Reform*, 7(2): 185–92.

Kiehne, E. (2016) 'Latino critical perspective in social work', *Social Work*, 61(2): 119–26.

Kim, D.-H. and Loewenberg, G. (2005) 'The role of parliamentary committees in coalition governments: keeping tabs on coalition partners in the German Bundestag', *Comparative Political Studies*, 38(9): 1104–29.

Kimberlin, S.E. (2010) 'Advocacy by nonprofits: roles and practices of core advocacy organizations and direct service agencies', *Journal of Policy Practice*, 9(3–4): 164–82.

Kingdon, J.W. (2003) *Agendas, Alternatives and Public Policies* (2nd edn), New York: Longman.

Kirbiš, A., Flere, S., Friš, D., Tavčar Krajnc, M. and Cupar, T. (2017) 'Predictors of conventional, protest, and civic participation among Slovenian youth: a test of the civic voluntarism model', *International Journal of Sociology*, 47(3): 182–207.

Kittilson, M.C. (2019) 'Gender and electoral behavior', in S. Franceschet, M.L. Krook and N. Tan (eds) *The Palgrave Handbook of Women's Political Rights*, London: Palgrave MacMillan, pp 21–32.

Kjeldesen, A.M. (2013) 'Dynamics of public service motivation: attraction-selection and socialization in the production and regulation of social services', *Public Administration Review*, 74(1): 101–12.

Klammer, U., Leiber, S. and Leitner, S. (eds) (2020) *Social Work and the Making of Social Policy*, Bristol: Policy Press.

Kleider, H. (2018) 'Redistributive policies in decentralised systems: the effect of decentralisation on subnational social spending', *European Journal of Political Research*, 57(2): 355–77.

Klofstad, C.A. (ed) (2016) *New Advances in the Study of Civic Voluntarism: Resources, Engagement, and Recruitment*, Philadelphia: Temple University Press.

Koeske, G.F., Lichtenwalter, S. and Koeske, R.D. (2005) 'Social workers' current and desired involvement in various practice activities', *Administration in Social Work*, 29(2): 63–84.

Kolivoski, K.M., Weaver, A. and Constance-Huggins, M. (2014) 'Critical race theory: opportunities for application in social work practice and policy', *Families in Society*, 95(4): 269–76.

Kondra, A.Z. and Hurst, D.C. (2009) 'Institutional processes of organizational culture', *Culture and Organization*, 15(1): 39–58.

Kooiman, J. (2003) *Governing as Governance*, London: Sage.

Kriesi, H. (2004) 'Political context and opportunity', in D.A. Snow, S.A. Soule and H. Kriesi (eds) *The Blackwell Companion to Social Movements*, Malden, MA: Blackwell Publishing, pp 67–90.

Krings, A., Fusaro, V., Nicoll, K.L. and Lee, N.Y. (2019) 'Social work, politics, and social policy education: applying a multidimensional framework of power', *Journal of Social Work Education*, 55(2): 224–37.

Krumer-Nevo, M. (2016) 'Poverty-aware social work: a paradigm for social work practice with people in poverty', *British Journal of Social Work*, 46(6): 1793–808.

Krumer-Nevo, M. (2020) *Radical Hope: Poverty-Aware Practice for Social Work*, Bristol: Policy Press.

Krumer-Nevo, M. and Barak, A. (2006) 'Service users' perspectives on the benefits system in Israel: a participatory action', *Social Policy & Administration*, 40(7): 774–90.

Kulke, D., Kindler, T. and Kohlfürst, I. (forthcoming) 'Politische partizipation im kontext sozialer arbeit – ein trinationaler blick auf politische einstellungen und beteiligungsformen von studierenden der sozialen arbeit in Österreich, Deutschland und der Schweiz' [Political participation in the field of social work – a trinational perspective on political attitudes and forms of participation among social work students in Austria, Germany and Switzerland], *Österreichisches Jahrbuch für Soziale Arbeit (OeJS)* [*Annual Review of Social Work and Social Pedagogy in Austria*], 4.

Kutsar, D. and Kuronen, M. (eds) (2015) *Local Welfare Policy Making in European Cities*, Cham: Springer.

Kwon, S. and Guo, B. (2017) 'South Korean nonprofits under the voucher system: impact of organizational culture and organizational structure', *International Social Work*, 62(2): 669–83.

Ladi, S. and Tsarouhas, D. (2020) 'EU economic governance and COVID-19: policy learning and windows of opportunity', *Journal of European Integration*, 42(8): 1041–56.

Lai, C.Y. (2004) 'Organizational survival and development strategies and social workers' political advocacy', unpublished PhD dissertation, Chinese University of Hong Kong, Hong Kong.

Landry, R., Amara, N. and Lamari, M. (2001) 'Utilization of social science research in Canada', *Research Policy*, 30(2): 333–49.

Lane, S.R. and Humphreys, N.A. (2011) 'Social workers in politics: a national survey of social work candidates and elected officials', *Journal of Policy Practice*, 10(3): 225–44.

Lane, S.R. and Pritzker, S. (2018) *Political Social Work*, Cham: Springer.

Lane, S.R., Ostrander, J. and Rhodes Smith, T. (2018) '"Politics is social work with power": training social workers for elected office', *Social Work Education*, 37(1): 1–16.

Lavee, E. and Cohen, N. (2019) 'How street-level bureaucrats become policy entrepreneurs: the case of urban renewal', *Governance*, 32(3): 475–92.

Lavee, E., Cohen, N. and Nouman, H. (2019) 'Reinforcing public responsibility? Influences and practices in street-level bureaucrats' engagement in policy design', *Public Administration*, 96(2): 333–48.

Lawless, J.L. (2015) 'Female candidates and legislators', *Annual Review of Political Science*, 18: 349–66.

Lawless, J.L., Fox, R.L. and Baitinger, G. (2014) 'Women's underrepresentation in U.S. politics: the enduring gender gap in political ambition', in S. Thomas and C. Wilcox (eds) *Women and Elective Office: Past, Present, and Future* (3rd edn), Oxford: Oxford University Press, pp 27–45.

Leigh Bliss, D. and Ginn, H. (2021) 'Expanding presence of social work advocacy on the national stage', *Journal Social Work Education*, 57(3): 432–44.

Leighley, J.E. and Vedlitz, A. (1999) 'Race, ethnicity, and political participation: competing models and contrasting explanations', *Journal of Politics*, 61(4): 1092–104.

Leighninger, L. (2001) 'Social workers as politicians', *Journal of Progressive Human Services*, 12(2): 71–7.

Levin, L., Goor, Y. and Tayri, M.T. (2013) 'Agency advocacy and organisational development: a feasible policy practice alliance', *British Journal of Social Work*, 43(3): 522–41.

Lim, Y., Maccio, E.M., Bickham, T. and Dabney, W.F. (2017) 'Research-based service-learning: outcomes of a social policy course', *Social Work Education*, 36(7): 809–22.

Lindenmeyer, K. (1997) *'A Right to Childhood': The U.S. Children's Bureau and Child Welfare, 1912–46*, Urbana, IL: University of Illinois Press.

Lindquist, S.A. (2017) 'Judicial activism in state supreme courts: institutional design and judicial behavior', *Stanford Law and Policy Review*, 28(1): 61–108.

Lipsky, M. (2010) *Street-Level Bureaucracy: Dilemmas of the Individual in Public Services* (30th anniversary expended edn), New York: Russell Sage Foundation.

Locke, E.A. and Latham, G.P. (2004) 'What should we do about motivation theory? Six recommendations for the twenty-first century', *Academy of Management Review*, 29(3): 388–403.

Lombard, A. and Viviers, A. (2020) 'The micro–macro nexus: rethinking the relationship between social work, social policy and wider policy in a changing world', *British Journal of Social Work*, 50(8): 2261–78.

Lorenz, W. (1994) *Social Work in a Changing Europe*, London: Routledge.

Lowndes, V. (2005) 'Something old, something new, something borrowed ... How institutions change (and stay the same) in local governance', *Policy Studies*, 26(3–4): 291–309.

Lowndes, V. and Roberts, M. (2013) *Why Institutions Matter*, London: Red Globe Press.

Lowndes, V., Pratchett, L. and Stoker, G. (2006) 'Local political participation: the impact of rules-in-use', *Public Administration*, 84(3): 539–61.

Lu, J. (2015) 'Which nonprofit gets more government funding?', *Nonprofit Management & Leadership*, 25(3): 297–312.

Lu, J. (2018) 'Organizational antecedents of nonprofit engagement in policy advocacy: a meta-analytical review', *Nonprofit and Voluntary Sector Quarterly*, 47(4S): 177S–203S.

Lundälv, J. (2019) 'The challenges of writing opinion pieces in social work: a national online survey of Swedish social workers' experiences of influencing public opinion', *British Journal of Social Work*, 49(6): 1395–414.

Lustig-Gants, S. and Weiss-Gal, I. (2015) 'Why do social workers become policy actors?', *Journal of Policy Practice*, 14(3–4): 171–90.

Lymbery, M. (2014) 'Social work and personalisation: fracturing the bureau–professional compact?', *British Journal of Social Work*, 44(4): 795–811.

Lyons, K. (2003) 'Dame Eileen Younghusband (Jan. 1902–May 1918), United Kingdom', *Social Work and Society*, 1(1): 159–70. Available at: https://ejournals.bib.uni-wuppertal.de/index.php/sws/article/download/264/324

MacIndoe, H. and Beaton, E. (2019) 'Friends or foes? How managerial perceptions of the political opportunity structure shape nonprofit advocacy', *Public Performance & Management Review*, 42(1): 59–89.

Madama, I. (2013) 'Beyond continuity? Italian social assistance policies between institutional opportunities and agency', *International Journal of Social Welfare*, 22(1): 58–68.

Mahoney, J. and Thelen, K. (2010) 'A theory of gradual institutional change', in J. Mahoney and K. Thelen (eds) *Explaining Institutional Change: Ambiguity, Agency, and Power*, Cambridge: Cambridge University Press, pp 1–37.

Makaros, A. and Moshe Grodofsky, M. (2016) 'Social workers' conflict of loyalty in the context of social activism: the case of the 2011 social protests in Israel', *Journal of Community Practice*, 24(2): 147–65.

Makaros, A. and Weiss-Gal, I. (2014) 'Comparison of the social and professional ideology of caseworkers and community social workers in Israel', *British Journal of Social Work*, 44(1): 100–16.

Makaros, A., Baum, N. and Levy, S. (2020) 'Policy practice is important but ... Voices of social service departments directors', *Journal of Policy Practice and Research*, 1(4): 1–16.

Mandelkern, R. (2021) 'Neoliberal ideas of government and the political empowerment of economists in advanced nation-states: the case of Israel', *Socio-economic Review*, 19(2): 659–79.

Mandelkern, R. and Rosenhek, Z. (2021) 'The politics of welfare state financialisation: the case of Israel's "saving for every child" programme', *Critical Policy Studies*, 16(1): 60–78.

March, J.G. and Olsen, J.P. (2008) 'Elaborating the "New Institutionalism"', in R.A.W. Rhodes, S.A. Binder and B.A. Rockman (eds) *The Oxford Handbook of Political Institutions*, Oxford: Oxford University Press, pp 3–20.

Martin, G. (1976) *Madam Secretary Frances Perkins*, Boston: Houghton Mifflin.

Martinez-Román, M.-A. (2013) 'Social workers affecting social policy in Spain', in J. Gal and I. Weiss-Gal (eds) *Social Workers Affecting Social Policy: An International Perspective*, Bristol: Policy Press, pp 121–42.

Mattocks, N.O. (2018) 'Social action among social work practitioners: examining the micro–macro divide', *Social Work*, 63(1): 7–16.

Maynard-Moody, S. and Portillo, S. (2010) 'Street-level bureaucracy theory', in R.F. Durnat (ed) *The Oxford Handbook of American Bureaucracy*. Oxford: Oxford University Press, pp 252–77.

McAllister, L. and Stirbu, D. (2007) 'Developing devolution's scrutiny potential: a comparative evaluation of the National Assembly for Wales's subject committees', *Policy and Politics*, 35(2): 289–309.

McClendon, J., Lane, S.R., Ostrander, J. and Rhodes Smith, T. (2020) 'Training social workers for political engagement: exploring regional differences in the United States', *Journal of Teaching in Social Work*, 40(2): 147–68.

McCullagh, J.G. (1987) 'Social workers as advocates: a case example', *Children & Schools*, 9(4): 253–63.

McDonald, C. and Reisch, M. (2008) 'Social work in the workfare regime: a comparison of the U.S. and Australia', *Journal of Sociology & Social Welfare*, 30(1): 43–74.

McDonald, C., Harris, J. and Wintersteen, R. (2003) 'Contingent on context? Social work and the state in Australia, Britain and the USA', *British Journal of Social Work*, 33(2): 191–208.

McLaughlin, A.M. (2009) 'Clinical social workers: advocates for social justice', *Advances in Social Work*, 10(1): 51–68.

McLaughlin, A.M., Rothery, M. and Kuiken, J. (2019) 'Pathways to political engagement: interviews with social workers in elected office', *Canadian Social Work Review*, 36(1): 25–44.

McNutt, J. (2011) 'Is social work advocacy worth the cost? Issues and barriers to an economic analysis of social work political practice', *Research on Social Work Practice*, 21(4): 397–403.

Medzini, M. (2017) *Golda Meir: A Political Biography*, Munich: De Gruyter Oldenbourg.

Meehan, P. (2018) '"I think I can … maybe I can … I can't": social work women and local elected office', *Social Work*, 63(2): 145–52.

Meehan, P. (2019) 'Political primacy and MSW students' interest in running for office: what difference does it make?', *Advances in Social Work*, 19(2): 276–89.

Meehan, P. (2021) 'Water into wine: using social policy courses to make MSW students interested in politics', *Journal of Social Work Education*, 57(2): 357–71.

Meeuwisse, A. and Swärd, H. (2007) 'Cross-national comparisons of social work – a question of initial assumptions and levels of analysis', *European Journal of Social Work*, 10(4): 481–96.

Mellinger, M.S. and Kolomer, S. (2013) 'Legislative advocacy and human service nonprofits: what are we doing?', *Journal of Policy Practice*, 12(2): 87–106.

Melzer, A. (2017) 'Involvement in policy practice: the role of public service motivation, public service motivation fit to job, organization, and support of the organization', unpublished thesis, Tel Aviv University, Israel.

Mendes, P. (2003) 'Social workers and social action: a case study of the Australian Association of Social Workers' Victorian branch', *Australian Social Work*, 56(1): 16–27.

Mendes, P. (2007) 'Social workers and social activism in Victoria, Australia', *Journal of Progressive Human Services*, 18(1): 25–44.

Mendes, P. (2013) 'Social workers affecting social policy in Australia', in J. Gal and I. Weiss-Gal (eds) *Social Workers Affecting Social Policy: An International Perspective*, Bristol: Policy Press, pp 17–38.

Mendes, P., McCurdy, S., Allen-Kelly, K., Charikar, K. and Incerti, K. (2015) 'Integrating professional social work identity and social justice advocacy: an analysis of the Australian campaign to restore Medicare rebates for accredited mental health social workers', *Journal of Social Work*, 15(5): 516–36.

Meyer, D.S. and Minkoff, D.C. (2004) 'Conceptualizing political opportunity', *Social Forces*, 82(4): 1457–92.

Meyer, J.W. and Rowan, B. (1977) 'Institutionalized organizations: formal structure as myth and ceremony', *American Journal of Sociology*, 83(2): 340–63.

Midgley, J. and Livermore, M. (eds) (2009) *The Handbook of Social Policy* (2nd edn), Thousand Oaks, CA: Sage.

Miller, D.B., Jennings, E. and Angelo, J. (2021) 'Social workers as elected officials: advocacy at the doorstep', *Journal of Social Work Education*, 57(3): 455–63.

Miller, S.E. (2010) 'A conceptual framework for the professional socialization of social workers', *Journal of Human Behavior in the Social Environment*, 20(7): 924–38.

Ministry of Welfare and Social Services (Israel) (2010) 'Report of the Committee to Draw Up a Proposal for the Reform of the Local Social Welfare Services', February (in Hebrew). Available at: https://molsa.gov.il/About/OfficePolicy/Documents/FINALREPORTREFORMV2010.pdf

Mmatli, T. (2008) 'Political activism as a social work method in Africa', *International Social Work*, 51(3): 297–310.

Mondak, J.J. and Halperin, K.D. (2008) 'A framework for the study of personality and political behaviour', *British Journal of Political Science*, 38(2): 335–62.

Mosley, J.E. (2010) 'Organizational responses and environmental incentives: understanding the policy advocacy involvement of human service nonprofits', *Social Service Review*, 84(1): 57–76.

Mosley, J.E. (2011) 'Keeping the lights on: how government funding concerns drive the advocacy agendas of nonprofit homeless service providers', *Journal of Public Administration Research*, 22(4): 841–66.

Mosley, J.E. (2013) 'Recognizing new opportunities: reconceptualizing policy advocacy in everyday organizational practice', *Social Work*, 58(3): 231–9.

Moth, R. and Lavalette, M. (2019) 'Social policy and welfare movements "from below": the Social Work Action Network (SWAN) in the UK', in U. Klammer, S. Lieber and S. Leitner (eds) *Social Work and the Making of Social Policy*, Bristol: Policy Press, pp 121–36.

Mullaly, B. (1997) *Structural Social Work: Ideology, Theory, and Practice* (2nd edn), Toronto: Oxford University Press.

Müller, M. and Pihl-Thingvad, S. (2020) 'User involvement in social work innovation: a systematic and narrative review', *Journal of Social Work*, 20(6): 730–50.

Munro, E. (2011) *The Munro Review of Child Protection: Final Report*, London: The Stationery Office.

NASW (National Association of Social Workers) (2017) 'Code of ethics'. Available at: https://socialworkers.org/About/Ethics/Code-of-Ethics

Necel, R. (2019) 'Advocacy in action: theory and practice of social work', *Polish Sociological Review*, 208(4): 511–25.

Newman, J., Glendinning, C. and Hughes, M. (2008) 'Beyond modernization? Social care and the transformation of welfare governance', *Journal of Social Policy*, 37(4): 531–59.

Nothdurfter, U. and Hermans, K. (2018) 'Meeting (or not) at the street level? A literature review on street-level research in public management, social policy and social work', *International Journal of Social Welfare*, 27(3): 294–304.

Nouman, H. (2020) 'Between majority and minority: a model for understanding and promoting culturally competent policy practice in multicultural societies', *British Journal of Social Work*, 50(2): 506–24.

Nouman, H. and Azaiza, F. (2021a) 'Personal, professional and political: minority social workers as policy actors', *European Journal of Social Work*, DOI: 10.1080/13691457.2021.1977248.

Nouman, H. and Azaiza, F. (2021b) 'Challenges underlying the involvement of social workers from minority groups in policy practice', *Australian Social Work*, DOI: 10.1080/0312407X.2021.1992459.

Nouman, H., Levin, L. and Lavee, E. (2019) 'Working through barriers: shaping social workers' engagement in policy practice', *British Journal of Social Work*, 50(4): 1107–25.

Nygård, M. and Jakobsson, G. (2013) 'Political participation of older adults in Scandinavia – the civic voluntarism model revisited? A multi-level analysis of three types of political participation', *International Journal of Aging and Later Life*, 8(1): 65–96.

OECD (Organisation for Economic Co-operation and Development) (2015) *In It Together: Why Less Inequality Benefits All*, Paris: OECD Publishing.

OECD (2020) 'Social expenditure (SOCX) update 2020: social spending makes up 20% of OECD GDP', November. Available at: https://oecd.org/social/expenditure.htm

Ólafsson, S. and Stefánsson, K. (2019) 'Welfare consequences of the crisis in Europe', in S. Ólafsson, M. Daly, O. Kangas and J. Palme (eds) *Welfare and the Great Recession: A Comparative Study*, Oxford: Oxford University Press, pp 15–42.

Oliveira, C.R. and Carvalhais, I.E. (2017) 'Immigrants' political claims in Portugal: confronting the political opportunity structure with perceptions and discourses', *Ethnic and Racial Studies*, 40(5): 787–808.

Olsson, J. (2020) 'Institutionalism and public administration', *Oxford Research Encyclopedia of Politics*, 27 October. Available at: https://doi.org/10.1093/acrefore/9780190228637.013.1458

Onyx, J., Armitage, L., Dalton, B., Melville, R., Casey, J. and Banks, R. (2010) 'Advocacy with gloves on: the "manners" of strategy used by some third sector organizations undertaking advocacy in NSW and Queensland', *Voluntas*, 21(1): 41–61.

Orjuela, C. (2018) 'Mobilizing diasporas for justice: opportunity structures and the presencing of a violent past', *Journal of Ethnic and Migration Studies*, 44(8): 1357–73.

Ornellas, A., Spolander, G., Engelbrecht, L.K., Sicora, A., Pervova, I., Martínez-Román, M.-A. et al (2019) 'Mapping social work across 10 countries: structure, intervention, identity and challenges', *International Social Work*, 62(4): 1183–97.

Ostrander, J., Lane, S.R., McClendon, J., Hayes, C. and Rhodes Smith, T. (2017) 'Collective power to create political change: increasing the political efficacy and engagement of social workers', *Journal of Policy Practice*, 16(3): 261–75.

Ostrander, J., Bryan, J., Sandler, A., Nieman, P., Clark, M., Loveland, E. et al (2018) 'The political participation of first year social work students: does practice specialization matter?', *Journal of Sociology & Social Welfare*, 45(3): 39–60.

Ostrander, J., Bryan, J. and Lane, S.R. (2019) 'Clinical social workers, gender, and perceptions of political participation', *Advances in Social Work*, 19(1): 256–75.

Ostrander, J., Kindler, T. and Bryan, J. (2021) 'Using the civic voluntarism model to compare the political participation of US and Swiss social workers', *Journal of Policy Practice and Research*, 2(1): 4–19.

Ostrom, E. (1999) 'Institutional rational choice: an assessment of the institutional analysis and development framework', in P.A. Sabatier (ed) *Theories of the Policy Process*, Boulder, CO: Westview Press, pp 21–64.

Palattiyil, G., Sidhva, D., Pawar, M., Shajahan, PK., Cox, J. and Anand, J.C. (2019) 'Reclaiming international social work in the context of the Global Agenda for Social Work and Social Development: some critical reflections', *International Social Work*, 62: 1043–54.

Papp, Z. and Russo, F. (2018) 'Parliamentary work, re-selection and re-election: in search of the accountability link', *Parliamentary Affairs*, 71(4): 853–67.

Parker, R. and Bradley, L. (2000) 'Organisational culture in the public sector: evidence from six organisations', *International Journal of Public Sector Management*, 13(2): 125–41.

Pastor Seller, E., Verde Diego, C. and Lima Fernandez, A.I. (2019) 'Impact of neo-liberalism in Spain: research from social work in relation to the public system of social services', *European Journal of Social Work*, 22(2): 277–88.

Pató, B.S.G. (2017) 'Formal options for job descriptions: theory meets practice', *Journal of Management Development*, 36(8): 1008–28.

Patterson, D.A., Cronley, C., West, S. and Lantz, J. (2014) 'Social justice manifest: a university–community partnership to promote the individual right to housing', *Journal of Social Work Education*, 50(2): 234–46.

Pawar, M. (2019) 'Social work and social policy practice: imperatives for political engagement', *International Journal of Community and Social Development*, 1(1): 15–27.

Pawar, M. and Pulla, V. (2015) 'Medha Patkar's environmental activism and professional social work: mass legitimacy and myopic structures', in Y. Nilan and M. Deena (eds) *Subversive Action: Extralegal Practices for Social Justice*, Waterloo: Wilfrid Laurier University Press, pp 77–97.

Paxton, P., Kunovich, S. and Hughes, M.M. (2007) 'Gender in politics', *Annual Review of Sociology*, 33: 263–84.

Payne, M. (2002) 'The role and achievements of a professional association in the late twentieth century: the British Association of Social Workers 1970–2000', *British Journal of Social Work*, 32(8): 969–95.

Pefer Talbot, E. and McMillin, J.A. (2014) 'The social work reinvestment initiative: advocacy and social work practice', *Social Work*, 59(3): 201–10.

Pence, E.K. and Kaiser, M.L. (2022) 'Elected office as a social work career trajectory: insights from political social workers', *Journal of Social Work Education*, DOI: 10.1080/10437797.2021.2019639.

Perkins, F. (1946) *The Roosevelt I Knew*, New York: Viking Press.

Perry, J.L. and Vandenabeele, W. (2015) 'Public service motivation research: achievement, challenges, and future directions', *Public Administration Review*, 75(5): 692–9.

Perry, J.L., Hodeghem, A. and Wise, L.R. (2010) 'Revisiting the motivational bases of public service: twenty years of research and an agenda for the future', *Public Administration Review*, 70(5): 681–90.

Phillips, N., Lawrence, T.B. and Hardy, C. (2004) 'Discourse and institutions', *Academy of Management Review*, 29(4): 635–52.

Pierson, P. (1995) 'Fragmented welfare states: federal institutions and the development of social policy', *Governance*, 8(4): 449–78.

Pierson, P. and Skocpol, T. (2002) 'Historical institutionalism in contemporary political science', in I. Katznelson and H.V. Minler (eds) *Political Science: The State of the Discipline*, New York: W.W. Norton, pp 693–721.

Poindexter, C.C. (1999) 'Promises in the plague: passage of the Ryan White Comprehensive AIDS Resources Emergency Act as a case study for legislative action', *Health & Social Work*, 24(1): 35–41.

Polsby, N.W. (1968) 'The institutionalization of the U.S. House of Representatives', *American Political Science Review*, 62(1): 144–68.

Polsby, N.W. (2001) 'Legitimacy in British policy-making: functional alternatives to the civil service', *The British Journal of Politics and International Relations*, 3(1): 5–35.

Postan-Aizik, D., Shdaimah, C.S. and Strier, R. (2020) 'Positioning social justice: reclaiming social work's organising value', *The British Journal of Social Work*, 50(6): 1652–68.

Powell, M. (ed) (2007) *Understanding the Mixed Economy of Welfare*, Bristol: Policy Press.

Powell, W.W. and Rerup, C. (2017) 'Opening the black box: the micro-foundations of institutions', in R. Greenwood, C. Oliver, T.B. Lawrence and R.E. Meyer (eds) *The Sage Handbook of Organizational Institutionalism* (2nd edn), London: Sage, pp 311–55.

Prakash, A. and Gugerty, M.K. (2010) 'Advocacy organizations and collective action: an introduction', in A. Prakash and M.K. Gugerty (eds) *Advocacy Organizations and Collective Action*, Cambridge: Cambridge University Press, pp 1–28.

Pratchett, L. and Wingfield, M. (1996) 'Petty bureaucracy and woolly-minded liberalism? The changing ethos of local government officers', *Public Administration*, 74(4): 639–56.

Pritzker, S. and Lane, S.R. (2014) 'Integrating policy and political content in BSW and MSW field placements', *Journal of Social Work Education*, 50(4): 730–9.

Pyles, L. (2014) *Progressive Community Organizing: Reflective Practice in a Globalizing World* (2nd edn), New York: Routledge.

Rainey, H.G. and Steinbauer, P. (1999) 'Galloping elephants: developing elements of a theory of effective government organizations', *Journal of Public Administration Research and Theory*, 9(1): 1–32.

Ravasi, D. and Schultz, M. (2006) 'Responding to organizational identity threats: exploring the role of organizational culture', *Academy of Management Journal*, 49(3): 433–58.

Rayner, J., Williams, H.M., Lawton, A. and Allinson, C.W. (2011) 'Public service ethos: developing a generic measure', *Journal of Public Administration Research and Theory*, 21(1): 27–51.

Reeser, L.C. and Epstein, I. (1990) *Professionalization and Activism in Social Work: The Sixties, the Eighties, and the Future*, New York: Columbia University Press.

Reisch, M. (2002) 'Defining social justice in a socially unjust world', *Families in Society*, 83(4): 343–54.

Reisch, M. (2014) 'U.S. social policy in the new century', in M. Reisch (ed) *Social Policy and Social Justice*, Los Angeles: Sage, pp 5–42.

Reisch, M. (2017) 'Why macro practice matters', *Human Service Organizations: Management, Leadership & Governance*, 41(1): 6–9.

Reisch, M. (2018) 'The year 1968: the turning point when US social work failed to turn', *Critical and Radical Social Work*, 6(1): 7–20.

Reisch, M. and Andrews, J. (2001) *The Road Not Taken: A History of Radical Social Work in the United States*, New York: Brunner-Routledge.

Reisch, M. and Jani, J.S. (2012) 'The new politics of social work practice: understanding context to promote change', *British Journal of Social Work*, 42(6): 1132–50.

Richan, W.C. (2006) *Lobbying for Social Change* (3rd edn), New York: Haworth Press.

Ritter, J.A. (2008) 'A national study predicting social workers' levels of political participation: the role of resources, psychological engagement, and recruitment networks', *Social Work*, 5(4): 347–57.

Ritz, A. (2015) 'Public service motivation and politics: behavioural consequences among local councillors in Switzerland', *Public Administration*, 93(4): 1121–37.

Ritz, A., Brewer, G.A. and Neumann, O. (2016) 'Public service motivation: a systematic literature review and outlook', *Public Administration Review*, 76(3): 414–26.

Ritz, A., Schott, C., Nitzl, C. and Alfes, K. (2020) 'Public service motivation and prosocial motivation: two sides of the same coin?', *Public Management Review*, 22(7): 974–98.

Rocha, C. (2000) 'Evaluating experiential teaching methods in a policy practice course: the case for service learning to increase political participation', *Journal of Social Work Education*, 36(1): 53–63.

Rocha, C. (2007) *Essentials of Social Work Policy Practice*, Hoboken, NJ: Wiley.

Rocha, C., Poe, B. and Thomas, V. (2010) 'Political activities of social workers: addressing perceived barriers to political participation', *Social Work*, 55(4): 317–25.

Rodems, E.S., Shaefer, H.L. and Ybarra, M. (2011) 'The Children's Bureau and passage of the Sheppard–Towner Act of 1921: early social work macro practice in action', *Families in Society*, 92(4): 358–63.

Roh, C.-Y., Moon, M.J., Yang, S.-B. and Jung, K. (2016) 'Linking emotional labor, public service motivation, and job satisfaction: social workers in health care settings', *Social Work in Public Health*, 31(2): 43–57.

Rollins, W. (2020) 'Social worker–client relationships: social worker perspectives', *Australian Social Work*, 73(4): 395–407.

Rosenthal, M. (2018) 'Agenda control by committee chairs in fragmented multi-party systems: a Knesset case study', *Israel Studies Review*, 33(1): 61–80.

Rothman, J. (2007) 'Multi modes of intervention at the macro level', *Journal of Community Practice*, 15(4): 11–40.

Rubinstein, A. and Medina, B. (2005) *The Constitutional Law of the State of Israel* (6th edn), Tel Aviv: Schocken (in Hebrew).

Rush, M. and Keenan, M. (2014) 'The social politics of social work: anti-oppressive social work dilemmas in twenty-first-century welfare regimes', *British Journal of Social Work*, 44(6): 1436–53.

Sadeghi Avval Shahr, H., Yazdani, S. and Afshar, L. (2019) 'Professional socialization: an analytical definition', *Journal of Medical Ethics and History of Medicine*, DOI:10.18502/jmehm.v12i17.201

Saeid, M. (2019) 'The social construction of social workers' involvement in policy practice: the "right to electricity" case study', unpublished PhD dissertation, University of Haifa, Israel.

Sainte-Marie, B. (1964) *Universal Soldier,* Vanguard.

Salsberg, E., Quigley, L., Mehfoud, N., Acquaviva, K., Wyche, K. and Sliwa, S. (2017) *Profile of the Social Work Workforce*, Washington, DC: The George Washington University Health Workforce Institute and School of Nursing.

Salsberg, E., Quigley, L., Mehfoud, N., Acquaviva, K., Wyche, K. and Sliwa, S. (2020) *Profile of the Social Work Workforce*, Washington, DC: The George Washington University Health Workforce Institute and School of Nursing.

Saulnier, C.F. (2000) 'Policy practice: training direct service social workers to get involved', *Journal of Teaching in Social Work*, 20(1/2): 121–44.

Saxena, A. and Chandrapal, S. (2021) 'Social work and policy practice: understanding the role of social worker', *British Journal of Social Work*, DOI:10.1093/bjsw/bcab073.

Scanlon, E., Hartnett, H. and Harding, S. (2006) 'An analysis of the political activities of NASW state chapters', *Journal of Policy Practice*, 5(4): 41–54.

Schein, E.H. (2010) *Organizational Culture and Leadership* (4th edn), San Francisco: Jossey-Bass.

Schiettecat, T., Roets, G. and Vandenbroeck, M. (2018) 'Hide and seek: political agency of social workers in supporting families living in poverty', *The British Journal of Social Work*, 48(7): 1874–91.

Schlozman, K.L. (2010) 'Who sings in the heavenly chorus? The shape of the organized interest system', in L.S. Maisel and J.M. Berry (eds) *The Oxford Handbook of American Political Parties and Interest Groups*, Oxford: Oxford University Press, pp 425–50.

Schlozman, K.L., Brady, H.E. and Verba, S. (2018) *Unequal and Unrepresented: Political Inequality and the People's Voice in the New Gilded Age*, Princeton: Princeton University Press.

Schmid, H., Bar, M. and Nirel, R. (2008) 'Advocacy activities in nonprofit human service organizations: implications for policy', *Nonprofit & Voluntary Sector Quarterly*, 37(4): 581–602.

Schmidt, V.A. (2020) 'Theorizing institutional change and governance in European responses to the COVID-19 pandemic', *Journal of European Integration*, 42(8): 1177–93.

Schram, S.F. (2015) *The Return of Ordinary Capitalism: Neoliberalism, Precarity, Occupy*, New York: Oxford University Press.

Schwartz, S.H., Caprara, G.V. and Vecchione, M. (2010) 'Basic personal values, core political values, and voting: a longitudinal analysis', *Political Psychology*, 31(3): 421–52.

Schwartz-Tayri, T.M. (2020) 'The willingness of social work students to engage in policy practice: the role of personality traits and political participation predictors', *British Journal of Social Work*, 51(7): 2381–98.

Schwartz-Tayri, T.M., Malka, M., Moshe-Grodofsky, M. and Gilbert, N. (2020) 'Integrating micro and macro practice: an evaluation of the policy advocacy course', *Journal of Social Work Education*, 57(3): 464–77.

Scott, W.R. (2008) 'Approaching adulthood: the maturing of institutional theory', *Theory and Society*, 37(5): 427–42.

Sery, A. and Weiss-Gal, I. (2021) 'Social work senior managers as street-level policymakers', *British Journal of Social Work*, DOI: 10.1093/bjsw/bcab191.

Shepperd, D. and Pritzker, S. (2021) 'Political advocacy without a choice: highlighting African-American political social workers', *Advances in Social Work*, 21(2–3): 241–58.

Sherraden, M. (1991) *Assets and the Poor: A New American Welfare Policy*, Armonk, NY: M.E. Sharpe.

Sherraden, M., Stuart, P., Barth, R.P., Kemp, S., Lubben, J., Hawkins, J.D. et al (2015) 'Grand accomplishments in social work', American Academy of Social Work and Social Welfare, Working Paper No. 2.

Sherraden, M.S., Slosar, B. and Sherraden, M. (2002) 'Innovation in social policy: collaborative policy advocacy', *Social Work*, 47(3): 209–21.

Sherwood-Johnson, F. and Mackay, K. (2021) 'Building knowledge for policy and practice based on service user and carer experiences: a case study of Scottish adult safeguarding research', *Journal of Social Work*, 21(5): 1182–202.

Shewell, H., Schwartz, K. and Ongaro, K. (2021) 'Social work faculty engagement in social policy practice: a quantitative study of the Canadian experience', *The British Journal of Social Work*, 51(4): 1277–95.

Shier, M.L. and Handy, F. (2016) 'Executive leadership and social innovation in direct-service nonprofits: shaping the organizational culture to create social change', *Journal of Progressive Human Services*, 27(2): 111–30.

Shin, J. (2020) 'Gender differences in perceptions of policy advocacy activities among top executive leadership: focusing on two types of South Korean social work organizations', *International Social Work*, DOI: 10.1177/0020872820962216.

Sicora, A. and Citroni, G. (2021) 'One, not one, or one hundred thousand? Voices of social workers in international comparison', *European Journal of Social Work*, 24(1): 60–70.

Silkin, A. (1973) 'Green papers and changing methods of consultation in British government', *Public Administration*, 51(4): 427–48.

Simon, B.L. (1994) *The Empowerment Tradition in American Social Work: A History*, New York: Columbia University Press.

Simpson, G. (2013) 'Social workers affecting social policy in England', in J. Gal and I. Weiss-Gal (eds) *Social Workers Affecting Social Policy: An International Perspective*, Bristol: Policy Press, pp 39–58.

Simpson, G. and Connor, S. (2011) *Social Policy for Social Welfare Professionals: Tools for Understanding and Engagement*, Bristol: Policy Press.

Sirkis, L. and Moskovitz, Y. (2015) 'Policy changes activities of the "water forum"', *Meidaos*, 78: 66–72 (in Hebrew).

Smets, M., Aristidou, A. and Whittington, R. (2017) 'Towards a practice-driven institutionalism', in R. Greenwood, C. Oliver, T.B. Lawrence and R.E. Meyer (eds) *The Sage Handbook of Organizational Institutionalism* (2nd edn), London: Sage, pp 365–91.

Smith, L.G. (1982) 'Mechanisms for public participation at a normative planning level in Canada', *Canadian Public Policy/Analyse de Politiques*, 8(4): 561–72.

Smith, R. (2019) 'Social work as policy innovator: challenges and possibilities in the UK', in U. Klammer, S. Lieber and S. Leitner (eds) *Social Work and the Making of Social Policy*, Bristol: Policy Press, pp 21–36.

Sommerfeld, D. and Weiss-Gal, I. (2018) 'The policy practice of hospital social workers in Israel', *Society & Welfare*, 38: 729–56 (in Hebrew).

Specht, H. and Courtney, M.E. (1994) *Unfaithful Angels: How Social Work Has Abandoned its Mission*, New York: The Free Press.

Spolander, G., Engelbrecht, L., Martin, L., Strydom, M., Pervova, I., Marjanen, P. et al (2014) 'The implications of neoliberalism for social work: reflections from a six-country international research collaboration', *International Social Work*, 57(4): 301–12.

Stevenson, W.B. and Greenberg, D. (2000) 'Agency and social networks: strategies of action in a social structure of position, opposition, and opportunity', *Administrative Science Quarterly*, 45(4): 651–78.

Stotzer, R.L. and Tropman, J.E. (2006) 'Professionalizing social work at the national level: women social work leaders, 1910–1982', *Affilia*, 21(1): 9–27.

Strandberg, C.T. and Marshall, G. (1988) 'Politics and social work: the professional interface', *The Social Worker*, 56(3): 113–16.

Streek, W. and Thelen, K. (2005) 'Introduction: institutional change in advanced political economies', in W. Streeck and K. Thelen (eds) *Beyond Continuity: Institutional Change in Advanced Political Economies*, Oxford: Oxford University Press, pp 1–39.

Strier, R. (2009) 'Community anti-poverty strategies: a conceptual framework for a critical discussion', *British Journal of Social Work*, 39(6): 1063–81.

Strier, R. (2019) 'Resisting neoliberal social work fragmentation: the wall-to-wall alliance', *Social Work*, 64(4): 339–45.

Strier, R. and Bershtling, O. (2016) 'Professional resistance in social work: counterpractice assemblages', *Social Work*, 61(2): 111–18.

Strier, R. and Feldman, G. (2018) 'Reengineering social work's political passion: policy practice and neo-liberalism', *British Journal of Social Work*, 48(3): 751–68.

Strøm, K. (1998) 'Parliamentary committees in European democracies', *The Journal of Legislative Studies*, 4(1): 21–59.

Swank, E.W. (2012) 'Predictors of political activism among social work students', *Journal of Social Work Education*, 48(2): 245–66.

Talbot, E.P. and McMillin, J.A. (2014) 'The Social Work Reinvestment Initiative: advocacy and social work practice', *Social Work*, 59(3): 201–10.

Taliaferro, J.D. and Ruggiano, N. (2013) 'The "L" word: nonprofits, language, and lobbying', *The Journal of Sociology & Social Welfare*, 40(2): 151–69.

Tartakovsky, E. (2016) 'The motivational foundations of different therapeutic orientations as indicated by therapists' value preferences', *Psychotherapy Research*, 26(3): 352–64.

Taylor, J. (2010) 'Public service motivation, civic attitudes and actions of public, nonprofit and private sector employees', *Public Administration*, 88(4): 1083–98.

Taylor-Gooby, P., Leruth, B. and Chung, H. (2017) 'The context: how European welfare states have responded to post-industrialism, ageing populations and populist nationalism', in P. Taylor-Gooby, B. Leruth and H. Chung (eds) *After Austerity: Welfare State Transformation in Europe after the Great Recession*, Oxford: Oxford University Press, pp 1–26.

Teare, R.J. and Sheafor, B.W. (1995) Practice-sensitive social work education" An empirical analysis of social work practice and practitioners, Alexandria, VA: Council on Social Word Education.

Thelen, K. (2004) *How Institutions Evolve: The Political Economy of Skills in Germany, Britain, the United States, and Japan*, Cambridge: Cambridge University Press.

Thompson, J., Menefee, D. and Marley, M. (1999) 'A comparative analysis of social workers' macro practice activities: Identifying functions common to direct practice and administration', *Journal of Social Work Education*, 35(1): 115–24.

Thorén, K.H. and Salonen, T. (2013) 'Social workers affecting social policy in Sweden', in J. Gal and I. Weiss-Gal (eds) *Social Workers Affecting Social Policy: An International Perspective*, Bristol: Policy Press, pp 143–59.

Timor-Shlevin, S. (2021) 'Contextualised resistance: the mediating power of paradigmatic frameworks', *Social Policy & Administration*, 55(1): 802–14.

Torczyner, J. (1972) 'The political context of social change: a case study of innovation in adversity in Jerusalem', *Journal of Applied Behavioral Science*, 8(3): 287–317.

Toubeau, S. and Wagner, M. (2015) 'Explaining party positions on decentralization', *British Journal of Political Science*, 45(1): 97–119.

Tower, L.E. and Hartnett, H.P. (2010) 'An Internet-based assignment to teach students to engage in policy practice: a three cohort study', *Journal of Policy Practice*, 10(1): 65–77.

Trætteberg, H.S. and Grødem, A.S. (2021) 'From national activation legislation to local practices in Norway – why the same law gives diverse practices', *International Journal of Social Welfare*, 31: 154–64.

Trappenburg, M., Kampen, T. and Tonkens, E. (2020) 'Social workers in a modernising welfare state: professionals or street-level bureaucrats?', *British Journal of Social Work*, 50(6): 1669–87.

Trattner, W.I. (1984) *From Poor Law to Welfare State: A History of Social Welfare in America* (3rd edn), New York: The Free Press.

Twelvetrees, A. (2008) *Community Work* (4th edn), Basingstoke: Palgrave Macmillan.

Tzadiki, T. and Weiss-Gal, I. (2021) 'Team managers in local social services in Israel as bottom-up social policy-makers', *Journal of Health and Human Services Administration*, 43(4): 324–45.

Vandenabeele, W. (2007) 'Toward a public administration theory of public service motivation', *Public Management Review*, 9(4): 545–56.

Van der Heijden, J. (2011) 'Institutional layering: a review of the use of the concept', *Politics*, 31(1): 9–18.

Verba, S., Schlozman, K.L. and Brady, H.E. (1995) *Voice and Equality: Civic Voluntarism in American Politics*, Cambridge, MA: Harvard University Press.

Verschuere, B. and De Corte, J. (2015) 'Nonprofit advocacy under a third-party government regime: cooperation or conflict?', *Voluntas*, 26(1): 222–41.

Virtanen, P., Laitinen, I. and Stenvall, J. (2018) 'Street-level bureaucrats as strategy shapers in social and health service delivery: empirical evidence from six countries', *International Social Work*, 61(5): 724–37.

Vito, R. (2020) 'How do social work leaders understand and ideally practice leadership? A synthesis of core leadership practices', *Journal of Social Work Practice*, 34(3): 263–79.

Vráblíková, K. (2014) 'How context matters? Mobilization, political opportunity structures, and nonelectoral political participation in old and new democracies', *Comparative Political Studies*, 47(2): 203–29.

Wainwright, J. (2009) 'Racism, anti-racist practice and social work: articulating the teaching and learning experiences of Black social workers', *Race, Ethnicity and Education*, 12(4): 495–516.

Webster, M. (2021) 'Human rights and housing unaffordability: applying policy practice engagement to a wicked problem', *Aotearoa New Zealand Social Work*, 33(4): 31–46.

Weidman, J.C., Twale, D.J. and Stein, E. (2001) *Socialization of Graduate and Professional Students in Higher Education: A Perilous Passage?* (ASHE-ERIC Higher Education Report Volume 28, Number 3), San Francisco: Jossey-Bass Higher and Adult Education Series.

Weingast, B.R. (2002) 'Rational-choice institutionalism', in I. Katznelson and H.V. Minler (eds) *Political Science: The State of the Discipline*, New York: W.W. Norton, pp 660–92.

Weir, M. and Skocpol, T. (1985) 'State structures and the possibilities for "Keynesian" responses to the Great Depression in Sweden, Britain, and the United States', in P.B. Evans, D. Rueschemeyer and T. Skocpol (eds) *Bringing the State Back In*, Cambridge: Cambridge University Press, pp 107–64.

Weiss, I. (2005) 'Is there a global common core to social work? A cross-national comparative study of BSW graduate students', *Social Work*, 50(2): 101–10.

Weiss, I. and Welbourne, P. (eds) (2007) *Social Work as a Profession: A Comparative Cross-National Perspective*, Birmingham: Venture Press.

Weiss, I., Gal, J. and Cnaan, R. (2004a) 'Social work education and professional socialization: a study of the impact of social work education upon the professional preferences of students', *Journal of Social Service Research*, 31(1): 13–31.

Weiss, I., Spiro, S.E., Sherer, M. and Korin-Langer, N. (2004b) 'Social work in Israel: professional characteristics in an international comparative perspective', *International Journal of Social Welfare*, 13(4): 287–96.

Weiss, N.J. (1990) *Whitney M. Young, Jr., and the Struggle for Civil Rights*, Princeton: Princeton University Press.

Weiss-Gal, I. (2008) 'The person-in-environment approach: professional ideology and practice of social workers in Israel', *Social Work*, 53(1): 65–75.

Weiss-Gal, I. (2016) 'Policy practice in social work education: a literature review', *International Journal of Social Welfare*, 25(3): 290–303.

Weiss-Gal, I. (2017a) 'Social workers' policy engagement: a review of the literature', *International Journal of Social Welfare*, 26(3): 285–98.

Weiss-Gal, I. (2017b) 'What options do we have? Exploring routes for social workers' policy engagement', *Journal of Policy Practice,* 16(3): 247–60.

Weiss-Gal, I. and Gal, J. (2008) 'An exploration of social workers' involvement in policy-practice: the role of social and professional values', *Journal of Social Service Research*, 34(4): 15–27.

Weiss-Gal, I. and Gal, J. (2014) 'Social workers as policy actors', *Journal of Social Policy*, 43(1): 19–36.

Weiss-Gal, I. and Gal, J. (2017) 'Where academia and policy meet: a cross-national perspective', in J. Gal and I. Weiss-Gal (eds) *Where Academia and Policy Meet: A Cross-National Perspective on the Involvement of Social Work Academics in Social Policy*, Bristol: Policy Press, pp 243–62.

Weiss-Gal, I. and Gal, J. (2019a) 'Social work academia and social policy in Israel: on the role of social work academics in the policy process', in U. Klammer, S. Lieber and S. Leitner (eds) *Social Work and the Making of Social Policy*, Bristol: Policy Press, pp 89–104.

Weiss-Gal, I. and Gal, J. (2019b) 'Social work educators and social policy: a cross-professional perspective', *European Journal of Social Work*, 22(1): 145–57.

Weiss-Gal, I. and Gal, J. (2020) 'Explaining the policy practice of community social workers', *Journal of Social Work*, 20(2): 216–33.

Weiss-Gal, I. and Levin, L. (2010) 'Social workers and policy practice: an analysis of job descriptions in Israel', *Journal of Policy Practice*, 9(3–4): 183–200.

Weiss-Gal, I. and Nouman, H. (2016) '"Money makes the world go around": social workers in parliamentary finance committees in Israel', *Journal of Social Work*, 16(4): 393–411.

Weiss-Gal, I. and Peled, E. (2009) 'Publishing voice: training social workers in policy practice', *British Journal of Social Work*, 39(2): 368–82.

Weiss-Gal, I. and Savaya, R. (2012) 'A hands-on policy practice seminar for social workers in Israel: description and evaluation', *Journal of Policy Practice*, 11(3): 139–57.

Weiss-Gal, I., Gal, J. and Schwartz-Tayri, T.M. (2017) 'Teacher, researcher and ... policy actor? Social work academics' involvement in social policy', *Social Policy and Administration*, 51(5): 776–95.

Weiss-Gal, I., Gal, J., Schwartz-Tayri, T., Gewirtz-Meydan, A. and Sommerfeld, D. (2020) 'Social workers' policy practice in Israel: internal, indirect, informal and role contingent', *European Journal of Social Work*, 23(2): 203–14.

Welbourne, P. (2011) 'Twenty-first century social work: the influence of political context on public service provision in social work education and service delivery', *European Journal of Social Work*, 14(3): 403–20.

Werkmeister Rozas, L., Feely, M. and Ostrander, J. (2019) 'Social work, problem definition and policy change in the US: the case of sex-trafficked youth', in U. Klammer, S. Leiber and S. Leitner (eds) *Social Work and the Making of Social Policy*, Bristol: Policy Press, pp 37–52.

Wiggan, J. (2012) 'Telling stories of 21st century welfare: the UK Coalition government and the neo-liberal discourse of worklessness and dependency', *Critical Social Policy*, 32(3): 383–405.

Witt, H., Witt, R. and Brisby, K. (2020) 'Does policy practice class increase social work students' planned political engagement?', *Journal of Policy Practice and Research*, 1(3): 77–95.

Wolk, J. (1981) 'Are social workers politically active?', *Social Work*, 26(4): 283–8.

Wyers, N.L. (1991) 'Policy-practice in social work: models and issues', *Journal of Social Work Education*, 27(3): 241–50.

Zhang, L., Zhao, J. and Dong, W. (2021) 'Street-level bureaucrats as policy entrepreneurs: action strategies for flexible community governance in China', *Public Administration*, 99(3): 469–83.

Zilber, T.B. (2012) 'The relevance of institutional theory for the study of organizational culture', *Journal of Management Inquiry*, 21(1): 88–93.

Zubrzycki, J. and McArthur, M. (2004) 'Preparing social work students for policy practice: an Australian example', *Social Work Education*, 23(4): 451–64.

Index

References to figures appear in *italic* type;
those in **bold** type refer to tables.